HORSEMAN

HORSEMAN

Memoirs of Captain
J. H. Marshall

EDITED BY
GEORGE MILLAR

THE BODLEY HEAD
LONDON   SYDNEY
TORONTO

© George Millar 1970
ISBN 0 370 01327 1
Printed and bound in Great Britain for
The Bodley Head Ltd
9 Bow Street, London w c 2
by C. Tinling and Co Ltd, Prescot
Set in Monotype Baskerville
First published 1970

CONTENTS

ILLUSTRATIONS

Introduction

JOHN HOWARD MARSHALL was a man who lived his life for and on horses. And as he also lived by them, that is by selling them, he was an acute observer of the human race. Just as a good sheepdog is happy only when it has sheep to work, so Captain Marshall was content when he had at least one horse to handle and to sell. He preferred working on his own to working for others, partly because he liked to take all the risk and all the profit, partly because selling was for him a subtle process, and the more difficult the sale the more pleasure he derived from it, though he might pretend otherwise.

He never, as it happened, sold me a horse. But he was breaking young horses for me—big, strong, blood ones too—when he was eighty, and he helped me to sell two or three. He was a wonderful man to have at your shoulder when a potential buyer appeared and the Captain, as he puts it in his Memoirs, heard 'the distant roll of drums and tramp of infantry'. In a flash he knew how to treat the customer: with a flood of talk, or almost none; jovially, or in a 'well, if you don't know a snip when you're offered it, more fool you' sort of way.

Numerous men and women in England today earn their living with horses. Some, particularly in the hunting, eventing, and jumping scenes, earn money much as Captain Marshall did. But most of them, at any rate of those I have watched with interest and admiration, have other sources of income. What they manage to make from horse-coping is only a welcome supplement, a reward for skill. Captain

Marshall had to sell horses to live, and he lived long and well. If that is not clever, tell me what is. Few of those with whom he dealt perhaps realised that he was a well-read, studious, and humorous man, one who would have done well in any business or profession. But there, he was a natural actor, just as he was a natural adventurer who, to the day of his death, took pleasure from the danger inherent in his trade.

By nature he was canny, and kept close hold on his money and his confidences. In the course of setting down his Memoirs I met people who had known him in Leicestershire and London and in the Sparkford Vale and Staffordshire. I learned from some of them that the Captain had been vastly popular with the ladies. Not a hint, not a whiff of that ever passed his lips. Nor, when he was taming our wild young horses or talking to me about his past, do I recall him using any word that could remotely be termed bad language. In all the time I knew him—this only struck me the other day— I remember him laughing frequently at himself, but never at anyone else. He had no children but he liked children and was as skilful with them as with young horses. Many a one he taught to ride, and for nothing, although he preferred teaching horses to teaching people. He went to church on Sundays, and told me without either pride or embarrassment that he believed in God, the Church of England, and the Crown. Despite his many terrible falls and breakages, old age did not cripple him, and, as he aged, he was able, with increasing experience and undiminished determination, to continue doing what he had done from the unnaturally early age of ten. Just imagine it: seventy-one years of horse-breaking!

Personal masculine elegance is an elusive quality, and possibly a rare one in an England that used to be full of it. Captain Marshall was never, so far as I know, a rich man, yet even in working rig he was always a picture, always himself, always different from any other man. Every bit of tweed or wool or cord or silk that he hung on his lean shape looked right, individual, unflashy. He never failed with hats: his slightly voluminous tweed caps, his summer Panamas, his horizontal bowlers, his vertical tall hats from Mr Herbert Johnson's. Every cubic Marshall centimetre was worth looking at. Then he was incredibly clean and systematic. His bootroom, his stables, his harness room, his wood pile, his muck heap, all were immaculate. To everything its place, its polish, or its saddle soap.

At intervals during 1968 when both of us could spare the time I would go to his house in Cattistock, the next village over the ridge to the west of us, and for an hour, two hours, he would tell the story of his life to me and to an unobtrusive tape recorder. Mrs Marshall, small, neat, and lively, considerably younger than her husband, made us comfortable with all kinds of attentions and afternoon tea or drinks as hour and custom suggested. Border terriers snuffled round our legs, and when I left I was always pressed to carry away fresh eggs laid by the Captain's game fowl, Old English birds, and bantams. I looked forward to such visits, and left them invigorated, as though I had breathed in energy from that young-old horseman.

That December he died in his sleep with absolute unexpectedness. In his stables below the deathbed stood a thoroughbred mare, aged three, that he had broken for polo and was schooling with stick and ball. He was in his eighty-first year.

Captain Marshall's husky voice with its slight Leicestershire accent came from the little machine so jauntily that I have set down his story as he spoke it. He talked horsey language, which is not my language, and it may be that here and there I have committed errors which he, had he lived, would have rectified. If so I apologise to him and to the reader.

Sydling Court, 1969   G.M.

Lord Lyon

WHEN the alarm clock rang Sam and Mitchell lay for a minute half awake in the bedroom above the coach house that the three of us shared. Then they rose silently, gathering their clothes. I pretended to sleep, letting them get a start in the·day's affairs, listening to the rookery in Home Field, to the clatter of wooden buckets in the stable yard, to Maggie Wrench, the housemaid, treading from room to room lighting coal fires, filling scuttles, black-leading grates. Breakfast smells came up the back stairs and along the landing.

It was a special morning. I had to put on uniform and feared a hostile reaction from my brothers. I was fifteen, Mitchell sixteen, and Sam seventeen. Yet they continued to treat me as though I were a nipper. I'd been in the Army as long as they because, when I was fourteen, Captain E. G. T. Thompson, yeomanry adjutant of the South Notts Hussars, had enrolled me and had persuaded Trent College to let me off work to attend the annual camp outside Nottingham. I took my own young horse there, Lord Lyon, and that first year the pair of us nearly won both the jumping and the tent-pegging. Hickling, where we lived, was between Nottingham and Leicester, and Sam and Mitchell had joined the other local regiment, the Leicestershire Yeomanry. My uniform, in consequence, was anathema to them. The blue coat with any amount of yellow cording and the yellow-piped breeches had been tightened by the master tailor until

I could scarcely breathe in the one or sit down in the other. The pillbox hat with elastic to go under the chin was an excrescence, a pimple that offered neither shade nor shelter. And the boots were stout enough to repel buckshot. It was the stiffest gear I ever rode in, and to walk in it was a penance.

I stamped down the back stairs, shaking the chestnut treads as though I wore armour, and into the kitchen, glowing and steamy, where my martial appearance raised cries of pleasure and admiration from the staff. Cook, Mrs Murgatroyd, said she was making braised duck sandwiches and brandy snaps, and what other favourites would I like in the picnic basket for the races?

My boots were slippery on the Staffordshire bricks paving the yard. Lord Lyon was being quartered by a man and a boy. He was a stone-grey gelding, aged five and standing fifteen hands three inches. His dark tail was shot through with silver. They worked on him with hay wisps and stable rubbers. The depths of his coat glimmered.

Breakfasting alone, I looked more often than usual at the watercolour of the famous gentleman rider Bay Middleton winning a race on Lord of the Harem. The two other pictures were less apt to my situation, one being a portrait in oils dated 1827 of a horse by Cadland, and the other an engraving of the Earl of Lonsdale. He sat a grey horse, one gloved hand held high, and warned his followers, 'Seeds gentlemen, PLEASE.' I ate bacon, eggs, butter, and honey produced on our farm. The coffee came from London and the long, flat breakfast rolls came warm from the oven of Mr Harriman the Hickling baker.

When I rode Lord Lyon out of the yard, the day lay bright ahead of me. We three older boys had the major share of work on the farm, particularly with the many hunter horses bred, bought, broken in, schooled, hunted and sold. Our father kept us so busy that the plan for this day seemed beautifully simple. I had to ride on twelve miles to Lord Harrington's point-to-point meeting at Woodborough

Hall, win the yeomanry race, and jog him home. He was a sound, brave, and well-mannered young horse. It would take a goodish one to beat him. We generally had rather more than twenty in our stables. My father was always buying and selling. Sometimes he would sell them before he got them home to Hickling, sometimes he would sell them before he'd even bought them. . . . But the five-year-old was surely mine. This was how we came to have him.

Captain Gordon Wilson, who was known as 'Father O'Flynn' Wilson after he won the Grand National on the outstanding horse of that name, lived with his brother Herbert at Brooksby Hall, later Admiral Beatty's hunting box, and he gave my father a grey mare.

'She's been blinded in the nearside eye and I can't hunt her any more,' he said. 'But she's a good'n, not too old to breed, and she might do you well, Sam.'

The Wilsons were a marvellous pair to hounds, and if they said Stella, as the one-eyed mare was called, was good, no hunter could have a fairer recommendation.

'You take to this mare, Howard,' my father said. 'See to her. Call her your own.'

She was a funny one. If you went near her blind side she could be mean, but I got used to working in front of her good eye, even putting on her bridle from the off side. Soon after we got her Major H. T. Barclay, a bang-up Leicestershire swell in the grand manner, fetched back from training his splendid handicapper Bendigo, putting him at the disposal of any Quorn or Belvoir farmers who had mares.

'Bendigo got back to Gaddesby Hall yesterday teatime, for I've just met his handler, Wheatear, in the Harboro',' my father said to me. 'Did I hear you say that one-eyed mare's in season? Well, ask Hibbert to get out a trap, and the pair of you lead her over right away, and when you've got her covered give this to Sol Wheatear.' He drew a sovereign from the round gold case on the end of his watch chain.

Stella was Bendigo's first mare and she duly foaled a little black one, her only foal. She had a bad time of it. Her pains began at midnight. He was born on her blind side and she was queer with him, not knowing what had happened to her. She let me into the box, but nobody else. I rubbed and rubbed him till he was dry. 'Leave well alone now, boy, and get to your bed,' my father said. But I persevered until she learned to nuzzle him round to her good side and he, clever foal, had a suck. From then on she mothered him well enough. Why Father named him Lord Lyon I don't know.

He was a well-grown colt when I led him with his mother to Melton Mowbray Show and the pair won their class. Melton's eight miles from Hickling. My father had numerous entries, cattle, sheep, pigs and poultry as well as horses, and we went there and came back in a glorified sort of Noah's Ark cavalcade. He said to me when I'd put up their rosettes. 'Well done, Howard. Don't go feeling smart though, for all you did was let the pair of them win.' No credit, thought I, for the work of turning them out. 'So next you'll take 'em to Newark,' he said. 'Newark's a *good* show.'

'How do I get 'em there?'

'God gave to you two legs, boy, and to each of them four. It's no more than twenty miles to Newark, and plenty of grassy side roads to stop in and let 'em graze. There'll be two or three others going and you'll walk with them.'

We set out in the dark to do the 48-mile Newark day (for Newark is twenty-four, not my father's 'twenty', miles from Hickling). The foal arrived in the ring fresh and bright, and they were in the money though they did not win. My father overtook us in a trap on the way home.

'Are you tired, boy?' he called.

'Yes, Father.'

'Then just set that mare's rope round her neck. She and her foal will follow the others home. You get in here. Look sharp now. Whoa! Stay at this horse's head. The *seat* needs moving back.' He was always particular about balancing.

The seats on his carts and traps were adjustable, with little hardwood stops. 'Jump up.' And we were away in luxury, the scarlet-silk-lined fur rug generating warmth round my legs.

I took Lord Lyon to Melton Show the following year and he won his yearling class. He was hard to fault as a yearling because he was better grown then than later, he had plenty of bone, and he had Bendigo's neck and shoulder. Before he went into the ring Mr Harry Gale, who had forgotten more about horses than most men know, said, 'You've got 'im looking well, yoong Marshall, you've got 'im looking extra.' I was going through his tail with a body brush. 'Joost put a roober over 'im,' Mr Gale advised. 'No need for a broosh on a coat like that. A nice bit of a roober is all you want. Ah! he's looking a treat, he's *doing*.'

That was the sort of interest we got from our elders. They were quick to blame, but their praise was manna in the wilderness.

And now here was Lord Lyon, aged five and full of beans, walking over to Woodborough to be a racehorse. Bright uniforms and star horses were common then in that part of the Midlands. Nobody would turn his or her head to look as we passed, pillbox hat and all.

The point-to-point course was cut out into a natural bit of hunting country. It came back in a big circle to finish near the start. A row of bookies had already been set up when Lyon and I walked in. Drags and traps and gigs were positioning themselves near the roped-in paddock and parade ground. I was passing quietly behind them when a voice arrested me. 'Think he'll give you a win, lad?'

'Oh no, Mr Maher.' It was one of the things we had been taught, to say no rather than yes where horses were concerned. My interlocutor was, to any boy, one of the greatest men in England, Danny Maher, the American jockey who won the Derby on Sir James Miller's Black Sand.

'Why, it's one of the Marshall lads from Hickling,' he said.

'It was the young horse took my eye. A good looker, eh George?'

George Williamson, the steeplechase jockey who had won the Grand National (on Manifesto) and every other major steeplechase in Europe, shared Cropwell Court with Mr Maher. It was a house down a drive off the Newark-Nottingham road. The two jockeys had bought it from Lawyer Wildes, a heavyweight who hunted with a fistful of violets in the buttonhole of his red coat. Mr Williamson now stood with a group of the racing people round the tail of a drag where there was an arrangement of bottles, glasses, sandwiches, cold game, and fruit. Matt Williamson was there, who rode mainly in Belgium, and Colonel Birkin, and the Percy Woodlands, all famous and all friendly.

'Small but quality,' George Williamson said. 'He'll take some beating if he's fit, but he carries a fair bit of meat, mind.'

'What's his story?' Danny Maher asked, stroking the grey's cheek. He had the smallest hands I ever saw on a man, yet they said he could hold any horse alive. I told him briefly what I have told you, thinking what a good-looking, dapper, intelligent little man he was. I had often seen him in the hunting field, for although our land was half in the Quorn half in the Belvoir we were handy for the South Notts, or Lord Harrington's Hunt as it was then known, in whose country Danny was a landowner and a covert owner. Such a covert too! You never saw its like. It had been planted entirely of privet and although it was no more than two acres the foxes adored it. A sure find. His lordship used to send a whipper-in round the far side and ride quietly up to it, his white whiskers flapping either side of his chin. A toot on his horn. Hounds went in like a broadside. No prickles there for tender skins. Imagine having two such men as Maher and Williamson in one ordinary country house for the whole hunting season—though of course George would be away race-riding a good deal. Then, in spring, when the hunting ended Danny would leave the Court in the hands of servants. The stud of hunters would be at grass until the flies became bad, when they would be stabled by day and turned out at night. In that respect our country was a strange one: while we were at our busiest with haymaking and harvest and the livestock, many of our best friends and neighbours would be far away, planning to return only in the autumn with the start of foxhunting and the fall of the leaf.

'And is he yours then, or your father's?'

'He's mine, Mr Maher.' I had never thought of Lyon as a saleable horse. He was more like a brother. And mine he would stay, I thought as I rode him into the Woodborough Hall stable yard. Big as it was, the yard was packed with traps and horses. My father had reserved a place for Lyon in one of the stud groom's boxes.

The yeomanry race was second on the card. It was run at catch weights over eleven stone seven. My brother Sam, who loved a race and was already experienced (or thought he was), had weighed me on the jockeys' scales in the cloak-room at home, and what with clodhopper boots and the ordinary hunting saddle I was a pound or so on the safe side. I stood six feet already, at fifteen, but then, as now, I was thin, with smallish bones. Sam and Mitchell had come with my father in the trap. Sam was riding at that time mainly for a fellow called Ransom who had a farm on either side of the road as you came out of Nottingham for Melton, and who seemed to have the knack of breeding or buying point-to-pointers. But he had nothing running that day. Sam had a ride in the third race though, on a novice belonging to a Pytchley farmer. I found our trap by the paddock, drank one glass of beer and wolfed down a lot of duck sandwiches and brandy snaps. Sam could scarcely pick at anything. He was highly strung over his racing. Once later, when each of us had a ride in the same adjacent hunts' race, we were galloping easily side by side across a plough when Sam screwed in his saddle and snarled, 'Don't you get within a field of me at the finish or I'll make you wish you were dead.'

There were ten runners in my race. A man called Josh Piggin, the devil of a one to go, was in it, and so was Sergeant 'Fiery' Cross, who sat straight up and stiff like a pair of scissors across a horse. I could hear the bookies shouting, but whether I was favourite or started at ten to one, I was too green to know. I would not say that I was icy cool, but nor was I agitated. The race passed for me in a sort of daze, not like a good run in the hunting field, much inferior to that. More like being at a dance where the music was good and there were dozens of pretty girls. I sat still on Lord Lyon, nursing his mouth and looking between his ears. Sergeant Cross was outside me for a longish time and Piggin was inside, brushing the flags with his boot. Cross's rigidity wore his horse down and he dropped back. Fence after fence streamed under us and then I saw Piggin was beginning to work. He went ahead of us a shade, breaking his rhythm, and then fell astern inch by inch until I no longer saw him. I felt the little horse take a breather, and then he found himself again and went on, stronger than before, over the last three fences. I had asked him no serious questions. He had told me no lies. He pulled up at a touch and a feel of the leg and walked gaily among the traps and the people. When I had weighed in I led him back to his box, made him comfortable, got him to stale, and gave him a bite to eat and some warmed water.

Lyon and I had a stream of visitors. Danny Maher was in the first batch. He came with Percy Woodland, who won the Grand National on Drumcree and who also won the big 'steeple' at Auteuil. His brother, Bill Woodward, married George Williamson's sister, and they were neighbours of ours.

'Good boy,' Mr Maher said. 'And your grey, well, I like him, I like him very much. I'm not trying to play you, see? You're big on that horse already, and you're still growing. He's just the compact, bold sort for me, and if you let me try him with hounds and we go well together. I'll give you your own price on him. What do you say?'

'If he went to anyone I'd like him to go to you, Mr Maher. But I don't want to sell.'

'I see.'

The grey glanced at all the people who came, and went back to his hay. My father was in and out repeatedly. He did not find time to talk to me, but when he caught my eye he gave me a wink. After I'd collected my cup, a silver rosebowl, and stowed it in the boot of our trap, I saddled up and we walked and jogged back home, me dozing and dreaming on his back as evening turned to darkness and the dew settled in my uniform and hung on my eyebrows under the pillbox.

His legs next morning were cool without swelling or puffiness—youth is a miracle. The morning was sunny and lazy. Time seemed to hang behind the gilded hands of the clock above the stable roofs. A wild mare had been harnessed to a gig. She stood sweating on the neck, squirming, pawing to go, with a man either side hanging on to her head. My father came into the yard, florid, heavy-moustached, his height made higher by a whiteish-grey square-topped box hat, the outdoor darkness of his skin accentuated by a white silk cravat. His leggings were wide over his feet, a fashion set by the popular Duke of Connaught. From his chequered waistcoat he drew his gold Benson's hunter, opened it with the magic that a watch then possessed, and said to the mare, 'We're late, my girl. You'll have to shift.' She showed him the white of her nasty eye, looking ready to kick him and the gig to bits. As my father was usually late, and in his search for horses he was always catching trains, we took it that he enjoyed the act of rushing to a station, and felt it worthwhile to be beaten fairly by the clock and the punctuality of the trains.

'We're late. Where's Albert? Bertie!'

Albert Mitchell Marshall was my second brother. He

detested the first of his names, and my father used it as a tease. Mitchell was to go as a passenger to Broughton Station and then bring the gig back.

'Cut on down to the field gates at your best pace, Mitchell,' my father said. 'And don't expect me to hang about waiting for you to get aboard. We're late.'

Mitchell shot out of the yard, light as a fly on his feet.

'Howard!' My father was pulling on his pigskin driving gloves. He didn't look round at me. 'Had your breakfast?'

'No, Father.'

'Lord Lyon all right, no knocks, no cuts? Good.' A string of farming instructions followed, numerous jobs I was to do that morning and how they were *not* to be done. He gently put his foot on the step and mounted into the gig. Feeling him behind her, the mare was boiling over. 'Whoa my girl, whoa my lady.' His voice with horses was soft. 'You still there, Howard?' he asked, never taking his eyes off the mare struggling for her head, the two men hanging on to her for all they were worth. 'Now listen. . . . Danny Maher wants a day's hunting on Lyon. So just lead him out today to stretch his legs and first thing tomorrow you'll lead him from a trap over to Cropwell Court. You hear me?'

'Yes, Father.'

'Leave Lyon there with Mr Maher or his stud groom and come straight home in the trap. I'll want you to meet me in the evening, seven o'clock in Melton at the Bell. And another thing . . . you did well yesterday when you told Mr Maher the grey was your own and not for sale. Don't go getting a swollen head now, but if he's sold and passes the vet, you'll have put at least fifty guineas on the price of him. You're my boy.' Then he hissed at the two struggling men, '*Now let her go!*'

They jumped back, and under my father's hands the raging mare walked quietly down the road. That was a special trick of his. He could do as he liked with almost any horse (and any boy). Now, though, he was in too much of a hurry to rub in his bit of showmanship, and after only a dozen sedate paces he gave her the office and she flew like a witch in a gale. His horses could usually go. If they couldn't go, he sold them. If they could, he sold them.

Next day I took Lord Lyon over to Cropwell Court. He never came back. I used to see him now and then carrying Danny in the hunting field. His heels and his tail were what one usually saw. Well, I suppose Danny hunted him out and then he'd be fed to Lord Harrington's hounds. He was a sensible, brave little horse.

2

Hickling Manor

I was born in 1888 at Hickling Manor, the fifth of eleven children.

If you turn off the Melton Mowbray to Nottingham turn-pike at Upper Broughton it's a mile and a half to Hickling, which is in the lowest part of the vale, eight miles north of Melton and twelve south of Nottingham. My father farmed an outlying hundred and fifty acres at the western end of the ridge known as Hickling Standard. That bit was well into Quorn country and included Curate's Gorse, one of the best fox coverts in England. He farmed by the house another hundred and fifty acres in Belvoir country, and there owned another famous draw, Sherbrooke's. The boundary separating the two hunts is the River Smite which there, in its upper reaches, is little more than a brook. Our land was the typical clay of Leicestershire, mostly permanent pasture hard grazed, with yawning perimeter ditches and black hedges cut tight and solid. We specialised in down-calving heifers, mainly Lincoln Reds, and put the Shorthorn bull to them—it was nearly always 'roan on red' with us, and if you say there's a finer grazing country than that in the world, I won't believe you. Our milk was made into butter, cream, and Stilton cheese. Often Father bought in neighbours' milk, Mrs Doubleday's for instance, because he sold our Stilton to London where he had a contract with a restaurant near the Stock Exchange called, I believe, the Palmerston. Locally it was thought risky business to let all your best cheese go to one London buyer. But Father enjoyed risks, and in that quarter they never let him down or we should soon have known of it. He also ran a flock of Lincoln Longwools, to which he put Hampshire Down rams bought at Wilton Fair. Then he had pigs and poultry and grew some oats, wheat, and potatoes. So although his heart was in horses, foxhunting, and the hunter trade he had a productive and balanced farm, and it was solidly built—the brass handles countersunk in all the stable doors, shining, everlasting, seemed to typify the quality and husbandry of the place. The brook, busy with our white ducks, went round Home Field. There were hens and bantams and ornamental gamebirds all about the yards and the grass, as was common in those days. Our house was alive with dogs, greyhounds and pointers and a setter or two. . . . I think I've described a paradise for any animal-loving boy to be reared in. That's what it was. Yet there was trouble. There always is.

My father's passion for sport, his delight in risking his neck and the necks of those closest to him, were not admired by my mother, a gloriously pretty woman from the rectory at the next village, Long Clawson. Her grandfather, old Mitchell, was a tea broker with an office in Throgmorton Street. He bought the living at Clawson for my grandfather, his son Tom. Tom Mitchell had two daughters and a son, all three of whom were regarded as matrimonial catches. Lawyer Elborne of Nottingham bowled over one of the girls and my father bagged the other. As for the son, Albert Mitchell, he was one cause of the trouble between my handsome and headstrong parents.

Young Albert admired my father, especially the way he could pilot any horse across any country. Father used to mount him. I don't suppose there was often a time when there were not too many fresh horses in his Hickling stables. One day the pair of them were out hunting. My uncle was smoking a pipe. The horse flung up his head, ramming the pipe down Uncle Bertie's throat, and the amber stem splintered inside him. My father put him in a trap behind a galloping mare and raced him to Nottingham Hospital. There were no X-rays then, and he died. The effects of that accident, though it happened four years before I was born, were to alter several lives, mine included.

No doubt my parents had fallen in love with each other. Nothing unusual in that. I suppose my mother felt that when she married Sam Marshall of Hickling she would soon soften and change him. . . . People concealed their feelings in Victorian times, and those feelings therefore pulsed all the stronger. I was aware from early days that, although nothing was ever declared, and neither would run down the other to us children, there was a split between them. From their big, ever-growing family and the circle of their friends each seemed to gather supporters, as though picking a side to play against the other. I was my father's boy. I was grateful to my mother for her care and sympathy. But I knew my father better. I belonged to him as Sam and Mitchell did. The three of us were thrown together by our interests, pursuits, and duties. But three is a bad number and they were hostile to me. I only cared about my father.

My nanny, Miss Randall, was reluctant to leave me. She felt I was being abandoned to some fate or other. She often came back to Hickling, and Mother would tell me she was the best nanny and nicest woman a child ever had to look after him. She attributed my strong constitution to Miss Randall's habit of getting me outdoors so early that the dew fell on my face. It sounds ungrateful, but to me my nanny was no more important than any other woman, and a darned sight less so than, say, Mrs Murgatroyd, the cook, or Ethel, the between-maid. The same applied to my early governesses, both active young ladies who did nothing to stifle my pre-occupation with animals. One came from Nottingham, and the other was from the Grantham side of the Belvoir country and was a good girl on a horse. I've forgotten their names.

There's an advantage in being born into a big family.

A new baby is for ever turning up to take the heat off you, and so you get peace. Most children are fussed over far too much, and that is partly because parents now prefer, understandably enough in days of economic stress, to have only one or two children. If you've eleven you can regard the little blighters as expendable, and in the end that's better for them.

No child ever had such a kick-off as I had, born in the heart of England with fresh food to eat and animals all around: able to spend a whole morning with the weaned calves, seeing that the weakling got his share of the milk until he drew strength from it and held his own; able to hold a baby piglet in my arms and feel its heart beat against mine; able to feed a vixen under the potting shed night after night until at last she'd come when I called and would let me sit close and touch her fur; able to bring a hedgehog indoors and keep it in the day-nursery; able to watch the great, slow-moving work-horses in all their moods of energy, fatigue, hunger and somnolence; able to dam the Smite for eels and watch until a tail fanned. A smooth grab, and he was on the ground behind you. Then you had to be smart to catch him or he'd go through the long grass like a snake in *The Jungle Book*. One hard winter we had a miracle. An eel about two feet long got frozen into a puddle in our road. We children used to go and look at him nearly every day. There he was, embalmed in solid ice, half beautiful, half horrid. Then the thaw came and he went slithering across the softening ground into the brook. It was the kind of thing you could imagine happening in India or Persia, some magic country.

When we caught an eel we slit him down the backbone, ringed round the head, and pulled the skin off like a stocking. Then we cut it in flat rings which we fried in goose grease with some fennel and chives thrown in at the finish. The eel rings would jump in the hot frying pan.

In spring our white ducks on the brook kept up a continuous quacking and flapping. Is anything whiter than a

white English duck or yellower than its beak? Most people
coming to the house were asked. 'Would you like a couple
of duck to take home with you?' Anybody, even a stranger
who rode in with a horse on trail, was likely to leave with
a present of ducks or fowls. Those were the days of plenty.
Nor was the plenty dear. Three shillings and sixpence a
couple, that's what we used to get for our shining white ducks.
Jack Mann the carrier, who lived our side of Hickling village,
used to buy them for that and take them to Nottingham
market. Bet you don't find ducks like those in Nottingham
today; they'll be deep-frozen, with no taste, and breasts on
them like the cuirasses of the Household Cavalry.

In the Midlands, the expression 'an Englishman's home
is his castle' seemed to ring true. The houses stood four-
square on mounds, large-windowed, large-doored, well-
heated, looking the country slap in the face and saying,
'I'm me. I belong here.' Our house was like that. I don't
mean that it was the biggest house even in Hickling—the
vicarage was a whopper—or that it was important because
it was down a bit of a drive. I mean that without being
pompous it asserted itself, and had important features.

The hall, for example. You went through the west porch
and the brown-grained front door and stood in a hall that
cut right through the house. The floor was tiled in black
squares and red squares. There was a rather dim hanging
light bought, I believe, in Kabul by some relation or other.
The stairs were cleverly tucked in for a few spiralling steps
and then climbed straight across the north wall past a window
offering a useful view of the stable yard. All those dark doors
opening off, the pattern of the floor, the rubies and scarlets
of the lamp, the trophies of the chase on the walls, the rack
of whips and sticks, the silver salver on a dark old walnut
table, it was a mysterious place, our hall. I always thought
of it when I read about mosques or catacombs or St Peter's or
St Latimer Without or the Inquisition. Don't ask me why.

Both the drawing-room and the dining-room had french

windows with low box-seats. You stepped over the seats, even
a toddler could do it, and you were out on the lawn fringing
the south elevation. If it was winter, the windows were bolted
so that the coal fires could probe the air with heat, and at
dusk the thick pinewood shutters and the almost thicker
dark red curtains were closed, the brass rings rumbling across
the massive brass rods. That was another impression. . . .
Our house, our land, our stackyards, our cattle, our servants,
our relations with village and county, our respect for the
Church, they all seemed imperishable, like the handles of the
stable doors, like those curtain rods and rings. My father was
a god to me, running my world, producing his boundless
wealth. If anybody had told me that Father every day grew
nearer being an old man, or that the Empire had probably
already passed its zenith, I'd have thought him nuts.

Step across the french window's box-seats in summer and
you were in the tropics. I never remember a summer when
the sun did not sizzle the hay as soon as it was cut, when the
scent of queen of the meadow was not overpowering beside
the brook, when the mating dragonflies did not hang as
though stuck in the thick air, when the south wall was not
smothered in apricots, quinces, and vines. The lawn on that
side of the house was bordered by a ha-ha. A plank bridge
crossed it to Home Field. A wired-in tennis court and a
croquet lawn had been stolen from the field. There were
chestnuts, elms and beeches round the north-west and east
sides. The other boundary of that part was the Smite, whose
banks in places were as high as the walls of this room. Every
horse or pony we had used to jump it.

George Harriman the baker was nearly opposite our drive
gates. I thought he was the best baker in England, though he
had his enemies in the village. *They* said that too often his
bread was burned, and that, when it was, Mrs Harriman
used to wrap it up extra well before passing it over the counter, and remark, 'I like them well cooked, don't you?' His
loaves were tinned, and when they rose up over the edge

they fluffed out a bit. His bakery was scrubbed out absolutely white. The day-by-day cleanliness of the place struck you when you rode past and heard the crickets that then lived and made their strange rattling behind the ovens of rural bakeries. If you sought out a cricket he looked like a beetle, and ran like one. Everything was spotless in that place, the baskets, the woodwork, the walls, the floors, the windows, the baker's cart and the horse or pony that drew it. George also kept the village shop and post office.

A footpath edged with blue stones ran through the village, and the path itself was tight cobbled with small, round stones that, by their colour and size, couldn't have come from anywhere nearer than the River Dove, on the far boundary of Nottinghamshire. (I've ridden a horse up the Dove for miles with a guide who knew the potholes; not many can say that I think.) If you came down the cobbled path to Harriman's gate, you found two deep grooves worn in the stone where the baker's cart crossed it. Talk about Greece and Ancient Rome and its chariots! What about ancient England? Years later I was to bring a horse back from the war in France and sell it to that bakery, to George Harriman's son John. I let the horse go too cheap. I'm by no means a sentimentalist, but I wanted to think of that horse further deepening those grooves.

Hickling was a self-supporting community. There was nothing we couldn't do. Covell, our postman, was a cobbler by day, an artist with the hammer. I don't say he could make you a pair of patent-leather dancing pumps, but for boots he couldn't be bettered. Then we had Granville Hopkinson, known as Old Hoppy, our saddler, the best in England and a very strong churchman (C. of E.). Our blacksmith was Alwyn Shelton and our wheelwright William Burnett. We had wooden wheels and iron tyres in those days. There was nothing worse than driving with a loose tyre. I've seen the hoop come off and go rolling past the horse's head, and then one was running on the felloes, the wooden pieces between the spokes. Mr Burnett was wonderfully skilled. He'd light a circular fire, lay the iron hoop on it, hammer it on to the wheel hot, shrink it by pouring on cold water. Then one or two good plugs in all the way round and it was on to stay, you hoped. With his little spokeshave he could turn out in a jiffy the most perfect spoke you ever saw. And when it came to painting spokes with those touches of yellow or red or white, he was an artist.

Such skills were country-wide, and much appreciated. The thought and money that ordinary middle-class people now put into the choice and purchase of a car then went into Burnett's kind of craftsmanship. Any trap was a fascinating object, apart from its usefulness. Take one little detail: a trap had a leather front, a dashboard we called it, as you now call the panel with instruments on your car. Just here, on the dashboard, was a socket to put your whip in. And the socket was made with a spring inside to hold the handle and keep the whip standing erect and yet instantly detachable. . . . Of all things ever made by hand, traps, carriages, and harness seemed to me the most remarkable. Consider the pole to take a horse to the end of his collar, to steer the carriage, and carrying a little strap across the back for him to sit into and stop the carriage, and everything so shaped and refined and correct. I've seen Mr Burnett pull away the stand upon which the shafts of one of our traps or dogcarts were supposedly resting and they'd remain hanging in midair, so perfect was the balance. 'Put a halfpenny on the tailboard, Master Howard.' And the shafts would slowly rise until he stretched up a hand to pull them back and I repocketed my halfpenny.

Ah, what things we youngsters had to learn from our elders! How fortunate we were! It was not like nowadays. When I was a youngster, all of them were either making something or doing something, and from the age of ten I was usually making something myself—a horse. How fortunate we were in England, too! God bless the dear old Queen!

We had a meeting in the village hall for her Jubilee in 1897. Schoolmaster Wilkinson and Farmer Collishaw (the one with the windmill that bruised our oats and ground our wheat) had an argument until Mr Skelton the vicar brought them up short. It was to be a day of jubilation, with a prize Shorthorn steer roasted outdoors, old ale in barrels set high on stands, and a band, and dancing, and sports for the children.

In those days the children of England could run and jump, and Mitchell and myself were the runniest and jumpiest in Hickling. We'd been taught how to do it by Thomas Rose, a man all springs and sinews who'd been a professional runner, and who had an exotic daughter—what a lovely girl! He lived in the first house above our gates. Miss Emily Corner came next, and she played the organ in church. Then Mann, the carrier, who left every morning except Sunday for either Melton or Nottingham in his substantial waggon with two draught-horses. When we were getting older, strangers used to come to Hickling and ask to see Mitchell and yours-truly jumping the walls and gates and stiles, not on horses, but off our own feet. Once a circus proprietor came to my father, offering to take his two boys on in an act and pay *him* for it. 'I'd call 'em the yuman hostriches,' he said. How Father laughed. Mother did not see the joke.

Opposite the Harrimans was the compact house and farmsteading of Mrs Elizabeth Doubleday. They farmed alongside our Home Field, and they milked and made fine Stilton. Mrs Doubleday was very devout. Once, much as she'd say, 'Good day to you,' she said to me, outside the post office, 'Honour thy father and thy mother,' and then she made it even better by adding, 'That's a nicish cob you're on, boy, except he dishes on the off fore.'

Twice each Sunday we went to church. Our cortège usually was a long one with our parents in the van followed by whoever happened to be staying, all us children, and our governesses and a nanny or two. One wet Sunday evening we were waiting in the church porch while our coats were hung up. A ginger kitten rubbed against my shin. Without thinking I picked him up. Once at my chest he dug in with four sets of claws. Our party was getting under way. There was no chance of disengaging. I put my arms around him and followed into the bright church throbbing with the organ. My parasite, horrified by everything he saw and heard, dug his claws deep through my coat and shirt and into the flesh below.

In so numerous a family there are seating rules. On that particular Sunday it was my turn to go last into church and sit at the end of our family pew. I kept trying to get the kitten loose and could not until I hit on an idea. There were walnut shells in my pockets. . . . We had a fine walnut tree on the west side of the garden, and a bowl of green walnuts often stood on the sideboard near the port and sherry decanters. The shells opened easily with the gentlest pressure of thumb and forefinger, and the nut inside was sweet and juicy, quite unlike the dried-out imported nuts sold in Nottingham. I'd been at the walnut bowl that morning. I went to work on the kitten's feet, one by one. As soon as I prized one loose I pushed a half shell over it.

When I'd shod him all round, the kitten jumped for the aisle and darted about, clattering like castanets on the tiled floor. Mr Tom Skelton, up front, was reading the lesson. After pausing to see who was misbehaving he thought it best to continue. John Hives, the verger, gave chase, and his assistant and brother Billy Hives thought to open the main doors, when the interrupter soon tapped his way out.

After the service I ran on ahead to see to the baked potatoes. It still rained. On Sundays, after luncheon, the maids were off duty, and for Sunday supper we ate cold meats and game and baked potatoes which were left in the oven before we went to church with just enough fire in the range to do them nicely. It was a massive iron range with strappings of polished brass and steel and a long jack for spit roasting. The main oven had a trough under the door and a special ladle so that the juices running out of the joints could be basted back over or used for gravy. That evening I ran extra fast. I had time to fill the Crown Derby tureen with spuds, take the red earthen jar down to the beer-and-cider cellar and fill it with ale for Father, and draw drinking water for the rest of us from the pump in the yard. The pump had two spouts; one gushed rain water that was used for the tack and for laundering, but the other sucked from a spring so deep and cold that if you gave it a hundred strokes during a heat wave you'd get water that frosted the glasses. Generally there were some Crown Derby dishes lying on the flagged part of the yard where the greyhounds, fussy eaters, had been offered their milk and meat. We didn't think of such china as valuable, though we were taught it mustn't be broken. It was a crime to break anything, to waste anything. China was there to be used.

Our tables were too solid of leg and back to groan, but they must have known the food was there. Great joints of meat on dishes with little legs and channels down the middle to a pool at the lower end for the gravy, and geese and fowls and ducks and game of all sorts in season. Piles of fresh vegetables and fruits and home-made butter and the heavy cheese, sometimes soaked with port. You would not credit the amount most of us ate then. Four meals a day, and I know I couldn't eat one such today. But Sunday supper was one of the best because it was informal, a picnic, and because we had just come out of church. Father would carve and then each of us would take a great round hot potato and put it on a side plate, bash it open with the heel of his fist, and fill it with butter, salt, and pepper fresh ground in the coffee mill.

During supper I was examining the scratches on my hands. Nothing had been said about the kitten incident. I looked up and saw Father observing me. He twigged. A smile just lurked round his moustache. So I went behind them all at the table and laid my arms about his neck over the back of his chair. Men smelled good in those days, of soft leather and tobacco and the open, like broom or heather.

*   *   *

One blustering March evening he found me reading before the morning-room fire.

'You'll do,' said he. 'Get some clothes on, untie the pony from the rail in the yard and bring the trap round here. . . . Drive on,' he said when he'd climbed in and tucked the rug round our legs. 'Right on up to Top Barn fast as he'll go. There's dirty weather on the way. I want to get those ewes down in-by and yarded.' When we reached the field he called impatiently, 'Have you frozen solid, then? Come, on get round them, and bring them slowly to the gate. Slowly, mind.' I began to push them while he called, and he managed to edge the leaders through the gate. He kept glancing at the sky, black, chill, and greasy. 'These should have come in-by yesterday,' he said. 'I told you before I left for Derby. I can't be everywhere all the time.' (That was one of his favourite dodges, parking the blame on whoever happened to be handy.) 'Don't hurry them, Howard. Humouring's quickest in the end with any old sheep.'

I tell you I was frozen. I could have strangled every one of those in-lamb ewes. Now it was snowing. There was a whistle in the wind.

'Not afraid of the dark, are you?'

'No.' I took a squint through the squashy snowflakes at the scurrying clouds, a terrifying sky.

'Well then, I'll cut on back with the trap and send Hibbert up to give you a hand. Take them nice and quiet, mind, or they'll get stubborn, and we'll never shift them this night.' He turned up the wide collar of his coat and pushed his hat more firmly on. The trap rolled away.

The ewes before me were heavy in lamb and heavier with wetness. Most of them had a good shake, and some began to stroll after the disappearing trap. But they would not have been sheep if the other half had not made up their minds to move in the opposite direction. I cursed my father's absorption in greyhounds (for the coursing at the Hussey-Packe place between Loughborough and Leicester), gundogs (for the farmers' shoot in the Smite valley), and hound puppies (walked for the three hunts he favoured); not a sheepdog would he have on the place. I cut a switch from the hedge, swept the road with it in front of the fat ladies and shouted at them, 'Hi, hi! Ho, ho! Oh, oh, oh!' This set them in motion, and the road running downhill all the way, and the leaders being hard pushed by those behind, they soon worked up a lumbering gallop. Here was a do! The farther they went, the more they galloped, and the faster the front ones travelled, the harder the others pedalled to keep up. I stood in horror for a minute, hoping my father might not be within miles. He had been particularly proud of their lambing percentage the year before, as one after the other they dropped their twins and triplets. I pelted down the slushy gravel road after them, running in a stench of sodden sheep, the snow stinging my eyes. I tried hanging back, They wouldn't stop. They kept up their gallop until at last the pace slowed and they began changing leg in a very unwholesome manner. At that point the grass verge was a wide one deeply serrated by cattle steppings. Some of them staggered, then fell. They fell faster until perhaps half were down. Then there was a tremendous clap of thunder which seemed to knock all the rest over. I shall not easily forget those struggling falls.

When Hibbert showed up, nothing that we could do would make them move. There was a stack of hurdles nearby. We hurdled them into the road for the night and then walked on down to the yard, where my father was busy with straw and hay and lanterns. He glared at me.

'You never said how to stop them from behind,' I said.

'Nor I did,' he answered with a hoarse chuckle. 'Is that

you, Hibbert? Will the ewes do for the night, then?' Hibbert reassured him. 'Get in that trap, boy,' he said. 'I can hear your teeth dance. D'ye feel cold or hot?'

'Cold.'

'You're all right then. It's when you're hot and should be cold there's summat up.' He took me straight into the scullery, leaving Hibbert to put away the pony. 'Drop all those wet clothes off you, Howard, here on the stone,' he said. 'I'll get a mustard bath for you in the kitchen, where it's warm.'

Soon I was in the tin bath with scalding water up to my chin and a strong smell of the mustard he'd added. My father stood in front of the range, its doors opened so that the fire gleamed orange on his back, and steam rose from him. My mother came in with a huge bath towel and my thick dressing-gown and flannel pyjamas. She hung them all on the back of a basket chair, displacing my father from his stance before the fire. She had a red spot in either cheek.

'On a night like this,' she said. 'You might have killed him. Boys aren't there to do the work of men; little boys like him. He's only nine.'

To my vast relief he didn't take her criticism seriously. 'Can't they just?' he said. 'Boys can do anything if they'll only try.'

*   *   *

My father was an enigma. He once said to Sam and Mitchell, 'Now you let him alone, you young devils. He's a small boy, and I won't have him knocked about.' I thought, What? He's sticking up for me. It'll only do harm. . . . For those two were a sore trial to me. I reckon their bullying and teasing turned me into what the Antipodeans call a loner. But I was never unhappy.

Young children are conscious of plenty, of prosperity. We seemed to possess the earth. It wasn't only all the animals and the food. Every piece of linen in the house was

ironed, starched, mended. The laundry went off in a trap to
Broughton every Monday and was fetched back on the
Friday, and that was apart from all the washing done by the
horde of women about the house. How they scrubbed and
polished and swept and baked and preserved! That smell of
raspberry or strawberry jam simmering in coppers! We were
allowed to taste the coloured foam that Mrs Murgatroyd
occasionally skimmed off with a giant spoon. In winter, when
the shutters were closed and the curtains drawn, we read or
played in front of mountainous fires. Coal was there in
plenty, and everyone on the farm or in the stables had it as
part of his wages. When he needed more, a wagon with
two horses was sent off to one of the Nottingham pitheads.
The coal shone like quartz, and had gold seams in it. Our
house was lit with oil lamps and candles. Everyone econo-
mised in candles, it was an English fetish. The back stairs were
as dark as a bag, and the hall was always spooky.

My mother remained a Long Clawson person at heart,
and she had favourites there whom she would employ at
Hickling. One of those was Roger Mann, a carpenter and
painter who was also a Wesleyan preacher. I was helping my
mother pick apricots (for brandy) when Roger arrived
trundling his tools in front of him in a hand-cart. 'I preached
'em on hell fire, Mum,' he said, describing his Sunday
doings. 'I made the buggers think, I did.' Mother didn't
seem to notice the odd word. I added it to my vocabulary.
The first time I used it there was a shindy and a half and even
my father seemed angry. I never used it again, but I noted
that Roger Mann was allowed to use words forbidden to me.
Another of Mother's pets was our gardener, W. Key. It was
the age of flowerbeds filled with arrangements of annuals.
He was a favourite with us, too, so brown and wrinkled with
his calloused hands and the strings tied under his knees. He
was said to drink quantities of herb beer, and any afternoon,
wet or fine, you might come on him in some unexpected
corner curled up in his barrow and snoring. His hat looked

like an old, old mushroom. I learned from his case too because there was a lot of drunkenness in those days, and everybody professed to be very down on it, except in Bill Key's case. They seemed to find *his* drinking habits endearing rather than reprehensible. Grown-ups!

John and Jane Morley lived in our prettiest cottage, a red one in Home Field. Jane worked in the house, and also went to Mrs Doubleday's to wash, and John turned his hand mildly to anything on the farm, in the stables, or in the garden. They were already old when I was a toddler, and aimed most of their misgivings at the railways, which they said were ruining the English as a race—much as people today run down television or the trade unions or the health service. John prefaced nearly every remark with 'Jane says. . . .' Jane, on the other hand, would begin, 'John says. . . .' Mother always said the Morleys were the most devoted couple in the world, and an example of the Bible's 'Blessed are the meek, for they shall inherit the earth'. Then one day my father said, 'It isn't a case of that at all, my dear. John and Jane won't inherit anything, though they deserve to, and with them it's "Blessed the married couple who are childless, for they shall love one another with a pure heart. . . ." ' Poor Mother.

Then there was our treasure, Hibbert, who turned his skilled hand to everything and was a true friend to us all without an ounce of soft soap or suction pump in his nature. Many a sharp word or angry look each of us had from him, yet he always got on with the difficult things. How often when I've been tired I've ridden into the yard thinking, 'Lord above, this horse is going to take no end of doing, and then I must dress that mare's foot.' And when I came to the mare her foot had been done. 'Who did it, Joe?' 'Why, Mr Hibbert, before he went on.' Well, now Hibbert has gone on, and that will be one more good'n in Heaven.

Cricket was the only ball game I ever had a fancy for, if you exclude polo, and that came later. As soon as I could

walk a bit I'd pretend to be a part of the village game. . . .
Mr Titus Littler was the vet at Clawson, and what a warrior
he was! One afternoon, driving past, he put his reins down
and stopped to watch our game. Shelton the blacksmith,
a great hitter, was at the wicket. He took a pull, half lofted,
and after one bounce on the baked clay the ball tried to
bury itself in the ribs of the vet's strong cob. He jumped
straight in the air, then made off for home, fast as he could
gallop, with the vet in the bottom of the gig. Mitchell and I
climbed bareback on a couple of ponies and galloped after
them all the road to Clawson. The cob swung into his own
drive, the gig on one wheel, and then, carried by his momen-
tum, plunged into the shrubbery. Mr. Littler picked himself
off the floor with a grunt and shook himself. Gig, cob, and
driver looked inexpressibly comic in those dark foreign
bushes. Seeing the pair of us watching, he gave the cob such
a pasting with his whip and his tongue, and drove off on
his rounds, back Hickling way.

Even better than cricket or eel-fishing was haymaking.
Our hay was cut by a pair of horses in a grass-mower. They
went out at three in the morning and stopped about ten,
when the heat of the day began. I think the summers were
better then than now, for I don't recall a difficult haymaking.
The hay was turned after a few days to dry some more in the
sun and then, without knocking it about as they do now, it
was ricked in the field it had been taken from. The ricks
were immediately thatched with reed. As soon as I was big
and strong enough I used to cut the hay from the rick as it
was wanted. I'd get on the south side in a niche I'd cut
halfway up. It was possible to be really warm there in mid-
winter, and to feel tangled with the bounty of nature.

I find myself, as I get old, remembering things I thought
to have gone for ever, ways of doing things that certainly
have gone, and attitudes of mind that have gone, and the
old Queen and the Royal Navy spread all over the world
keeping the Pax Britannica. What a shout of delight went

up among us (far from the sea though we were) when the Navy was mentioned, or the Brigade of Guards. You'd have thought we were a band of savages (and perhaps you think that in many ways we were).

3

Early Rides

I HAD my first ride, not counting du Maurier, our donkey, at the age of four. My father had a mealy-coated Irish hunter called Sinbad the Nailer. That horse was pigeon-toed, came from County Galway, and was the boldest, smartest ride across a country that ever was seen. He was roughish, for he had a mind of his own, and his mouth was one-sided because he'd been a hunt-servant's horse (and you know what they're like, good luck to them, jab, kick, bravest-of-the-brave) when he first carried me, and it happened like this.

Mother had me in the yard hanging on to her hand (Sam told me some years later) when I saw my father mounted on Sinbad and about to ride round the cattle, sheep, and out-lying horses. I set up a wailing as brats do, and when they told me to shut up and asked what was amiss I declared that I wanted to be up on top of Sinbah (as I called him, not then being able to get out a 'd'). So my father, laughing, scooped me up with one hand, shoved me in front of him on the crupper with a small cushion under me, and trotted off down the drive.

When you left our drive and crossed the single street of Hickling village, a line of gates and stiles climbed up to the Melton turnpike, probably eight or nine of them with grass fields in between. Father opened the first gate, but he didn't open another. He cantered on and jumped stile after stile with me held in front of him. I'd feel his body come forward and then see the stile swishing below Sinbad's hooves.

42

Imagine the delight any boy would feel at that. Boys enjoy scenic railways with their twists and sudden breath-catching descents. But you can't compare an old scenic railway with a real, live horse going over a stile. From that day I pestered for more of the same entertainment, and although my mother got up to all sorts of dodges to prevent it, my father was still jumping me about the farm in front of him when I was six or seven.

As for Sinbad the Nailer, I didn't hunt him till I was thirteen. He took some holding, and he was supposed to be touched in the wind, and therefore not to be trusted to a callow boy. I think my father actually loved that horse. It was the only one he wouldn't sell, and he used to declare he wouldn't sell him because he couldn't warrant him sound. To hunt him with the Quorn or the Belvoir was, I can tell you, an unforgettable experience. There was nothing that horse did not know or could not do, from hopping over a tricky one to galloping into a spread. His gallop was just a steady progression. But brave! I tell you if he'd been alive and kicking today he'd be up with those Yankee astronauts, examining the moon. (I doubt if he'd have thought much of it, though, no brooks, only craters, and how that horse enjoyed jumping a glint of water!) I know that when I left for the Army at the age of sixteen Sinbad was still being got up for hunting and going in the van, and he must have been five years older than I was. Touched in the wind indeed!

Before graduating to horses I rode du Maurier, sitting first in a basket saddle and towed by Miss Randall, and then sitting up more or less properly in a Champion & Wilton, and steering him on a snaffle, or driving him in a Raleigh car. My father had bought the Raleigh at the Royal Show. What a beauty! It was American (never tell me those people are not craftsmen) and it was made of hickory with lance-wood shafts that you could almost bend over each other. It had a corduroy back to the seat, and cushions of piped corduroy. You sat facing frontwards, and the reins ran out over a silver guard. In this exotic vehicle the donkey pulled me to the near meets. I was driving one of my sisters the first time I saw and heard hounds running from close at hand. We'd driven out on the Clawson road. Near our own covert, Sherbrooke's, we heard them coming in full voice and the horn in the background blowing Gone Away-ay-ay. The hounds crossed in front of us, maybe a dozen yards away. The donkey stood and flapped his huge ears, unafraid. We heard the field, galloping. The leaders took the fence into the lane just as they came to it, landed, collected, and legged their horses at the open ditch and fence on the far side, over and away. Sinbad and my father were at the back end of the thrusters' gang. He saw us sitting behind the donkey, who had begun to bray. My father's mouth opened but we couldn't hear his words. Sinbad soared over that ditch and fence. I remember the muscles gathering in his quarters. I think in those very young days I learned the lesson of fox-hunting, the great divider. It divides the brave from the mediocre, the skilled from the clumsy, the real enthusiast from the trumped-up case.

I wonder what sort of effect du Maurier had on our riding. I mean, let's face it, Sam, Mitchell, and myself turned into absolutely first-class nagsmen, able to tame most things and drive almost anything over almost anything. Yet we all of us had rocky beginnings with that donkey. He was all right with a saddle and bridle on when he was coming home. Going the other way was often difficult. He had a will of his own, and it was a will of steel. Bareback, none of us could stay long on him. My father used to amuse his friends by having the three of us take the donkey into Home Field, remove the bridle, and ride him. They'd have bets which would stay on longest. I always thought Mitchell the best runner and the best rough-rider of the three of us. He it was who found the answer. One day when Father had had a convivial luncheon party and the guests included that peer among dealers and livery keepers, Mr Harry Beeby of Melton Mowbray, we were told to lead out the donkey. Wagers were heavy. Normally the three of us rode du Maurier on these gladiatorial occasions in order of age, and as I came third and the edge had been taken off him by my two predecessors, I won more often than they. But that time Mitchell had gone round the corner when Sam was bucked off, so I took his place, and after a struggle was decanted. Mitchell then jumped on du Maurier *facing backwards*, one hand sunk in the wool on the animal's wither, the other in the wool on the quarters. He remained there, secure, until the donkey rubbed him off against a pear tree. I always reckoned it was a put-up job, because I found out afterwards that Mr Beeby had slipped Mitchell a fiver out of his winnings.

My first pony was a long-tailed Welsh mare standing thirteen hands. We called her Creamy, that being her colour, poor girl. She deserved a better name, for she carried most of us in sequence, went exceptionally well in harness, and was a trump with hounds. Clever! There can seldom have been her equal. You can't beat the Welsh pony blood. Driving from Nottingham to our place, once off the turnpike you went down a steep hill before Parson's Thorns, with some of our farm spread out below you. She would put her little hind legs together and *slide* down that long hill, allowing the weight of the trap to push her on, and only occasionally putting in a few pitter-pattering steps to hold her balance, rather like those funny short toe-runs you'll see skaters make. As a hunter she knew everything except patience and humility. I swear *she*, more than anyone else, taught me the thrill of the chase. She was a maniac. It was her life-stream. Like a first-class foxhound, she cared infinitely more for the sport than for her food. Talk about a fidget by the covert-side. Once she got going and her blood was aboil nothing would stop her, and mind you, I'm talking about Leicestershire. If an obstacle was too big to jump she could swim and climb and slither and even crawl through. I've been on her when she's perched on a bank and *bitten* her way through a bullfinch. Of course when they were galloping in a fast hunt she couldn't keep up. Once she and I were careering down the Grantham Canal towpath when Parson J. P. (Jeremiah) Seabrooke from Waltham-on-the-Wolds (about six miles from us and a favoured Wednesday Meet of the Belvoir) came seething up behind on a huge hunter.

'Clear the path, wretched child,' he roared. 'Or I'll ride you into the Brook Kerith.'

I pulled the pony off into the hedge and the Reverend tore past. No sense in taking chances with him when hounds ran. He was one of the thrusters in that flying hunt and the Quorn and the Cottesmore as well.

There aren't many parsons in England today, worse luck, like the Reverend Seabrooke, so I'd best say a few words about him. A manlier or a tougher gentleman you'd never see, and to meet his eye was like meeting the point of a sword. He was a member of the Belvoir Hunt Committee, and he was a Justice of the Peace and a bachelor to boot. Before Waltham he'd been in Aldershot, and had created a legend for himself, and also a pack of harriers, which he hunted. His turnout and performance in the hunting field were alike impressive. He wore a black cutaway coat, one of Stultz's I think, white cord breeches of the most incredibly wonderful line, pale-topped boots (the sort said to be dressed with champagne and apricot puré, but I expect he was more scientific, or ecclesiastical), and an elegant form of Messrs Lock's tall hat, with an extra curl to the brim. His moustaches, white in my youthful days, hung either side of his firm mouth like twin ice-cream cones. He was a man, and it was an honour to clear his path. I never heard him in church, but I often heard him beside a covert.

Another parson in the same hunt, was the Rev. F. M. P. Sheriffs of Caythorpe, near Grantham, and by golly, he went well and spoke well, and must have drawn many a sinner into God's fold. He'd come to the Belvoir from the Quorn, and loved to talk about the legendary huntsman, Tom Firr, possibly the greatest man across any country that ever lived. Mr Sherriffs had a way with boys. He was born in Dublin, his mind was supple, his sympathies were ready, and his speech was music. When hunting, he was a less formidable character than Parson Seabrooke, and not quite so elegant and well-mounted. But he was great all the same, and he went like a bomb. Goodness, since those days I've seen some parsons, and I've thought if only they could be more like those two courageous men.

Since I've mentioned the canal, I'd better explain that much of our local hunting was affected by it. The Grantham Canal wound across the vale from Nottingham to Grantham, and passed Hickling village close to the northward. Kaye Wood, where we had drawn that day, is a tight little place over the canal near Colston Bassett, where a neck of the Belvoir country runs into the South Notts, or Lord Harrington's as we knew it. If hounds ran across the canal, as they usually did, one normally made for the swing bridge, but some of the keener hands were in such a hurry they'd ride through the canal. They were in an extra fluster to get on because once the fox had crossed the canal you could bet your life he'd run the bank of the Smite for Kinoulton, next village into the Quorn country, and a neutral covert. If they pushed him through that, there would be a jumping festival over the pastures and up and across the Nottingham turnpike. . . . How did they get through the canal? In a few places you could ride until you came to the deep channel for the boats, then some horses would push off and swim across, which was a bit of all right. But others would just walk you downhill into the water, and then you had to duck, hold your breath, and hope your submerging wouldn't last too long.

*　　*　　*

When our pony Creamy began to get footy with the vast amount of roadwork she was asked to do, brave soul, we retired her and she produced eight foals in a row to thorough-bred stallions. Six of her foals made over sixteen hands, sold well, and went in the first flight in the best company in the world. Amazing that she got them so big.

Her fifth foal, a black gelding called Lazaretto, my father sold to our medico, Dr Swain. Lazaretto was a star, and I expect he was sent over to the doctor's stable at Clawson in settlement of a hefty bill. As the doctor rode about the country he had an amusing way of puffing out his cheeks, and he was for ever telling us to eat more rice pudding. 'It's better than all the coloured medicines in the world,' he would say. Doctors are very often endearing characters. He was. And when Dr Swain had reached his hundredth birth-day and the Belvoir hounds met at Long Clawson, the Prince of Wales visited him and gave him a present, a bottle of vintage champagne.

I had no more ponies after Creamy except ones that my brothers and I were breaking for other people or to sell. By the age of eight I'd graduated to horses. I remember being put on a big blood mare, between two others. My father was leading (mounted) on the near side, and George Smith on the off. They held her steady like anchors when she drove into her bridle. After some time, perhaps a whole, long morning, she settled, and they unbuckled the leading reins.

'She's all yours, Howard.'

She behaved. . . . I was highly strung, but my father taught me not to be nervous of horses, that almost every one of them had its key, and that when they misbehaved there was always a reason—usually some stupidity or clumsiness in handling. Father taught me how a horse should look and how a man, or woman, should look on him. He taught me it was the feel that mattered, the balance, the pulse, and that when you decide to be firm with any horse you must, for his own sake, be very firm. He was an artful teacher. Then I was lucky in having Sam and Mitchell ahead of me, both

J. H. Marshall's mother and father: Mrs Mary Elizabeth Marshall
and Mr Samuel Thomas Marshall—Sam Marshall of Hickling
(*by kind permission of Mrs Catherine A. Dennett*)

The Marshall children at Hickling Manor in 1904. Howard is standing on the back of the Raleigh cart, Mitchell is on the left and Sam at the head of du Maurier, the donkey. Creamy, now an old

as mad about horses as I was myself. . . . A boy can learn nearly everything just by watching and listening.

A great English skier called Bracken, Bill Bracken I think, once sat with me at Olympia in the horse lines and told me about a little consumptive English boy who was sent to Mürren in Switzerland for his health. For long months he had no strength to move on or from a wooden balcony. He watched the skiers flash by, some of them Swiss boys of his own age. At last the doctor told the boy he might try to walk a few steps. What did he do? He hired himself some skis, and he went off on them as though he had been born with them on his feet. He'd learned the trick, the pulse of the thing, by all those avid hours of watching. Walk? he could do better than that. And incidentally, the sport saved his life.

When I was ten I broke and backed my first hunter, a seventeen-hands black gelding called Othelloric, aged five and up to fifteen stone. That was the year we foaled Lord Lyon, too. I'd watched Sam and Mitchell breaking, and couldn't wait to try, and it was easy. I mouthed him and all the rest in a box, got him accustomed to harness, drove him in a breaking-cart about our paddock and then on the farm roads, backed him, schooled him, and got him fencing smoothly. Father sold him straight away for £280 to a cotton-bobbin wallah who hunted with the Meynell.

At the beginning of each summer holidays Father would say, 'You've any number to break, lads. You can use the ten-acre paddock and the traps in the corner. Take what you can get from the owners unless they've settled with me, as they should by rights. If an owner'll give you a fiver or a tenner or even fifty quid for breaking, so much the better. If he gives nothing, say nothing, but let me know at once. All I ask is, break horses. Don't break harness, and don't break shafts. And keep 'em on the grass. Shoes cost money.' Then he'd leave the three of us to get on with it, and an astonishing number of horses went through our hands. Now and then, usually when we imagined him to be far from Hickling, he'd appear and criticise everything we were doing. He liked to bring a couple of buckets of sawdust and make driving marks on the grass. 'Back him, Howard, till your wheels exactly cross this line,' he might say. 'Exactly. You're over. That's no good. Now stop. I mean stop when I say it, not in a week's time.'

One market day I'd gone to fetch Father from Broughton Station with a blood mare in harness that was more than a bit quick. As his train came in she did some fancy rearing in the shafts, and when he came out of the station she was standing right on end. He made for her head at once, and calmed her. When we'd moved the seat back he took the reins and fairly swept the mare along the top Nottingham turnpike, which was a mass of carts and wagons going to or from market. She didn't behave too well, and he was short-tempered with her and inclined to snarl at me. When we reached the gated Hickling road the mare was driving into her collar at last. I jumped out, opened the gate, shut it, and sprinted after them to get in over the tailboard.

'Come on. Run!' he shouted over his broad shoulder, trying to pacify his mare, and more interested in her than in me. I got a foot on the step, but I couldn't do it without a spill. I dropped back, gasping for breath. 'Run, when I tell you, you tortoise,' he said angrily. 'She won't wait, and no more will I.'

'I can't run any more.'

'Then we must leave you.' And so he did.

I ran down the footpath that cut across a neck of land, but as I got near the road again he streaked past, beating me by seventy yards. I thought I'd pay them out. If I failed to turn up at home they'd send out a search party, suddenly realising how useful and precious I was to them. I hung about in the woods for an hour or more and then strolled down to Hickling, where I called on the Roses and had tea with them. The elder daughter was called Lily Rose, which seemed a bit daft, but she really was charming and very pretty. Her father, the runner, was a tall, gaunt man who walked with an exaggerated swing of the arms. He must have been a goodish age then. He still practised jump-off starts, and even Mitchell couldn't hold him for the first thirty yards or so. Shortly before dinner I crept into our house by one of the back entrances, tidied myself in our room, and appeared in the dining-room just when my father was about to say grace. It must have been four hours since he left me stranded, yet nobody paid the slightest attention to me. I suppose he'd told them I was sulking. . . . Their indifference taught me a lesson every child should learn, but not many do.

*   *   *

Were I given a guinea for every hour I spent driving my father or being driven by him I'd now have some money laid by (perhaps). Much of his business at Melton was done sociably in the Harboro', the George, or the Bell. I never went into those places with him, but he knew he could usually find me in Mr Harry Beeby's livery yard.

'You're to make haste, Master Howard, Mr Marshall says. See to the mare's feet and to the gig, and bring 'em and yourself straight round to the Bell,' said the boots, with an air of self-importance.

'Her feet,' Mr Beeby said. 'What's Sam up to now then?'

The roads were still loose-surfaced. It was fairly common for a horse to pick up a stone. We all carried hoof picks as a matter of routine, and the moment a horse went a bit unsound we stopped him and looked for the trouble. When I drove Kit, the American mare, to the doors of the Bell Hotel a crowd was gathered there, and my father came forward at once.

'Now listen. I've wagered I'll drive to Leicester in under the hour carrying one passenger. I won't find anyone lighter than you; are you game? That's all right then. Just wanted to sort it out in case we spill and your mama starts beefing.

51

Have you looked everything over? Good.' He hardly glanced
at the mare and the straight-shafted Lawton gig. 'We leave
at the first stroke of two,' he said. 'The other parties to the
wager catch the two-six train, and will be waiting by
Leicester clock tower, where we finish.'

We took our places. He lit a cigar and pulled on his
wash-leather gloves. The clock struck and we were off,
trotting rapidly out of Melton. It's fifteen·miles from there
to Leicester and the last four of them, downhill from Syston,
were tricky driving for anyone in a hurry. The horse-drawn
trams could block you, and their rails were a dangerous
hazard. Our American mare had a queer gait. She went
cloppety-clop, cloppety-clop, cloppety-clop, clop, with a
kind of a jig to it. If you took a slight pull at her and then
let her go she'd dash on with redoubled purpose, and she was
always full of hard oats and beans, and fit for anything.
Then nobody could shoe them better and trimmer than
Alwyn Shelton of Hickling.

We flew to Syston. The hill dropped in front of us, the
tramlines gleaming, the granite sets dark and greasy. After
a major and daring swerve round two trams at the top he
put one wheel between the lines and sent her right into her
collar. He sat quite still, smiling into his moustaches, enjoying
every minute of it, his eyes dancing but all else frozen, save
his hands, giving gently to her mouth. Would she hold us
straight? If the wheel went into a tramline we were done.
Whew! But the American mare had luck to match her nerve.
We reached the clock tower at eight minutes to three. I
walked her about to cool her, and washed her mouth out,
while all of them settled the business end of it. I wondered
what my mother might have said if she could have seen the
three of us tearing down Syston hill.

I've always been discreet. Even at that age I had enough
sense to keep mum about Father's wager when we got home.

Now *there* (speaking of the one who really won the wager,
for what did either of us do but sit still and pray?) was a

mare that earned her keep. Didn't she do some work for us? She was never out of the shafts, never off the road, never sick, never sorry, a good doer and a flyer. Father had got her in a swapping deal with a big rubicund gentleman named Harrison, who lived at Saxondale, between Nottingham and Newark. He hunted with Lord Harrington's, but enjoyed a day with the Quorn when they met his side of the country. And then he'd drop in at Hickling for tea or a dram, and perhaps on occasion to do some horse trading. One such day as we rode home from the hunt Father said to me, 'Take Mr Harrison into the house when he's put up his horse and see he gets tea or coffee or anything else he may fancy. I'll be with him directly, but I must stop here a minute or two and have a word with the vicar.'

Mr Harrison put his horse in one of our boxes, took off his hat, and walked slowly round the stables, running his eye over every inmate.

'What's this one?' he asked, stopping dead before Robin Dudley, a grand-looking horse who refused when he tired.

'Sorry, Mr Harrison. I know nothing of him.'

He walked slowly on and stopped to look at Alexandria, a cream-coloured, well-made, well-set-up gelding aged eight. None of us had yet discovered how to stop him once he got galloping. 'What's this one, Howard? By Jupiter! he looks a good sort.'

'He does, doesn't he? Sorry, he's been here some little time, but I can't say I've had anything at all to do with him.'

He stopped again, this time in front of Fleet Street, a raking, generous sort of hunter for whom my father confidently and justifiably expected an extremely high price. 'What a picture!' said he. 'Here's one up to weight that looks as though he could gallop.'

'Best-looking hunter we have,' I agreed. 'I haven't had a ride on him yet, though I did hear someone speak very well of him.'

'Is he for sale?'

'They didn't say.'

'How long have you had him here and where did he come from?'

'I wish I could answer your questions, Mr Harrison, but I just don't know the answers. My father will be here in a few minutes.'

At last, having looked at every horse, he consented to come into the house. He stopped in the yard, fishing in the small pocket of his hunting coat. 'Here's half-a-crown, Howard, for saying, "I don't know." You won't go far wrong in life if you keep that up.'

Our father had drilled us all carefully in stable tactics, or whatever you choose to call it. 'Don't go blabbing to anyone, *anyone*, about the horses, d'you hear me? It's easy enough to say, "I don't know." And anyway, nine times out of ten you *don't* know.'

There was always an assortment of show traps and gigs in the coach house below our bedroom as well as a brougham for my mother's use in bad weather, a nice-looking curricle with a pole for a pair, and a drag. Many a hilarious drive we had in the drag, to or from hunting. And one was not so hilarious. The drag with Thomas Goodburn, the coachman, went off one evening to Widmerpool Station to pick up the hunting party. I was not one of them, I was away at school. Anyway, the party was in great spirits, and on the way home the drag ran over a heap of stones at the verge and overturned. Several of them were injured, and one man was killed, a nasty business. There had to be a coroner's court, but the accident was held to have been an act of God.

We had two ways of getting about. We rode or we drove. Horses were as natural to us as our feet and hands. When Mr Otho Paget brought his beagles up to us from Thorpe Satchville Hall, or Lady Lonsdale brought hers from Oakham, we never dreamed (unless the ground was iron-hard with frost or deep in snow) of following them on foot. We rode after them—though it was rare in that favoured country, where you could hunt the fox six days a week, to bother with any old beagles.

My father was one of the best shots in the county, and I went through a craze for that sport. Most country boys go through it, and some never get over it. In the old days when we had an Empire the residue of the gun-hungry ones could join the forces and have the prospect of bigger targets. I'd keep a shotgun in the trap, and I had a mare so sensible to drive that I'd leave her to potter along the road on her own while I beat round the hedge-rows and had the odd shot.

One morning I was driving Father to Broughton Station. As usual he was filling me up with orders, as though pouring them into a jug. 'I want you to do that, do you hear, Howard? Not anybody else, you. If anything goes wrong with that mare I hold you personally responsible. Understood?' (Very often he had asked another party to do it too.) As we neared the station he happened to look round and, with a compensatory movement, shifted one foot astern. With that foot he felt a hard object under the carpet. What a suspicious character he was? He bent down at once and pulled up my gun.

'I've spoken to you twice about this before,' he said in sultry tones. 'It won't do, my man. . . . One day you may be old enough and rich enough to have the sense to shoot only your own game and that of your friends by invitation. But if I let you shoot now, you wild varmit, you'll get yourself a name and you'll make trouble with neighbours. I'm impounding this weapon' (waving my dear old twelve-bore in the air) 'for your own good and mine.'

He could not, however, take the gun with him to Lincoln, so he left it with the station master. I stood by the train while he leaned out of an open window, talking, talking. 'Get Shelton to look at the new roan's feet. Tomorrow I'll ride Prince of Denmark, leaving home (tell Hibbert) just before ten. You'll come, and Sam, on Danny Dicer and

Borax. Second horses: Pinkerton, Silas Levy, and Andromeda
Mia. Got it? . . .' Strings of names, strings of orders. 'Oh,
and another thing, Howard. . . .' But the train was heaving
itself away, with slow puffs.

As I unhitched the mare the station master opened his
office window. 'Pssst!' I went over. 'Mr Marshall left me
your gun, Master Howard, to keep safe till he gets back late
tonight.' A long pause. 'You got any cartridges on you?'

'Yes.'

'To fit this gun?' He took the gun from a cupboard and
gave it to me. 'Step this way, I'll show you the shot of a lifetime. There's a covey keeps coming into my garden. Part-
ridges, see? They're in the pathway now. If you crawl
carefully to that bank and sight down the path you'll near
get the whole bang-jing.'

I did as he suggested, lay flat to the ground and drew a
bead through the tussocks. The birds were approaching in
two files, like soldiers. I fired twice, and (I'm ashamed to say)
killed sixteen out of seventeen. My accomplice helped me
pick them up. 'Best give me the gun back, Master Howard.
Here's four brace for you and four for me. When Mr Sam
sees the birds he'll relent about your having the odd pop, I
know he will.'

He knew wrong. When my father came home that night
there was hell to pay.

'Howard, come into the hall.' In the half-dark of the hall,
beside the rack of whips and cutting whips, he gave me a
dressing down, and he did it well. I had disobeyed him. He
was going to sell the gun and give the proceeds to the building
fund of Hickling Church. He did not care whether I ever
shot again, and as a matter of fact I never have, seriously.
He pointed out that I ought to be too busy to get up to
mischief. In summer, apart from hay and harvest, the water
tanker had to be taken round fields that had no brook, the
tubs of the store cattle had to be topped up with linseed cake,
the ewes were always in bother with foot trouble or the fly,

and there were horses (including Stella and her foal) to be ridden, doctored, schooled, broken, sold. In winter there was hunting, and in summer work and cricket. What more did I want, my father inquired. . . . And also, when I was little more than ten years old, there was school.

I was packed off as a boarder to Trent College, a grey cliff of a place across the Derbyshire border. Life there was a considerable penance. I had become geared to working on my own. Such of my two elder brothers' society as had been forced on me had made me wary of other boys. Because of my riding abilities, which were known in the school, I was regarded as something of a freak. I think the masters resented that (horse) side of my life, whereas the boys were amused, and in favour of it.

As an English schoolboy I was a bad bet. I can't wonder that my term times were merely sentences to be worked off before the Hickling holidays came again (when I would work ten times as hard, but at things I wanted to do). In my second year at Trent I won both the junior and the open high jump, beating the head of the school into second place. I had beaten my seniors with great reluctance, but the Headmaster at once called me into his study and gave me a dissertation upon the dangers of 'swollen head'. I was then twelve, and I thought him an ass, for I was a polite, shy, and nervous boy, and I was so very bad at the rougher sports such as football and boxing that a petty success in something so ordinary as the high jump was unlikely to swell my head. . . . Everyone, after all, goes to one school or another, and I don't think of my schooldays as important either to me or to anybody else. I'll round them off with a description of the last memorable episode in them:

It was the year that Mr James de Rothschild's St Amant, ridden by Kempton Cannon (not alas by my American friend, Danny Maher) won the Epsom Derby in a snowstorm. Yes, a snowstorm in June, freak weather, and it was even worse, of course, up north in Derbyshire with a wind growling round

the walls of Trent College. Six of us in G Dormitory had
subscribed three shillings and fourpence each. I had taken
the pound to old Kipling, who·did the boots, asking him to
get it on St Amant to win with Messrs Hibbert & Heap, a
Nottingham firm of bookmakers who had a branch office
at Long Eaton, near the college.

'You're on,' Kipling whispered to me at the noon break.
'Sixes. But he won't win.'

I made no reply, thinking that if St Amant failed no feelings need be hurt. When he *did* win, brave little horse, and
it was clear that Messrs Hibbert & Heap owed us seven
pounds (which then seemed a colossal sum), my co-investors
were unanimous that it would be putting unfair temptation
in Kipling's path to allow him to collect. Boys are suspicious
creatures, and riches defile. As the horsey member of the
syndicate, I was chosen to collect our winnings. The others
would cover up for me while I missed chapel and supper,
and would see to it that one of the big sash windows of the
form rooms on the ground floor was propped open for my
return to college. It was to be the second window on the
right as you faced the main doorway. I got out of it, and the
others closed it gently behind me. From a potting shed I
took a couple of potato sacks to wrap round the barbed
wire of the perimeter fence so that I could edge through it.

The night was horrible, black, wet, and hugely windy.
I got through the wire (my nickname at school was Squirma
Marshall), crossed the canal on the funny little dog-legged,
lock-keeper's bridge, made straight for the house of the
bookmaker's clerk, and rang the bell. He opened the door.
At first he didn't want to let me in. It was my youth that
plagued him.

'We're a reputable firm,' he kept saying. 'We're an honest
firm. You could get me shopped, you could. We don't do
business with squirts.'

'You accepted our bet through the College boot-man. You
knew perfectly well whose money it was. Now you must

settle or take the consequences. There are five others involved
and their parents are important people in Nottingham and
Derbyshire. My father knows everyone in the Midlands who
has to do with horses. You'll never hear the end of it if you
welsh.'

He kept me on tenderhooks for quite a while.

'You ought to be tucked up in bed. How did you get here?'
he asked.

'Climbed out of College and crossed the canal.'

'Lord Almighty!' Then he asked me to swear that if
discovered with the money I'd never say it came from him
or his firm. I swore it. He got out a small chamois-leather
bag and counted seven gold sovereigns from a wall safe
into it. The sight made me feel faint. 'What's the matter?'
he asked, looking closely at·me. 'You're devilish pale. Have a
snifter of whisky. That'll put you to rights.'

I'd never been nearer whisky before than on farmers'
breaths or lying about unwanted on sideboards. The taste was
vile. How could people swallow such stuff? Much of it trickled
down my chin and over my coat as I coughed and spluttered.
We shook hands, and he let me out into a turmoil of wind
and rain. I ran as fast as I could, tremendously uplifted by
my success with the money. When I came to the lock I
slipped on the sodden, greasy timber and all but fell into the
basin, which happened to be empty, and would have made
an enormous tomb. I'd crossed the canal and was on the
towpath, going alongside the school's barbed fence, when I
heard a strange, loud splashing, I don't know what it can
have been. I ran on and, in the darkness, missed my two
sacks. I stopped, dared not go back, and there and then
tackled the fence with its barbed-wire overhangs. I cut my
hands and tore my suit getting to the top, and when I was
trying to work out how to descend safely I was blown off
balance by the wind and rain, got caught up, and fell to the
ground inside the perimeter bit by bit with a noise of rending cloth. I lay on the sodden ground panting. First thought,

my bag of gold. 'Here it is.' I felt no breakages and my cuts were superficial. Springing to my feet, I galloped up to the school. Yes, they'd propped the window open with a piece of board. I jumped, caught the sill, pulled myself up. And then my right hand slipped on the wet wood, my shoulders twisted, knocking away the prop, and the huge sash came down like a guillotine, pinning me across the back of the neck. Not a move could I make, beyond taking most of the weight of my body with my arms. (I was able to get my hands through under the sash.) My situation could hardly have been more compromising. To sum up: there I was, trapped and longing for discovery, covered in mud and blood, stinking of whisky, my clothes severely torn, and a bag of illicit sovereigns in my trouser pocket.

My groans and howls alerted an elderly night watchman. He carried me to Matron's room, and woke her. Matron, not at all a bad sort and devilish handsome, had him carry me to the infirmary, where she dressed my cuts, doped me, took off all my clothes, and put me to bed in a single room with a cup of bouillon and some dry rusks.

By jove, the school was abuzz the following morning! Patrols of masters were out round the pubs and haunts of vice (apparently those existed, though I never knew them) trying to trace my movements of the night before. There was a conspiracy of silence. The Head had decided that the good name of the college was the first consideration. I was to be kept on my own until the doctor would allow them to obtain or flog the truth out of me.

In G Dormitory they were frantic. What had become of me? Why were all those masters snooping and asking stupid questions about women and drink? Where was the St Amant money? Had Kempton Cannon done his stuff in vain? My absence was glossed over by all those in authority; that could only mean that they had me incarcerated. Sooner or later they would break me down. Then all in the dormitory would be for it.

After eleven o'clock on the second night I was roused by Matron and taken in my camelhair dressing-gown to the Head's study, where she left me after giving my arm a squeeze that I suppose was meant to be reassuring. He sat not at his usual desk but at a side table. I was told to sit opposite him, with my back to the door. On the table lay a cane, dark and oily-looking, as though soaked in human blood, and also a small heap of sovereigns, which he kept turning over, relishing the feel of gold.

'This your money, Marshall?'

'Some of it, if it was taken from my pocket.'

'Where did you steal it? . . . Answer when you are spoken to. . . . Where did you steal it? . . . Well? . . .' He took out his pocket-watch, looked carefully into its face, stroked the taped handle of the cane with his fingers, and said, 'I shall give you exactly three minutes to come out with the truth.'

I found my tongue. 'I'll never tell you, never. You'll never find out from me.'

'Never find out, *Sir*,' he corrected me. 'Come, come. You have not been a satisfactory member of the school. But with your plunge into debauchery you seem to have lost such rudiments of good manners as you formerly possessed. Tell me, when did you first take to drinking whisky?'

I turned over in my head his assumption that I was a thief when I'd only been collecting what belonged to me and my friends, and his dirty trick of hauling me out of bed at nearly midnight, when I was propping my eyes from sleep. Soon I began to shake with rage, a most unusual condition with me. I picked a heavy leather-bound book from the shelves behind me and flung it with all my strength and fury at the gas light above his head. He gave a cry and the light went out. I opened the door, slammed it behind me, and ran, not back to the infirmary, but to G Dormitory, where I jumped into my bed and pulled the sheets over my head.

Soon I became aware of a friendly twittering round the bed. The dormitory was in ferment. A council of war was held when I'd simmered down. The five of them decided to stand by me through anything and take my part against the authorities. Each would swear if asked that I'd acted on the room's behalf, and had not behaved dishonestly or dishonourably. It was all very highfaluting and inspiring. Each was also pledged, since I had given my word to the bookie, never to divulge where the money had come from. . . . All those fine resolutions, which comforted me at the time and restored my faith in human nature, proved unnecessary. No move was made by authority, either against me or against the dormitory. All the same, I was glad that that was officially my last term. I was sixteen, and was to go into the cavalry. I cannot think why my school experiences had not shown me that the Army was an unpromising field for my endeavours. Boys are dense, and should be given much help by their parents.

One morning at breakfast during the ensuing summer I saw my father open the long envelope that I knew held the Trent College accounts and reports.

'Surly and violent at times!' he exclaimed. 'They call him surly and violent.'

'Call whom?' asked my mother.

'Howard, who else? Then here's another queer do: the college is never too ready to give anything away, yet they've credited me with seven pounds against the fees, and they write it off as a refund against an overcharge last term. . . . But there was no overcharge. It beats me. . . .'

'That money's mine,' I said. 'Or part of it is. They tried to make me say I stole it. They'll never know how or where I came by it.'

'Hoity-toity, won't they now?' When my father used that tone you had to be careful. 'That's a fair bit of money. So if I give you my word here, in front of your mother and several of your brothers and sisters, that I won't pass on any information you may give me, well, I think you'll out with it.'

'I will, I will,' I cried. 'And if the Head had put the

question to me that way it might have been difficult. He made it easier to keep my word because he set about me with insults and accusations.'

'To keep your word? Who to?'

'Why, to Hibbert & Heap.'

'*Hibbert & Heap!*'

'*Bookmakers!*' my mother said. 'You wicked boy.'

'The Derby,' I said. 'St Amant. The six of us in G Dormitory had a pound on at sixes.'

'Sixes on St Amant,' my father said. 'You did well, and you shall have your winnings, Howard. Be off now, all of you. I'll see you three boys in the yard in ten minutes.'

I stood outside when I'd closed the door behind me. My father was laughing. My mother was silent. Not a cheep out of her.

4

Foxhunting

WE three boys first went to London in the summer of 1900.

My father, in the Duke of Portland's sale at Welbeck, bought a hunter stallion called Sundorne, and as no quick deal with the horse seemed likely in the Midlands he thought to have a go with him at the Hunters' Improvement Society show in the Agricultural Hall, Islington. I don't know why, but he sent us three boys (aged, twelve, thirteen, and fourteen) down south with the stallion. Perhaps he thought each would keep the others in order on that interminable train journey. Perhaps he just wanted us out of the house. And guess what orders were given us.

'When you reach St Pancras—that's the big London station you've heard me speak of—just look out for old Sandy.'

None of us had been in London before. We were due to arrive after dark. But—'Just look out for old Sandy'. I don't know what Sandy's age would be then. Neither old nor young, I suppose. He was, when he put his mind to it, a good man with brood mares, but restless. He'd come up to Hickling about March and foal a few mares. As soon as Lincoln and Liverpool races were due, he vanished. If he did well at those meetings we saw no more of him that year. If he did badly he'd usually come back to us until the racing came local again, at Leicester and Warwick. A gem of a man but hardly, one would have thought, the most reliable guide to London.

It was after midnight when our goods train stopped in

LEFT: J. H. Marshall schooling Miss Muriel Dunn's 'Grey Mist', champion polo pony at Madison Square Garden (*by kind permission of Mrs C. M. Marshall*). RIGHT: Mr Godfrey Preece on 'Dr Garnier' in 1912 (*New York Times*)

J. H. Marshall on 'The Jumping Mare'
(*by kind permission of Mrs C. M. Marshall*)

Woolwich Department for Demobilisation. 'One second later and they would
have been in step' (*by kind permission of Mrs C. M. Marshall*)

some outer tentacle of St Pancras. In the gas lights' flicker we saw Sandy's face beyond the railings, and soon he was with us, accompanied by two dreadful-looking men in cloth caps who dragged a handcart. Sandy entered our box, and with a lot of hissing and murmuring made friends with our highly-sexed companion. Soon the pair emerged, Sandy apparently in control, and we walked out into the streets, the horse and his leader followed by the two ruffians dragging the corn and forage and rugs and our one small, Gladstone bag, and us three bringing up the rear and staring around us. This, then, was London, very dark, and smelling of soot and horses. Sandy led briskly up the hill, and after a mile and a half's walk we came to the Agricultural Hall. Never in my life, not even at Ypres, did I hear such a bedlam. Stallions and mares were whinnying and shrieking, all strangers and far from home in an iron, alien, and echoing vault. We slept with the horse in his box. In the morning we were working on him, getting him ready for showing and he and all three of us in a high state of nerves, when warm-hearted Mr Harry Gale hove up, well dressed and thoroughly in his element.

'Now then, you yoong Marshalls,' he said. 'Have ye got him all plaited oop, nicely fed and coomfortable in his toomy?'

Sam, as the oldest, said we couldn't get his plaits done to our liking. He was a tall horse. We took turns of standing with needle and thread on an upturned bucket, and each time he saw us getting to the end of a plait he flung us off. He wasn't a boy's horse. No stallion is.

'I'll hold him,' Mr Gale said at once. 'And when the four on us have him doone, I'll take him in and win the show for you. How's that?' What a relief that was to us!

Sundorne won a premium that day. He went to Mr Mumford, under whose ownership he travelled Leicestershire and covered some good mares, among them a Bendigo mare belonging to our friend and cousin the Melton farmer and gentleman rider, Dick Black. The resulting foal was called

E

Sunlock, and was nothing to look at, a leggy animal with four white socks.

It must have been in my last year at Hickling that Mitchell began to hunt Sunlock as a three-year-old. I suppose Dick Black was schooling one of their other horses, or had hurt himself either hunting or racing. I always remember Mitchell coming home from a day on him with the Cottesmore.

'I'll never ride another young horse like that one,' he said at dinner.

'Looked a bit of a camel to me,' said my father, who'd also been hunting, 'though I'll admit he was there at the end and we had some tidy fences.'

'He'd shoot into his fences and then seemed to have all the time in the world,' Mitchell insisted. 'And he landed as though on springs. I've been on good horses. I say that's a great young one.'

'Have it your own way,' Father said, disbelieving.

Dick Black won the farmers' race at the Melton Hunt meeting on him in 1913 and then, when Dick had gone off to France with his yeomanry regiment, Sunlock won the Grand National ridden by C. V. Smith. Sunlock broke his leg finally, racing at Sandown Park, and that was the end of him. As for C. V. Smith, he turned up again for us because he saved Mitchell's life by putting a tourniquet on his wounded leg under fire on the Somme. C.V.S., as we called him, afterwards broke his neck in a steeplechase. It's a great life, and it can be a short one.

*   *   *

W. Payne had one of the several liveries in Melton. He was an extra good old-fashioned horsemaster, and he had the loveliest stable yard imaginable, a yard that put thirty guineas on the value of any horse in it. When we were chock-a-block at Hickling we often sent a horse along to Payne's for breaking or schooling, or just tidying up. Most of such work was done, and well done, by Mr Payne's

66

homme de confiance, Podgy. Mr Payne also did funerals, and one day a hearse drove into our stable yard with two coal-black Belgian horses pulling it and two men in black (one of them Podgy) on the box.

'I'd have thought you'd have more sense than to bring that charnel outfit near my stables,' said my father, who was superstitious. 'Who've you been planting?'

'Squire Knowles of Colston.'

'What! R. S. Knowles is dead and I never knew it. I should have been there.'

'He's dead all right, else we shouldn't have planted him. Now, sir, I've come to get your green young horse and, as the young lady said to her mother-in-law at the wedding, "Take a good look at him afore he leaves this 'ere, for he'll never look the same again." '

A few weeks later when we arrived at Melton Show we saw Podgy slow-cantering a superb bay with a well-trimmed tail and the smoothest of actions. So thorough a job had been done that my father, of all people, failed to recognise the horse until Podgy rode up close behind him and said, 'Are you taking the ride, Mr Marshall, or shall I win on him for you?'

'Dang me, Podgy, you caught me out! Is that him then?' He got on, felt the youngster's mouth, and swung him off to win a strong farmers' class. That bay horse could gallop, and there never was a better man than my father to show a galloping hunter. He'd push them round against the rail just as fast as they could go. He always won on his gallop. If one of us boys was showing he'd yell from outside the ring, '*Send him on!*' The judges used to look around them, wondering what's up. In my opinion he overdid it, going on like that at a boy on a great strong well-fed hunter in a small ring. If you get one that's catching hold and he becomes un-balanced going into a tight corner on slippery turf and goes over the rail, he's going to hurt himself and maybe some spectators too. We said nothing and did our best. But he'd

be at you the second you left the ring. 'You didn't go half
fast enough for that horse. Dawdling round like a girl. Next
time you show one, gallop him, or never call yourself a son
of mine.'

*   *   *

It wasn't unusual for my father to buy a dozen hunters in
the Saturday sale at Wade, Sheppard, and Warner's Repository. He'd leave them standing there over Sunday and roll
up at Leicester on Monday morning in a drag filled with
men, boys, and saddles. When we'd got the strange horses
saddled, off we'd stream up the tramlines to Syston, making
for the Quorn meet. The horses were all warranted—he
never bought one that was not. We were proving them. If
they were unsound, or bad hunters, back to Leicester they
went, the Saturday deal nulled.

At 2 p.m. we'd rendezvous with him at some prearranged
place out in the country, possibly at a crossroads or on a
bridge or outside an inn. Not only would he know everything
about the horse he rode, he'd have an accurate opinion about
each of ours.

'You take that one straight back to the Repository,
Tommy, he's no good to us.'

'How'll I get home, Mr Marshall?'

'Never bother your head about that, son, we'll fetch you
somehow. Push on now, and no more hunting, mind.'
Tommy rode off, none too pleased. 'I've *sold* yours, Howard.
No bother, was he?'

'No, Father.'

'Nice easy fencer?'

'Not too bad.'

'Hack him on home, then. Give him to Hibbert. Tell him
he's sold to Colonel Blakely. When you've had your tea
and Hibbert's had time to make a job of the horse, ride him
on to the colonel's place, Quatre Bras.' (It was 2.15. We
were nine miles from home, which was another twelve from
Quatre Bras.) 'That's a valuable animal, Howard.' (One

wondered how much extra value he had accrued between Saturday and Monday.) 'Don't knock him about. Use up all your time. Go on all the grass you can find. Don't clatter him on the road, and remember, tell Hibbert to take trouble, and the colonel's one of the best, a payer on the nail. A nailer. Anyway, I'll probably be home before you leave for Quatre Bras.' (That was a favourite trick of his, to be imminent, to keep us saying to ourselves, He'll be here any minute.)

* * *

I was riding the sold horse through the night on the second leg of his journey to the buyer. I could see the glow of Leicester reflected in the cloud layer. All about the black, knobbled surface of the earth were fireflies, the lanterns of carriages and traps. In the loneliness of the night I was governed by my father's will and my own sense of duty, nursing the horse—he had had a very long day—smoothing his mane. A strong trotter came up astern. It was one of our gigs, sent to take me home, and the driver was furious.

'Good God! Are you only this far? You aim to keep me outdoors all night? Trot on then, damn you!'

'You give me that gig,' I said. 'You can walk this horse on for a change.'

'Not me. I'm going to the Bras. Shake that old file up or I'll leave for Hickling without you.'

He wouldn't dare. I rode on slowly, stubbornly.

When we got home my father was asleep by the dying fire in the morning room. 'Hungry?' He asked me.

'Yes, a bit.'

'Grab some cold pheasant and ham and murphies in the larder and get to bed. It's late. We'll talk at breakfast.' It was hard to please him. I think that he was trying to make us resourceful and independent. I call that kind of parent more unselfish than the type that cossets children, currying their favour. He looked quite different, sitting there in the small hours, older and bald. But if he'd been a hunchback with three eyes (come to think of it he did have three eyes) he'd still have had control of me. We had heard that when young he was very gay, yet to us he seemed almost inhuman except for his love of sport. He told us it was ridiculous to go gallivanting in owl-time, as he put it. When we wanted to stop out late, perhaps for some distant dance or party, we'd lay horse rugs on the Staffordshire bricks of the yard so that he wouldn't hear us drive out, and we would do the same when we came home.

*　　*　　*

Among the mounted foxes' masks and brushes on the walls at Hickling were many sketches by Basil Nightingale, the sporting artist, another friend of Father's. Nightingale was then celebrated, and he (or rather his work) will certainly be so again. He lived in Melton, and we mounted him when we hunted in our vicinity, for he was a dear, and we all loved him. He'd come to the nursery or the day nursery and ask us what animal we liked best, and draw it straight on the wall, and there it stayed.

Later on, when I was already a fledgling, he was having a day with the Quorn. They met at our place. Hounds had split in the afternoon hunt, my father going with one lot and Basil with the other. Time passed. Everyone was safely home except the painter.

'Where's Basil then?' Father kept asking. 'Has nobody seen Mr Nightingale. Meg Merrilees is a patent safety, though I wish now I'd put him on Sinbad.'

As it happened, Basil had taken a header into a brook. Merrilees had floundered in, and got herself wedged. Luckily her head was above water, but it took him a long time to get her out, and then longer to find his way back to our place in the dark, his hunting boots full of slime.

'Where did it happen?' he was asked when he'd been togged out in dry clothes and was getting some hot food inside him. He tried to describe the place, but lacked the born foxhunter's bump of locality and memory for names. 'I could draw it though,' he said. Out came the pencil, and on the damask table cloth with his 3B Venus he drew a brook, the side of a small wood, and part of a house beyond.

'Jericho!' my father exclaimed. 'I should've known it. The banks are hollow there for some way either side of your ducking, my friend.'

*   *   *

When the Quorn met at our house there was a full cask of ale set up in the yard and a table of eatables, while indoors more luxurious foods and drinks of many kinds were laid out. Our nearest Belvoir meet was at Mother's village, Clawson. I think we must have hunted about equally with the two packs.

Until I was ten the great Earl of Lonsdale was Master of the Quorn. He was an extraordinary person, a man's man, a lady's man, and a nobleman who was equally at home in his rightful places or among the so-called dregs of society. He sent us a brace of pheasants and a haunch of venison every Christmas. As for Lady Lonsdale, she knew the name and Christian name of every farmer's wife in the Quorn, yes, and the names and ages and prospects of the children. The Quorn was in a bad state when his lordship took it on, but he didn't half knock it into shape. Firstly he encouraged his wealthy subscribers to buy forage and oats and everything else they could from the local farmers; secondly he put the second horsemen in their proper place—on the roads. Before he came you'd get four hundred mounted madmen knocking down your fences and ruining your grass, and two hundred of those would be servants, the so-called second horsemen. I have never forgotten Lord Lonsdale's voice—he was the kind who could send a whisper halfway round the world and actually knock you over with his shout—nor his extraordinarily powerful yet lissom seat on a horse and the straight line he struck across our country. My father for a period had a standing order to find his lordship twelve chestnut hunters every twelvemonth. They took a lot of finding. Lord Lonsdale's standards were the highest, and although he rode light, he was a heavy man.

Despite the wonders of Lord Lonsdale, however, and our many good friends in the Quorn, the Belvoir was my favourite hunt. I shall never forget those Saturdays when the Belvoir came down from Holwell Mouth or Clawson Thorns to draw Sherbrooke's, a vintage field, having changed to their second horses for what was likely to be the hunt of the day. Sir Gilbert Greenall, only twenty years my senior and so only in his thirties, was Master. He had taken over the hunt when that superb huntsman, Frank Gillard, was retiring, and he chose Ben Capell to be Gillard's successor. Sir Gilbert was a topnotch breeder of hunters, hackneys, show hacks, and ponies, and the quality of his hunt servants' mounts had to be seen to be believed. It was a great hunt. They all have their ups and downs.

It is in the houses of hunting farmers that hunt servants, dropping in for a drink and a chat or some well-prepared fresh victuals, are at their most natural. I suppose we saw a side of Ben Capell little known to the subscribers for whom he produced sport to order, four days a week, in every sort of weather save frost and snow. Ben often wished the Marshall boys a thousand uncomfortable deaths.

Sherbrooke's was normally an afternoon or evening draw, and was right on the edge of the Belvoir country. It seemed to us amusing to induce the Sherbrooke's foxes to break covert across the Smite and make for Curate's Gorse. When the fox population seemed to favour Sherbrooke's we'd lay plenty of smelly dead hens or lambs or sheep in Curate's, to encourage fox-flow in that direction. Ben soon understood our mischief, for, being a good huntsman, he was also a detective, and after a hard day's hunting (how many people in England today can understand just what that ordinary phrase means?) he was totally averse to being drawn from Sherbrooke's deep into Quorn country and farther and farther from his well-strawed kennels at Belvoir Castle on some murky winter afternoon. We three boys would wait carefully posted so as not to miss a fox crossing the Smite and making off for Curate's. How we would halloa and yelp and howl! The hounds battered their way out of the thicknesses and flung themselves through the water with its evening skin of ice forming. Then that gallant field would come round the covert and ride straight and eager, a whole line of them at the brook. There never was a finer sight in all England. Poor Ben, of course, had to join issue and get in front of them, perhaps according us a gesture full of hatred as he galloped past. Huntsmen have their little artifices—they wouldn't survive two seasons without them—and Ben's trick from that boundary covert at that late hour would have been to pick up his hounds and blow them at a gallop towards Belvoir. He'd have given his field a few fences, and perhaps had the luck to sweep up an outlying fox in some hedgerow or patch of gorse, *en route* for home.

Once when things worked out as described above, the Belvoir bitches flew so that they pulled down their fox halfway to Curate's Gorse, and that time Ben came back all smiles. But the next time the fox ran, hard-pressed, smack through Curate's, up and over Fosse Way past Broughton Lodge, round Willoughby-on-the-Wolds to Willoughby Gorse, where they all but had him but, headed by a farmyard cur, he swung left-handed for Eller's and then ran west of south for three miles to Walton Thorns. They caught him not far from the Quorn kennels. Eleven miles as hounds ran, and a seven-mile point, all in enemy territory. Not a bad little evening hunt. Even Ben was secretly feeling pleased by the time he had done the long ride back to us.

'Which of you young devils is going to have this?' he said, as he rode into our stable yard uncoiling the kangaroo-hide thong of his whip and cracking it with a sharp echo. 'Gruel for these 'osses,' he ordered as he stiffly dismounted. 'Milk, and plenty of it—none of your skim now—for my hounds.' We put their horses in, took off their bridles, loosened their girths, and shook straw under them until they staled. Ben and his three red-coated assistants had long since stamped through to my father and mother, to be comforted with devilled chicken legs and steaming brandy punch. How pleasant it was to be able to rest and comfort those good-looking hunt horses, and to see the smart bitches lapping their warm milk and revelling in the clean, sweet straw! An hour later, off they all went, men, horses, hounds, cheerful as you could wish, and they had another ten miles to ride. I admired hunt servants so much, still do. I wonder I didn't decide to be one (too idle, I suppose); my second brother, Mitchell, did just that, and it led him to a good life in far-off places.

Those Belvoir and Quorn fields were a joy and also a puzzlement to country-reared boys. We lived and worked and rode in the Mecca of the sport, the cream of the galloping country. Each season, people who lived in palaces, castles, and mansions competed to occupy the smallest of Melton houses. We saw some of the greatest in the land. We learned that if the slender Prince of Wales had not (who had?) the skill across a country of the Earl of Lonsdale, at least he had the courage. We learned that when a hunting parson got hotted-up it was wise to clear his path. We learned that some bankers looked poor in comparison to their worst customers, and that some of Europe's most austere-seeming leaders could become soppy about a pretty or clever female, just like villagers, and that some of the splendid ladies who took hunting boxes had eyes for handsome males. If we heard or read that Americans or Frenchmen or Germans or Russians were not like ourselves in England, *we* knew differently, for we saw all those, yes and the occasional Indian or Pole or Hungarian, and even once a Siamese prince, hunting over our own fields and fences.

Many, no most, of their names and faces have left me now, yet even those I remember as shifting figures in a crowd have a place in my heart. Best of all was that Belvoir Saturday field late in the afternoon, when the timid and the lazy had long departed for home. There might be a mounted servant with us at the covertside, extra smart and clean with a tall cockaded hat and a big pigskin case, silver-mounted, mono-grammed, slung from his shoulder. He would spin the case to get glasses out and different sorts of drink. . . . Then a hound speaks, the pack confirms, a halloa from the whipper-in at one corner of the covert, Ben's horn. Gone Away-ay-ay! They slide off across country into the gathering winter evening gloom that they light up with their colour, their gaiety, and their courage. The brave and the bold. England was still great then. I remember E. W. Griffiths, the Mild-mays, the Wilsons, W. H. Wilkinson, Colonel W. E. Lawson, Major Lacock, Captain H. T. Barclay, W. Gale and of course his brother, Harry Gale, Harry Beeby and the race-riding Smiths, and Teddy Brooks whom it was such a joy to watch across a trappy bit of terrain. Vintage foxhunters.

Captain Barclay was the hell of a one to go. Most weekends he'd have six or a dozen of his own kind come up from London or over from the Continent to stay with him at Gaddesby Hall and hunt Saturday with the Belvoir and Monday with the Quorn. Some weekend! My father was a real goer. I always remember him feeling down for his girth as he sat Sinbad the Nailer by Sherbrooke's, and saying with the deepest interest and satisfaction, '*Now* we're going to have some fun, for here come Captain Barclay and his circus.'

How the horses were turned out! By present day standards (especially if you look at show jumping) they were perfection. The stud grooms at Melton were a race apart, deferential gentlemen to their employers, devils to their workmen. Mr Polendine, stud groom to the Countess of Cardigan at Egerton Lodge, was the smartest little beetle of a man. With all his personal elegance and importance, Mr Polendine would be up before dawn and banging on the stove, shouting at the lads above in his peculiarly clear and penetrating accents (a linseed voice, we called it then), 'Get those horses OUT!' And when the lovely Countess of Warwick left Warwick Lodge and Lord Hamilton of Dalziel took it with his hard-riding and absolutely splendid wife (one of the Burnham family), they had a treasure of a stud groom, a fellow named Wootton. That man could have been Prime Minister of a great government at the height of England's glory.

Houses had their runs of fame and fortune. I've spoken of Cropwell Court with its two great jockeys and of Thorpe Satchville Hall, where Otho Paget sold out to the brilliant if eccentric 'Banker' Loewenstein. At Warwick Lodge, Lady Warwick and the Hamiltons were succeeded by no less a personage than Ambrose Clark, the Lord Lonsdale of the U.S.A., a multi-millionaire who lived for sport. He only hunted from there for half of each season. Reg Hobbs, trainer of Battleship, was Mr Clark's factotum at Warwick Lodge, and until Christmas, before his boss arrived, he hunted all those gorgeous horses. Then Mr Hobbs became a trainer, and a great job he made of it.

Soon after Danny Maher and George Williamson moved into Cropwell Court, Danny decided that life on wet days in the Midlands was too slow by far. A billiards table must be installed. He consulted Harry Williamson, George's brother who was a Nottingham architect. He put builders in the house and ordered from Thurstons in Leicester Square the best table obtainable. There George Williamson sought the advice of Thurstons' chief expert at the time, 'Melbourne' Inman. Within a week the table was being installed at Cropwell, and the cushions were set by Inman himself. The day after his work was done was a Tuesday. Danny and George persuaded their Australian guest to stay for a day's hunting with Lord Harrington's, and as he refused to ride out with them, they put him in a curricle. At the end of the day George asked Mr W. H. Wilkinson, who hunted from Grantham and was on his way home there, and who particularly fancied himself with the cue, to bait his horse at Cropwell Court, take a dish of tea, and perhaps have a friendly game.

When W.H.W. was shown the new billiard room, one of the house party, a little Jewy man whom he took to be a jockey and whose name he heard but had barely registered was sliding the ivories round the table. W.H. was annoyed by the series of outrageous flukes brought off by the stranger. Dying to get his own hand on the table, he burst out at last, 'I'll play you three hundred up for a tenner.'

'Done.'

For a while Inman was content to fiddle about with impossible shots, and W.H., who was a good amateur, was well on the way to three hundred. Then, settling, and taking trouble, the Australian ran out with a long and exquisite sequence, and not the semblance of a chance in it.

'Inman, Inman, they *said* your name was Inman,' W.H. exclaimed. 'If you ain't the devil himself, you must be *Melbourne* Inman, sir, for I never dreamed such skill was possible, and I'd have given *fifty* pound to have seen it.' He paid up cheerfully, insisted on it, and they parted good friends, and often played together later.

It always amuses me to hear people describe a man as a typical foxhunter. There's no such man and no such foxhunter. The hunting field always was, and still is, an agglomeration of individuals, not types or archetypes. Let me tell you a little about W. H. Wilkinson, of whom I saw so much when I was a boy. He was twenty-two years my senior, and was a friend of my father and mother.

He lived then, and lived well, in Malvern House, Grantham. I don't think he ever had fewer than sixteen fine hunters in his stables. His grandfather, William Wilkinson, was a big Nottinghamshire farmer—that was where the pennies came from. W.H. never, so far as I know, put on a red coat. He always hunted in a perfectly cut and sewn pepper-and-salt coat, tall hat, patent-leather topped boots with little doorknockers on them, and the most perfect nut-brown breeches ever seen outside heaven. He looked every inch a workman, sat right down into his good horses, and where he could not or would not go was not worth going. . . . What an immense number of people he must have known, and if they all liked him as well as we did W.H. was a lucky man indeed. . . . He was a fanatic. I mean it. He was busy creating a record. Year after year, the weather being open, he hunted six days a week—and I understand he kept that up for twenty years. Nobody will ever equal it.

When W. H. Wilkinson, the 'Farmer's Boy' we jokingly used to call him, left Uppingham he rode for a while for Bob Chapman, a Cheltenham dealer. One day while he was employed there *he rode a hundred and fifty miles to have a hunt.* Yes, he hunted a full day with the Warwickshire and covered a hundred and fifty miles in the same day, getting to the meet and getting home from hunting. He left Cheltenham at four a.m. and rode very fast to Moreton-in-the-Marsh and on to Todenham, where he stabled his horse and mounted a galloping hack. After riding fifty-six miles he got to the meet at Kineton punctually, changed to a hunter, and enjoyed a full day's sport. (W.H. never went home till hounds did.) They ended up at Shuckburgh, which is near Rugby. He rode back to Todenham, and after dining there, he rode home to Cheltenham.

He *was* a formidable sportsman, and you could not meet a nicer man. From time to time he sent us boys a horse to break. We amused him, and I think he was genuinely fond of my father, and vice versa.

* * *

Another who sent us, or rather me, horses to break was Captain Frank Forester, Master of the Quorn for nineteen years from 1905. It was he who sent me Christmas Daisy, twice winner of the Cambridgeshire, and when he arrived the smart groom handed me a note from Captain Forester.

'Please teach this great horse to *enjoy* his hunting, F.F.'

Captain Forester rode thoroughbred horses, impeccably turned out, from his place, Saxelby Park just outside Melton. When Christmas Daisy arrived there from the Druid's Lodge gallops, they found him rather exuberant. Captain Forester had a mind to ask Dick Black to take the horse in hand. But Dick was unwell at the time so, as luck would have it (and that was my last hunting season at home), he came to Hickling and to me.

For the first eight days he did little but grind his teeth. He was seven years old and his whole life had been spent racing, or training to race. His one concern was how far he had to gallop, and against what or whom. Still, he was a lovely ride, such paces!

It was his mouth that needed sorting, and then his mind. When I had his confidence in the box, and had taught him to bridle properly, I rode him out round our farm with either Sam or Mitchell on Sinbad the Nailer as leader and teacher. We had the farm well laid-out for such schooling. Gorse was thickly plugged into the fences. Horses don't like prickles, and they'll jump cleaner over gorse than anything. We had a place or two with a ditch dug to face them, and others with dropping ditches to make them spread. We had the brook, and all kinds of timber obstacles and in-and-outs. . . . We started Christmas Daisy on tiddlers, but he was a natural fencer, and within a few days of his arrival I could slip him over the trickiest or biggest ones on his own. He very soon became a dream of a ride. I told my father that I dreaded parting with him.

'Give him a few days with the Belvoir, then' he advised, pointing out that once Captain Frank saw the horse out with the Quorn he would soon have him off me.

When Christmas Daisy first found himself in the hunting

79

field he reverted to his old racing ways. I had to skirt with him for quite a while. Then I managed more and more often to nick into good hunts with him. As soon as I felt the horse enjoying it, and saw his ears prick and swivel to the hounds, I knew my job was nearly finished, and I was sorry. To get into a hunt on such a horse was then my idea of heaven, and frankly, even at my present advanced age, it still would be.... All good things must end (or they would be less good) and one day when I was out with the Quorn on another horse Captain Forester beckoned me to his side.

'Where's Christmas Daisy?' he asked, very blunt, almost angry. 'You doing any good with him at all?'

I was stupid enough to say that he was going well, and that I'd had him out twice that week with the Belvoir.

'What the devil did you take him *there* for? Bring him out with us, Friday, without fail.'

I had the first run on the Daisy, that Quorn Friday, and hounds, drawing the second covert, were just beginning to speak, when Captain Forester beckoned.

'Make haste. Bring him here.' He didn't hunt those hounds himself because he'd smashed a thigh in a hunting accident (I think during his long spell with Irish packs) and he had to have constant treatment for that leg. He'd no strength in it, and use to hang on a horse. But he could go, and he had tremendous spirit. 'How are those leathers?' he asked, gruff as gruff. I sidled the Daisy up to a bank, and got hold of the captain's horse while he swung over from one saddle to t'other. He sat on the racehorse, getting his length and saying to the restive Quorn field, 'Hold hard now, hold hard there!' He twisted the thoroughbred round, trying his mouth and reactions to the leg. '*Now*, you can come,' he said to his subscribers, and cantered down the ride and through the covert, for hounds had just gone away from the other side. Christmas Daisy went beautifully for him, and Captain Forester loved him, as I had done. There was no mystery about that horse at all (though I earned a lot of bogus credit through him). If you left him *alone* he trained himself, and then, in addition to his grace, strength, and blood, he had the most important quality you can find in any hunter—he almost instantly became passionately addicted to foxhunting. . . . As for me, I never got another ride on him.

That season, my last as a boy at Hickling, Sam, Mitchell, and I rode pretty frequently for Mr Harry Beeby, the personality and dealer without whom Melton would not have been Melton. Usually he put us on wild green animals from Ireland, and it was surprising how well they went, and how few tosses they gave us. I remember driving over to his yard one morning, the three of us behind a fast thoroughbred mare that had scarce seen shafts before. We were late, and we hurried. Mr Beeby was standing in his archway, across the street from Melton churchyard.

'Your nags are gone on,' he called. 'Get to Wilde's Lodge as quick as you can. You can leave your trap there with Ebenezer—if there's any trap left by then.'

'Can't we give you a lift, Mr Beeby?' Sam asked, seeing that Mr B. was fully dressed for hunting.

'I wouldn't get up aside you in that rig for a thousand pounds,' he answered with a shudder. And we were later still at Wilde's Lodge, for on the way there the mare kicked the bottom out of the gig. Harry Beeby was to mean a lot to me when I was older, and Sam and Mitchell, both intent on becoming top-class horsemen, were rough-riding for him when I left Hickling.

One Quorn Monday Mr Beeby mounted Mitchell on a grey horse, a powerful heavy-weight aptly named Bullet. He had an obstinate bump to his brow and a mouth that could clamp fiercely on any ironmongery put in it. They met in gathering fog, near Melton. Hounds quickly ran with a tearing scent, the Bullet after them, absolutely unmanageable. As they approached the Midland Railway near Frisby both level-crossing gates were shut, but just as Mitchell thought his last moment had come, the gates swung open,

F   81

and he was through. On they went, the fog slowly lifting. He was just able to steer the mad hunter clear of two ponds full of ducks and fringed with wire. A series of fences. The grey horse did not deviate from his course, the jockey stayed with him. The Widmerpool Brook, after a terrifying steeple-chase of many miles, opposed Mitchell on the crackpot horse. At that point the Brook had no bottom, ran wide on the take-off side, and washed the clay banks under. Mitchell dug in his heels and Bullet just cleared it and, with a scramble, pulled his great hind legs to safety. Hounds had killed their fox in front of the landing, and Mitchell, first there, was given the brush.

On Tuesday morning Mitchell turned up at Beeby's yard opposite the church in Melton, properly dressed for hunting and none the worse for his scarifying experience of the previous day.

'You killed that grey 'oss Bullet,' was Mr Beeby's greeting. The grey had died of a broken blood vessel during the night, and a good thing too, I think, for *he* would have killed anyone less expert and less bold than Mitchell.

Another day I called at Mr Beeby's, as I normally did whenever I was in Melton and had a minute to spare. He met me in the yard at the door of a box, and he was very depressed.

'Oh, Howard,' he said, 'if only you had had the riding of this 'oss. I used to think brothers were brothers, alike in brain and performance, but it ain't so. I sent Mitchell away on this five-year-old yesterday to qualify him for the Belvoir. Ever such a keen owner too, and the horse would walk any hunt race in England. I ask you. . . . Hounds found in the Vale, at Jericho Court to be precise, and, as you know, the fastest hunt of the season ensued. I was there, and saw Mitchell and the 'oss in question. It was a steeplechase and they just went straight over everything, stick, stone, or water. The Honourable Wyndham and your brother were the only two followers in the field when hounds killed their fox, and they were given the brush and the mask respectively by Sir Gilbert. Now don't think, my dear boy, that I'm criticising any lad who can go as Mitchell does at the top of any hunt. I'm only pointing out, I asked Mitchell to *qualify* this very valuable young horse. Now come and see him.'

The five-year-old had two big knees, full of blackthorns. Needless to say, he did not run in that race, but he turned out well afterwards. There's an old saying: 'Never go into the stable today of the horse that you hunted yesterday.'

*　　*　　*

Because I enjoyed horses and foxhunting as much as my father and many other fortunate people did, I seldom in those days even noticed my mother's hostile reaction. But once when I was in the brougham with her on the Nottingham side of the country, we met Lord Harrington, mounted and followed by a groom, on the outskirts of Shelton. Recognising us, he stopped our coachman and leaned his face with its two wings of white whisker in at the window. After inquiring about the health of our father and the whole family, he said how much he hoped I'd soon be out with his hounds again, because any Marshall was welcome, and so on. . . . He seemed to me the most pleasant of old men, so old that I could not understand, in my greenness, how he managed to hunt his hounds beautifully. He rode on.

Mother asked me to shut the window. I pulled it up on its silk-bound velvet strap, and I hear the catch in her voice and saw the tears in her eyes. We sat, bumping against each other in that leathery, groomy, saddle-soapy atmosphere of closed carriages. (I cannot think why I was there with her—either it was a funeral, or a sickbed call, or I was convalescent.) I was insensitive and she was reticent. We said nothing to each other.

*　　*　　*

Parents, even in a family of eleven children, have favourites. While for some reason my father seemed to take to me more

83

than to the others (perhaps I was more *serviable*), mother's darling was Sam the handsome, the first born. But Sam was a demon on a horse, less artful, less patient than I was, and racing was his passion. When he was sixteen he had a shattering fall in a farmers' hurdle race on the old heart-shaped racecourse at Croxton Park, just south of Belvoir. He was so badly hurt that they dared not move him. (Roads were rougher then, and ambulances were uncouth by present standards.) He had to lie in the grandstand for a whole fortnight, wrapped in blankets. Mother visited him every day. Those must have been odd scenes, I have since thought, the handsome lady with her basket covered in white napkin, crossing the empty racecourse and ascending the empty stand to the pale youth stretched out on its terracing.

In my last year at Hickling, 1904, Sam had taken a fancy to Sondoroa, an absolute brute of a mare, a potential Gold Cup horse and a potential killer. All of us had had a go at her, even my father. Nobody could control her save Sam, and he only sometimes. Well, it was coming to point-to-point time, and Sam had been absent for three and a half hours, exercising Sondoroa.

'Get out a horse quick, Howard, and go and find Sam,' my father said at last. 'He's stuck somewhere. Maybe he needs a hand. Hope you'll find him. Go Clawson way, I should. I've an idea he rode off that side, and he promised me he'd stick to the roads.'

There was no need to labour the point. Mother was sitting with a face that might have been white-washed, tapping at the work table with her nails, her crochet lying across her knees.

I cantered through the gloaming towards Long Clawson. Coming out of that village there was (and still is) a narrow bit of metalled road opening out into wide verges with really deep drainage ditches (it's about the lowest part of the vale) and stiff fences behind them. I heard a horse coming at speed and saw sparks flying from the road before I made out the

mare. Then I heard her crash into one of the hedges, and
fall into the ditch below. And as she got rid of Sam and
jumped, possibly six feet to get out of the ditch, she kicked
him in the ribs and the back. I managed to pacify my own
horse, and to catch the mare, 'Whoa gal, whoa now. . . .' But
Sam lay still. I couldn't even hear him breathing. I believe I
was in tears.

A car jolted and rattled along the road. It was welcome
indeed, and its driver more so, for he was Doctor Atkinson
of Clawson.

'Let those horses go, Howard,' he said when he had examined my brother. We found a hurdle and together, inch by
inch, shifted his poor, flaccid body into the back seat of the
big open car. 'Now catch your horses again and cut on home,'
Doctor Atkinson said. 'Tell Mr Marshall I'm taking Sam
straight to Leicester Infirmary. Only hope I shan't get a
puncture on the way. Let's see, are you on the telephone?'

'My father won't have one.'

'Best ask him to come to Leicester then, right away.'

Sam was in the Infirmary for six months, and his health
was permanently affected. That horrible mare had kicked
away a bit of his liver, and they kept plugging it with silk
gauze, so he told us with gruesome relish any time that we
called to see him. He had never been strong, and I know
Mother hoped the doctor would order him not to ride again.
Whether the doctor did, I don't know, but nothing would
have kept Sam off horses. He'd have ridden if both feet and
both hands had been cut off. Mother was on a losing wicket
there. And she would have been with me. Even today, at
fourscore years and more, I need horses. They are oxygen
to me; my life and my amusement.

5

The 16th Lancers

W H Y did I leave Hickling? I belonged there. Why did I leave
it so young? I suppose I wanted to play my part in the world
and do my best for England, and I know I was curious to
see places and people. India was a magnet. I imagined myself
pigsticking, playing polo, and exchanging lethal shots in some
nullah with the brave Pathan. Then there was Captain
Thompson always talking about his regiment out there, and
telling my father I would get commissioned rank, marry
an heiress, win the Grand Military Gold Cup and the
Grand National, and become a *Field*-Marshal.

And why was I allowed to leave Hickling at the age of
sixteen? I'd been useful on the place since I was ten, or even
less. Apart from all the fun and the hunting, I had put in
months of slogging work on the horses and on the farm. I
had thought that my father loved me, and I know that in
his way he did. Why then did he push me so quickly away?
He never had me taught any trade or profession, unless you
count what he taught me about horses, and at that time the
horse trade was depressed. I suppose he felt himself swamped
by his family. There were too many of us and we were leaving
school while he was still young, able, and busy. In any event
he was a hard man and he wanted me to be hard. He pushed
me out, and I cannot honestly say that I was unwilling to go
until just the last moments of leaving Hickling, and even then
I was borne up by anticipation of the good things to come.
At the age of sixteen I was an optimist.

When I'd taken the King's shilling in Nottingham Drill
Hall they gave me a medical examination, a railway warrant,
and orders to go to Aldershot and report to the adjutant of
the 16th Lancers at the South Cavalry Barracks.

Outside Aldershot station I saw a clean and active sort
of man, and asked him my way.

'You come to join up?' he asked.

'Suppose so.'

'Then turn about and go straight back 'ome. You'll be
better off anywhere nor what you will be 'ere.'

'Having got this far I'll have a look at it.'

'It's your own funeral.' He told me he was a 16th Lancer
and a horse servant (army groom) to Colonel Tewson, who
was second in command to Colonel Gough.

Next morning I searched him out and found him with his
horses at the end of C Squadron block. He had a nice
charger and a couple of polo ponies in there, and I thought,
By golly! from what I've seen this is the best corner of the
God-forsaken hole. I wouldn't mind being on this caper
for a bit. (And at that time I had not got started with
normal duties, which were to prove even worse than I
expected.)

'I'll buy that suit off you when you draws your uniform,'
my new acquaintance offered.

'I don't think I'd better sell it, thank you. I've got several
brothers at home just about my size. Indeed I'm not sure it
doesn't belong to one of them.'

That day I was moved from the Intake Centre to my
alloted barrackroom. There were twenty-five of us, old
sweats and young ones, on iron cots round the wall, and in
the corner the troop-sergeant's bed. You pulled out the foot
of the cot, put three 'biscuits' on the frame, and what blankets
you had on top. There was one pillow, hard as concrete and
of about the same texture, covered with rough canvas, I
should think. The stabling was in long blocks with barrack-
rooms above surrounded by balconies. You could come out

of the barrackroom, lean over the balcony rail, and look across the great red drill square. The whole place, the noises, the smells, the proximity and intimacy of my strange fellows, struck a chill right through me so that now, more than sixty years on, I can feel it, even smell it, and shudder.

Those first barrackroom nights! The horses were directly below us tied with chains running through holes in the mangers to iron 'logs'. All night the chains rattled as the poor brutes pulled them up or let the weights pull them down. Around me men belched or snored or whistled or groaned or even sang in their sleep. I suppose the adverse impression that these surroundings made on me was deepened by my youth. Although physically I was tall and probably hardier than most of them there, I was still young enough to be wooden in my reactions to strange surroundings and people. During the earlier part of my life I'd been a form of slave to one beloved martinet, and had always been willing to see the rightness of his orders and his standards. But my father's toughness with us all had not prepared me for the opening purgatorial stages of life in a cavalry barracks, the fierce and bullying discipline, the degradations imposed on us by the lower echelons of authority, the stinks, the sordid food, the lack of privacy. My fellow recruits had been longer there and were much older, and townsmen to boot. I'd no companionship of any sort.

As for mod cons, the troop-sergeant would call, 'Hey you, Marshall! Tub orderly tonight.' It was a darned great tub with two handles, about the size of an eight-gallon beer barrel sawn in half. We had to fetch that from below, put a bit of disinfectant in the bottom, and carry it up to the balcony where it remained for the night just outside the barrackroom entrance. They called it, with startling originality, the 'piss tub'. If it was a Saturday night and the lads had drawn their seven bobs and gone out to find beer they would be singing round the tub and sometimes falling in it. Great joke! We got seven shillings, and a bit was kept back, deferred pay, to be made up to you when you'd done your seven years. That was what I had blithely signed on for—*seven years*. Ever since those days I've sympathised with any criminal who gets a sentence in terms of years. . . . Of course, when I'd signed on, I imagined myself sailing through a bit of interesting training (plenty of shooting with live rounds) and then pushing off for India, tigers, maharajahs, the King's commission. Imagination can betray. My first three months in that cavalry barracks hit my natural optimism such a blow that it never completely recovered.

'Fall in the meat squad! Left turn! Quick march!' Down to the butchery and the menial duties there. 'Spud fatigue, *you!*' Well, obviously, somebody had to peel spuds. God knows we ate 'em, and precious little else except suet and gravy and loathsome white bread with margarine, something I had not tried until then. The only time we saw horses was from eleven a.m. till one p.m. when we did 'stables'. And such horses, poor things! When the trumpet sounded FEED, they *did* kick up a din. They knew one o'clock to the split second. They bit at one another until they got it, and then they wolfed it in two ticks. Each horse had a small bucket of the oats ration, and a bit of hay was pushed into the iron rack beside his manger. Their hocks were all bunged up on the outsides where they had knocked the 'bales', and there had been festering cuts. When I looked into their faces, some cunning and surly, some desperate, some just unhappy, I knew the horses felt exactly as I did about our life as recruits. Not that the horses the recruits had under them were new to the place; they were the old stagers, and they found their lot intolerable, or almost so.

For the first three months I was being ground into shape (their shape) on the barrack square. I say nothing against foot drill except that I never could abide it. I know it can make soldiers and can make armies, but to me such stamping of heavy boots, such hoarse and aggressive commands, were even sillier than they were stupid. It mattered nothing what

I thought. First we drilled with the rifle, then the sword, and finally the lance, wearing the high lance-cap of the dress uniform.

But one afternoon, unexpectedly, a ray of Leicestershire light shone through. I was leaning on the balcony rail and looking forlornly over that grim square when I saw on it a man I remembered. He was walking out of the barracks in civvies. I went down those stairs like a greyhound.

'Mr Payne, what are you doing here?'

'Good grief? It's young Marshall from Hickling. What am I doing, well, I'm not in the Army, if that's what you mean. But you *are*. . . .'

'Yes, worse luck. We do nothing but wear out boots on the ruddy square.'

'You're the Christmas Daisy one, the one that sold that good young grey to Mr Maher, aren't you? Well, listen carefully now. I'm going to tell you what I'm doing here, and there might, I say *might*, be something in it for you. . . . I brought a batch of horses down here for Second Lieutenant Geoffrey Brooke, and I aim to stop with him for quite a bit before I go back to my business in Leicestershire.' He was Clifford Payne, and he had stables at Kirby Gate, and hired out horses. He was an uncle of W. Payne, a steeplechase jockey who lived at Weedon, and was no relation to our W. Payne, Podgy's employer, at Melton. 'Have you met Mr Brooke?' he now asked. 'No? Nor seen him jumping? Well, take my word for it, he's the coming man. With him on top any horse is twice what he was before. I happen to know he's looking for a soldier servant to school and break and help look after his string. I make no promises, but I'll give your name to him and I reckon you might suit him and he you. He's only a young gentleman, you know, no more than twenty-one, though he seems it.'

Then he took me to see Mr Brooke's horses. They were stabled at The Rifleman Hotel, just outside the barracks' gates, with their sentry boxes and well-raked gravel. There were some ripping good boxes, and the best lot of horses I had seen for a time. I was *very* glad I'd recognised Mr Payne.

*   *   *

'Riding school tomorrow.'

When those words were barked at us by I cannot remember which performing tomcat of an N.C.O. I'd done·three months on the barrack square at foot drill with two hours' stables a day, but most of my squad had done much longer, some of them as long as a twelve-month without getting on a horse. The funny thing was that if I asked them why they'd offered their services to the cavalry arm the usual answer was that they disliked walking and hated or feared the sea. There was no air force in those days.

We were ordered to parade outside the riding school, ourselves in breeches and puttees, our horses in blankets with surcingles round them (no saddles) and plain bridoon bits.

Mr Jock Lang, the riding master, inspected us and then, in tones of facetious refinement, delivered a standard but by no means stupid description of the horse as a conveyance. He was a smart little fellow, immaculate in Kiwi-ed boots and spurs, Sam Browne belt, moustaches. He wore an eyeglass. We'd been warned that he was an absolute so-and-so, and eyed him as though he were a poisonous snake. He had us lead round inside the riding school for a while, then halted us, facing him.

'Any of you fellows ever ridden befoah?' he asked.

No answer.

'Well, in your own time. . . . Mmm-ount!' He had a good many minions and quite soon everybody had been hove up on top. Most of us looked scared and uncomfortable.

'Walk mm-arch!'

Clever as monkeys and schooled to death, the horses went trailing round at the word of command whether the blokes had them by the head or not.

'Trrr-ot!'

The old horses jogged on round.

'Haaalt!'

Everyone fell off except me. I forgot to. The horses were quietly sniggering.

'Come out he-ah, young man, yes you, Lofty,' Mr Lang said in tones from which kindness was conspicuously absent. '*You* have ridden befo-ah.'

'Yes, sir.'

'Did I not inqui-ah if any of you had ridden befo-ah?'

'Yes sir.'

'Then are you a cheat or a li-ah?'

'Neither, sir. I feared you'd think I was showing off.'

'Neith-ah, sir,' he mimicked. 'A barrackroom law-yah. Come he-ah.' He put me through a few movements with the horse. I sat still and sat back, riding as well as I could, now that I was found out. My fellow recruits stood by their horses' heads, their eyes glassy, anguished.

'Fetch us three bah-rs,' Mr Lang called to his assistants. They set up one decent obstacle, neither low nor high, the battered bars laid on pegs. 'Come, Lofty. Canter your horse round and ov-ah.' My dobbin went round as though he meant it, and sailed the bars almost handsomely. An intake of breath from the squad. 'Round and ovah again,' Mr Lang said to me. I could see him unreefing his whip and I knew his plan well enough. As we came into the fence his thong shot out and round my horse's forelegs. He put in two short ones, hit the bars hard, and came down with me in the peat beyond. 'Now,' said Mr Lang, 'You must get that peat out of your eyes and your e-ahs and your neck, and brush down your clothes and report to the orderly sergeant, for you are to join the other squad tomorrow, so I understand.' He'd known all along that I could ride.

While my recruits' squad was beginning its eighteen-month stint in the riding school, the other squad was to pass out (if judged worthy) the following day. It was to be a parade in full dress uniform, an event for which they had long been working.

'Draw your passing-out parade kit at the store,' the orderly-sergeant said. 'And if you know what's good for you, make haste and get your turnout clean and sparkling, or you'll know all about it.'

From the time when I was seven years old I'd been cleaning tack, boning boots, burnishing bits and irons, doing things properly. I saw straight off that the stuff they pushed at me from the store was absolutely impossible. I spent half the night sweating at it in the passage under a gas jet. I finally crawled into bed sick with apprehension. I knew that nothing, NOTHING, was going to put suppleness and shine into that old, cracked, salty, discoloured leather and the heavily-vaselined dull metal. And that was only the start of it, since my weapons and my dress uniform as well as my person and that of my poor old dull-coated horse also had to be worked up to the peak of smartness. I was supposed to do in hours what the others had taken months over, and it just could not be done.

My appearance on parade next morning, the ugly one among all those smug ducklings, made Squadron Sergeant Major Mullins howl like a seal. 'You'd spoil any parade you heap! You'd disgrace any ride, you basket, you closet! Out! OUT! Go on, get out of it!' That was how he spoke to me.

Although I'd feared such a reaction, I put my horse away sadly and went up to the barrackroom to change into fatigue trousers and shirt. I joined my former squad of tyros at stables. But I hadn't been there long when I was suddenly engulfed in a wave of half-friendly, half-bullying sergeants and corporals. I couldn't imagine what they were trying to do to me. . . .

General Byng, G.O.C., Aldershot, took the passing out parade that morning, assisted by Colonel H. B. de la Gough. We little monkeys were not as stupid, of course, as the officers thought us. We used to hear the colonel's friends calling him 'Goughie, old boy', so Goughie he was to us. He lived to the age of ninety and got to be an Army commander. He was a good sort. While they were taking the parade, the colonel asked the R.S.M., Jimmy James, 'Where's that Marshall boy, the one I told you about, from Leicestershire? I don't see his name on this list.' What excuse was offered I don't know. Goughie spoke up sharply. 'Get him on parade at once. We'll see him alone when we've done with this lot.'

'Very good, sir.'

My treatment now was dramatically different from the previous day, when the carbuncle-faced storeman had flung at me the worst articles from his shelves and harness room. I was soon turned out in perfect guard-mounting uniform, stuff kept in glass-fronted cases, frequently cleaned by experts, and only used for ceremonial. Saddlery and weapons were to the same standard and meanwhile three men were hard at it strapping a troop-sergeant's horse, the best mount available.

Regimental Sergeant Major James, almost an intellectual to look at and very slack-kneed in his walk, preceded me into the riding school as No 1 Squad was being dismissed.

'Trooper Marshall present and correct, sir.'

General and colonel looked me over for a while in silence, then asked a few friendly questions. The R.S.M., behind them, glared horribly. They began to put me through it.

'Dismount!' I did it, avoiding the rifle butt and the hilt of my sword as well as managing the lance in my high dress cap.

'Prepare to mount . . . mount!' I was up again with lance serene, its end in the bucket strapped to my stirrup iron. I'd never previously held a lance on a horse except informally for tentpegging with the yeomanry, but all those long hours of lance drill on the square had familiarised me with the movements and taught me their rhythm.

'Walk march!'

'Trot!'

'Halt!'

'Canter from the halt and execute figure of eight, changing leg at the markers!' I set the sergeant's horse in motion, sat still, and he did it perfectly without aid or interference from me.

'Halt! Prepare for lance exercise. Point! . . . and go right through with it. . . . Left front, point! . . . Right front, point! . . . Left rear, point! . . . Right rear, point! . . . Thrust! . . . Parry! . . .

They moved away, the two officers, discussing me in low voices. The R.S.M. stood, holding me immobile by the force of his personality. They returned with smiles and compliments on my turnout and performance. Most of the compliments appeared to be directed (possibly with some justice in the circumstances) at the R.S.M. In any event I had passed out with only two brief sessions in the riding school, in which my less fortunate fellow recruits were to suffer for long months.

'Trooper Marshall transferred to No 1 Troop, C Squadron,' next day's orders proclaimed.

That was Mr Brooke's troop. Almost immediately he had me transferred from it to the Reserve Squadron where the remounts were. I enjoyed myself for the first time in the Army, schooling the remounts, mostly green youngsters from Ireland. I got better results than my mates who were, on the whole, made horsemen rather than born to it as I was, and soon they gave me the best horses. As you must know, the better a young horse the more tricky he usually is to break. It's a matter of spirit which, in the end, must come to terms with intelligence. While I was working in the Reserve Squadron I was perfectly aware that I was under observation not only from the Brooke-Payne lot but also from the adjutant. It had been planned that I should join the 16th Lancers at Aldershot because they were the depot regiment for the 17th Lancers, and sent out reinforcements and replacements to that regiment in India. I had seen more than enough of the trooper's lot at Aldershot. . . . For the cavalry officer India could plainly be a paradise; for the trooper it was emphatically, in my view, a hell. I would *not* go to India. Yet what if I were ordered to go? If it came to a contest with the will of the Army what chance would I have? I need not have worried.

Major-General G. F. H. Brooke, C.B., D.S.O., M.C., is now so famous in the horse world, it seems strange that when I first met him he was a second lieutenant and only twenty-one. He was a remarkable twenty-one, I can tell you, and already he had power in the regiment because of his string of horses and his superb horsemanship. When he asked me to become his No. 2 batman he had taken time to have a good look at *me* and I, having had an equal look at *him*, was delighted to join his entourage, and felt able to breathe. So long as I managed to satisfy him with my work they would never drag me off to some red-hot barracks surrounded by reeking bazaars. He had not taken me on as a valet, but to ride and school and help look after his hunters, jumpers, polo ponies, and young horses. Mr Barnaby was No. 1 batman, and Clifford Payne was acting stud groom, and keeping his own establishment at Kirby Gate going at the same time. With our dashing employer we made an exceptional team, and one that soon proved itself with telling blows for England in the world of show-jumping.

When I joined them Brooke was already doing well with a jumper called Combined Training. He was Barnaby's horse. I never had much to do with him. But two of my remounts proved to be stars: Alice and Harriet, he named them. We got Alice to jump seven feet. Three years running I took her to Olympia and Brooke won the Daily Mail Cup on her. Harriet was broken by Trooper Kinsella in the Reserve Squadron, and we saw she could jump like a flea. We won the Canadian Cup with her and the King George V Cup (All Nations). As for Combined Training, he was still jumping and winning in international company in the post-war years.

Geoffrey Brooke was batting one afternoon on the Cavalry Brigade cricket ground at Aldershot. He went to hit a ball on the leg side, slipped, twisted himself badly, and fell all of a heap. They carried him from the pitch and up the steps of the big pavilion. He sent for Clifford Payne and me because, as he had injured himself and would not be able to ride for a while, he had decided immediately to take a trip to Russia.

'I should have gone months ago,' he said. 'But horses are the very devil. You can never leave 'em. I shall be gone several weeks because I've something important to fix up. Everything I value here I leave in your hands, with absolute confidence. You know our horses and you know our standards. So long, both of you.' A Mess carriage was waiting for him at the foot of the steps, and we both noticed that he went down the long flight slowly, but looked perfectly sound, though the doctor said he should not be on his feet. He was a tough customer, and very aloof. I never got to know him, but I always liked him, and I owed him my release from that other Army life. More than that, as I drove him about a lot, I saw many things. Those were the days in a smart regiment for a dashing and successful young man like my boss. With him (and yet not with him) I learned my way about London. I soon knew the whereabouts of the clubs, the polo grounds, the hotels, the livery stables, Tattersalls, Weatherby's, the shirtmakers, the bootmakers, the tailors, the hatters, the jewellers, the restaurants, the houses of the great and the wealthy, and—certainly not least in the galaxy—Olympia in its jewelled days when the horse still reigned supreme, even in London.

We didn't learn until his return what he had gone to Russia to 'fix up'. He'd got married there to a baroness, and when they'd made a short stay in England she came with us to the Argentine.

A board of five officers led by General Sir Alex Godley had been chosen by the War Office to report on the suitability of Argentine horses for our Army in the event of war. The other members were, if memory serves, Major Beresford (later Lord Waterford), Captain Bayford, 8th Hussars, Lieutenant Montefiore, R.H.A., and Lieutenant G. F. H. Brooke. Always the man to improve the shining hour, the last-named officer asked me to go along in charge of two jumping horses, which I loaded on the *Asturias* at Southampton for Buenos Aires. The *Asturias* was a comfortable vessel, my two horses were in excellent quarters, and a good time was had by all.

Our personal target on arrival was the open jumping festival at the great exhibition to celebrate the country's hundred years of independence. The chestnut horse won us a couple of good events. He was a great raking animal, a little on the raw side and no easy conveyance. I always remember him soaring over the long jump as though he would never come down, and Brooke smiling on his back. We hadn't taken any of our better-known jumpers there for the good reason that my employer (as I thought of him, though technically he and I were both employed by King Edward VII, this was 1908) intended to sell the horses he took there and buy others. Sell them we did, and then travelled all over the country with the inspecting board. As we were in the market and representing the biggest buyers, or just about, in the world, the dagos couldn't do enough for us. Great were the rodeos and cattle-handling displays. Wild horses were saddled in crushes after being corralled. Riders were legged up over the top rail, the front timbers of the crush were withdrawn, and whoosh! the horse was sent forward with a clout over the quarters from an empty flourbag. The way those little dark men sat on and also their knack of falling off on to their feet was a miracle. I could never tire of watching them.

I had to pay a price for my holiday in the Argentine, not that it wasn't a working holiday, as we were acquiring horses here and there. The price was the toughest trip home

I ever had. Our passage was booked to Liverpool on an elderly freighter, the S.S. *Raphael*. My charges were twelve Argentine polo ponies, a grey pony belonging to Count Martinez de Hoz, and a grey thoroughbred by Guercillero out of Bacquita that Geoffrey Brooke had bought after we'd all seen him win convincingly on the Palermo track, Buenos Aires.

The *Raphael* belied her pleasant name. She was a sordid old tub. My horses were nailed into improvised stalls on the foredeck immediately aft of the forecastle head. The loading was nothing to do with me, and I was thankful, for they fought like tigers against the slings and they shrieked their heads off as the derricks plucked them from the quay. But once in their stalls they stood like so many Lord Fauntleroys, even the racehorse. The ship chugged and vibrated off into the airless night, developing a slow, creaking roll as we left harbour. A crew member was sick into one of my stalls, and I was so enraged that I went for him with my hunting whip. The bo'sun fortunately got in first, felled the offender with one to the jaw, ordered two others to carry him below, and then himself cleared the offending mess. He was a gem of a fellow, as Liverpool Irish as you could meet, hard, kindly, industrious, and a very devout R.C. He'd been a sailor all his life, and was due to retire with almost nothing put away, yet he was as cheerful as a robin.

One morning of fine weather they opened the hatches to air the holds and I nipped below because I've always believed, and still do, in giving horses a varied diet. Down there I found a lot of brown sugar that had spilled from sacks stowed between bales of wool. I fetched a couple of buckets and did trip after trip laying in a store of the stuff for my ponies. They loved it. Next time the hatches were opened I lost no time in going down. The cargo had shifted. The light was bad. As I walked between the wool bales I suddenly felt myself falling. I crashed down into the iron spaces of the lowest hold and lay unconscious there for most of a day and all that night. In the morning, though, I woke at my usual time, five a.m. (can you beat it?). I staggered about in the blackness until I found the iron ladder and some time later, after inch by inch climbing, I pulled myself over the hatch coaming and collapsed on deck in the sizzling sun. There was enormous relief at my appearance, and a celebration was at once thrown by the officers, partly, I believe, because nobody else on board wanted my job of looking after the ponies. They had searched down the holds and shouted and had decided I must have gone overboard, having taken rum, which struck me as funny since then, as now, I never drank much. I'd even been entered in the log as dead. The captain gave me the page as a souvenir, but I lost it with a lot of other papers and photographs when I was in hospital during World War Two. By golly, it was lucky for me and the ponies that the weather had stayed good during my slip-up! Otherwise, when they came for the wool and the sugar at Liverpool, the jolly dockers would have found a skeleton: the rats would have eaten eyes, hair, and flesh.

In the passage from Pernambuco to Madeira the decks became nearly red-hot. I paid a couples of lascars, black as the Ace of Spades, to sluice round my ponies' feet three times a day. Funny, the ponies did not take to their dark helpers, though after all they themselves came from a country where the humans are not exactly white, and later when I worked in North America I found that horses got on well enough with the Negroes there. The dull old wooden decks were soaked with barrel after barrel of oil, presumably to stop them drying out completely and going up in flames.

After we left Madeira everybody said we were for it. The sea got worse every day. As we rolled and wallowed our slow way into the Bay of Biscay I truly thought each time she plunged that she was going under. My worry for the ponies was so rending that I got little sleep. But those ponies never stirred, not even when she stood on her after-end and then plunged so deeply you swore she could never come up. Up she always rose, with a great wash of salt water over and round them, leaving a coating of brine all over their backs and thick in their manes and tails. Do you know, when it was at its worst and in full oilskins and sou'wester and seaboots I cowered with them, wondering how I could get a bit of dry food into them, they actually seemed to be enjoying it. My admiration for their fortitude was boundless. You never stop learning when you're with horses.

But it went on too long. The *Raphael* became an extended nightmare. Any farmer who has had a lot of stock out during a hard winter with forage running short will have known a fraction of the worry I felt for my charges. We were fourteen days overdue into Liverpool.

To my way of thinking there has always been one thing wrong with England. She is an island. Just think if she had not been. Firstly we would have been linked by land to the paradise that is Ireland. Secondly we should have had proper foxhunting all the way down through France to the Mediterranean and all the way east through the Low Countries, Germany, Poland, and Russia to the Manchurian frontiers. Then we should have had no wars. For the Chinese are a sensible race. They would have taken to foxhunting like mad. Imagine jumping all those brooks on the Willow Pattern plates; the bridges would not take a horse's weight, though no doubt fox and hounds would use them. . . . What fun, what sport, what fellowship! *And* what sales for Anglo-Irish blood hunters, the best sort of horse!

As soon as the old ship thrust her blunt nose into the Western Approaches my charges, so well behaved until then, must have got a whiff of land. They went quite crazy. I managed to keep them more or less in order until the banks of the Mersey became visible and then they really let fly. When we tied up in the dock at Liverpool every stall was matchwood lying on the dirty old deck. The ponies and the racehorse, all looking well, mark you, and damned pleased with themselves, were strolling about as they wished among the winches and coils of wire and rope. Fortunately during the voyage I had removed their shoes and kept the feet well rasped, so they had grip.

It was a grey January afternoon, though not cold, and, horror of horrors (did I say there was only one thing wrong with England?) it was a Saturday. The gangway was over in a flash and all the crew, captain, officers, deck hands, stewards, firemen, vanished instantly and thankfully ashore. They were followed by a few sick-looking rats. I was left alone with the ponies until the night watchman arrived, elderly, Liverpudlian, and sensible.

'There'll be no off-loading party for the horses and no horse gangway till Monday morning soon after nine,' he said. 'If I were you I'd throw down plenty of hay on deck, fill up their water troughs, and leave 'em alone. They'll be all right if they're left quiet, they're so pleased just to *be* here. You clear off till Monday. That's my advice.'

Not bad advice either, I thought. We made a rope boundary fence and I left them there on that queer, echoing steel paddock with steam blowing off all round and the screams of the gulls in their ears.

I took a taxi to the Adelphi Hotel where I booked a room and bathroom for two nights, spending about two month's wages on a small slice of comfort I felt I had truly earned. I had most of my meals in bed, soaked in three hot baths a day, and turned up on Monday morning feeling new. (I'd had a good look at them on the Sunday.)

We led them off and into a train bound for Rugby. That little train seemed like heaven to me and to the horses after the ship. At Rugby they were off-loaded and jogged in threes to Springfield Polo Ground where, in the intervals of catering for Geoffrey Brooke's hunting with the Pytchley, I set about their education. By May the Argentine ponies were beginning to play well, and when we sold them later at Tattersalls they fetched an average of a hundred and twenty guineas. Up to then the main costs on them had been as follows: five pounds to buy, five pounds to ship to England, and five pounds insurance. I think Mr Brooke felt they showed him a reasonable profit. One little bay mare, though, could not be sent for sale, as she proved to be in foal. Mrs Brooke later drove her in a governess cart. And when she foaled down do you know what she produced? A *mule*. It was a funny trip all round. She was the prettiest pony of them all and an old donkey had got at her. It happens in the best circles, doesn't it?

As for Robin Grey, the Guercillero racehorse, I took him to Persse's stables at Stockbridge to be trained but very soon Mr Persse (Persinperson, we used to call him) was on the telephone to Brooke saying the grey was a stumer, a foozler, and a frost, that he was so footy he would ·stumble over a leaf of grass. Down I went with the box to fetch him up to the cavalry school at Weedon, where we were based. All through that spring and summer we tried to get him to go, and to school him over fences, so you can judge he had the full treatment, patience, skill, cunning, blandishments, everything. With the start of cubhunting I used to slip over and ride him out with the Pytchley, hoping he'd take to the sport as Christmas Daisy had done. No such luck. He wouldn't move in the heavy going, and he wouldn't jump a stick.

The maddening aspect of it was that four or five of us had seen him register a splendid stayer's win on the Palermo track at B.A. and had had some productive bets on him too. But there they'd brushed the sand smooth before the race with a couple of bullocks drawing a heavy hurdle. He could go like fun on top of the ground with a bit of soft dust spurting under each foot and his head high and steady as though suspended in the atmosphere. But oh Lord! On the grass or, worse, in Midland mud, how he would labour! So we decided to off-load him. How it was done I can't quite remember, but certainly in the most ethical manner, and thankful I was to see the last of him. My Pytchley rides on him had been

purgatory. I could understand why Geoffrey Brooke did not
wish to be seen on a chronic refuser, but no more did I. That
sort of thing harms anyone's reputation. Anyway, the sequel
was fully up to the S.S. *Raphael* pattern, and amused us all
no end, at least I think it did. Robin Grey found his way into
the hands of that fine horseman, Major Faudel-Phillips,
who brought him out as a show hack—and sold him to the
Kaiser for a thousand pounds. That's the horse trade all
over: one man's poison is another man's meat.

Geoffrey Brooke at that time wanted to win the National
Hunt at Cheltenham and the Grand Military Gold Cup.
When he bought Robin Grey in the Argentine he had had
those two races in mind. As it happened he owned, while we
were doing our best with Robin Grey, a far more likely
animal, a St Simon horse. He'd been at Weedon that same
winter and Brooke and I had spent any amount of time
schooling, exercising, and hunting him. Unlike the grey, he
was absolutely Cheltenham class, bold, smooth, and stayed
on for ever, the dickens of a good potential steeplechaser.
He was sent to a Northamptonshire trainer, Beechner, to
be tuned up for the big Cheltenham meeting, and in his case
you may be sure we had no complaints from the trainer,
who was mad about him, particularly as the owner would
be riding him, and what an owner-rider!

One day as ill-luck would have it the hounds ran right
through Beechner's village. Geoffrey Brooke was, as usual,
in the first flight on a little mare that was cooked. He rode
into Beechner's yard and shouted to the lads.

'Get that horse of mine out. I must see the end of this
hunt, and my mare's done.'

'So's the hunt,' the head lad answered, coming at once
from his lair when he heard one of his charges menaced.
'So's the hunt, Captain Brooke. And your horse is watered
and fed. You can't take him.'

'Who says so? Can't I?'

'They're not running on. It's fizzled out. You might as

well stop on that nice little mare. Turn her into the wind and let her catch her breath.'

'I *must* have him,' Brooke said. 'Look at that hound feathering down the ditch. They *will* run on. Come on, quick, no more nonsense, out with my horse.'

So, muttering and reluctant, they pulled out the fine, sleek, sleepy creature. He rode him, with his usual matchless elegance, through the orchard where the hounds were snuffling about. They suddenly hit off a line. He jumped out of the orchard straight into a single strand of barbed wire that cut deep into both hocks. His fine young horse was ruined, and many expectations went with him. . . . That was one side of Geoffrey Brooke. He could get so hotted up, so overwound, that nobody could tell him anything. One minute he'd be the most civilised man on earth in relation to horses, and the next he'd be too bold.

Usually he was as cool as an Alp, as Buster Keaton. Jumping for example, what judgement, what nerve, what timing! When I say he was up to every trick in the trade I mean every honourable and sensible trick. I never in a long life with horses saw anyone to compare with him for getting any horse over any obstacle. And it was he, after all, who proved and then taught the forward seat at Netheravon. I have told you that when I first saw him he was twenty-one and a junior second lieutenant. He soon got his lieutenancy and then was adjutant to the Northamptonshire Yeomanry. That meant he could keep his horses (and their attendants, myself included) at Weedon and hunt with the Grafton and the Pytchley. He was given command of a regiment just before the 1914 war, commanded one in the line right through, and was obviously a wonderful fighting soldier. He emerged loaded with decorations, and landed up a major-general and A.D.C. to the King.

As a man he was separate, distrait. I never enjoyed his confidence, or got to know him as more than *the* man on any horse.

Colonel Gough ('Goughie') was often at Weedon and the polo grounds and I saw a great deal of him because he was immensely keen on schooling. He used to ride with a little check cord through the mouth, up the sides of the bridle and back to his hand. He could fetch them on their hocks like lightning with the cord. They didn't need it often. I must admit that when Colonel Gough, who had been partly instrumental in getting me off the grind of ordinary regimental duties, was being so nice to me I often wondered who and what the hell I was. Although still officially a 16th Lancer I was seldom in a Mess or in regular quarters. I drew the allowances and the pay, such as it was, but I was always schooling, hunting, or playing polo.

Officers then, before World War One, in crack cavalry regiments were enjoying the peak of their good times. Summer for them meant polo, Hurlingham, Ranelagh, Roehampton, and of course all the balls, racing, cricket, rowing, and other entertainments that went so well with polo. In winter there was hunting.

When we went to the Pytchley, Lord Annaly was Master and Frank Freeman hunted hounds, a great combination. It was a perfect galloping country then, with not a trace of wire in most parts, and my goodness how those Pytchley Fields did fly. Their hunters were bought to travel far and very fast, and they had to jump, and did. Much credit for that must go to the two great dealers in that country, the brothers John and Herbert Drage of Chapel Brampton. I met the Drages frequently through Brooke, but they already knew of me because Harry Gale, our friend from boyhood, was one of their buyers.

Two or three times I accompanied Brooke and Gough to the Bellvilles' house, Papillon Hall, Market Harborough, for foxhunting houseparties. The Bellvilles were, I was told, ground landlords of Harrods, so they had a bit of money. George Bellville was a 16th Lancer and a good polo player. He nearly always had a staff job, and when he retired from the regiment he took on the Mastership of the Woodland Pytchley. I particularly enjoyed Papillon Hall. One morning when they were looking for Geoffrey Brooke to school a young horse that was sticky at his fences, Colonel Gough said to Miss Bellville, 'You're wasting your energies looking for Geoffrey when Marshall's standing just behind you, and he's the man behind Geoffrey and the reason for most of his success. There's many a young one won't go for Geoffrey, if he's in one of his Godalmighty-let's-get-on moods, that *will* go for that modest young man behind you.' What he said was not true. I've told you what I thought of Geoffrey Brooke. He was the top. But it was nice of Colonel Gough to say it and it did me no end of a good turn because after that when any Bellville asked anyone from Weedon for the hunting they would say, 'Could you possibly get that young man of Geoffrey's to come along.' One afternoon there I was schooling a roan pony, a sweet little thing no more than fourteen hands but headstrong and puzzled, when a crowd of people came round the house, strolling about before luncheon, glasses of sherry in their hands. One of them hailed me.

'Are you not Howard Marshall from Hickling, the one that broke in Christmas Daisy for Captain Forester, the boy that won his first race when he was ten?' It was Mr Ambrose Clark, the American multi-millionaire I've told you about. What he said to the Bellvilles about me I don't know, but after that I was promoted to mess with the butler and the housekeeper when I was at Papillon, and they did themselves well and were very kind to me. Mr Clark also, when I was going to America with Geoffrey Brooke to jump with the victorious British team at Madison Square Gardens, not only gave me introductions and addresses in New York, but sent me a wad of dollars as well. That trip was so hectic, and I was so busy right through it with the horses, looking after others as well as our own, that I didn't have an hour to spare on my own interests and pleasures. Pretty well all I registered was that I liked Americans in their own country as I'd always liked them in mine (and we had seen a goodish number of them from Hickling), and that there was nothing the matter with New York either. One day during the jumping when I was working on a slight overreach Harriet had given herself, a tall Englishman stood watching me.

'Your name Marshall?'

'That's me,' I said, not looking up.

'I believe you know my brother Ambrose in London, Ambrose Preece.'

'Yes I do, and you'll be Mr Godfrey Preece,' I said, stand-up and shaking hands with him.

'You're busy now,' he said. 'But if you get any time off, come out to Long Island and look me up, or give a ring to Durland's Riding Academy, for I'm often there, morning, afternoon, or both.' He gave me his card which stated that he dealt in high-class riding and driving horses, and special-ised in polo ponies.

I was very conscious at that time that although I was enjoying myself and was having a good deal of success, I was still only a trooper (and a queer one at that) in a crack regiment, and I was absolutely at the mercy of G.B., who, had he wished, could have turned me back any minute to routine duties. I don't say he'd ever have done such a thing, quite the reverse. But I knew how quickly misunderstandings could arise between employer and employee or between two men, and both of us had hasty tempers. I knew where to find Mr Ambrose Preece, and the first Monday I could get off in London I went to Tattersalls, which was where I most liked going anyway. There he was, a small, rolypoly gentle-man in a brown bowler hat, very jolly, and obviously nobody's fool.

'Godfrey wrote me from Long Island, telling me how well you saw to those jumpers, young man.'

'I didn't do anything special.'

'If that's how you look at it, better still. We need con-scientious helpers in our business. I'd take you on any time.

Plenty of work for you, not in the livery either, schooling and travelling. More money than you get now, I'll be bound.'

'But how do I get out of the Army?'

'How much longer before your time's up?'

'Nearly four years.'

'There I can't help you. You must take that fence on your own, my boy.'

What I should have done, I now see, was to go to Brooke and tell him I wished to better myself. He'd then, I think, have helped me to get out of the Army or he'd have improved my situation in it. But he was an officer who went abroad a lot, and he was in Italy when I got into difficulties.

I did not desert, though I know there were rumours to that effect.

No, the whole thing was occasioned by an accident. What happened was this:

One night I went to a party south of Weedon, down Watling Street, the Towcester-London road. I travelled on my old bicycle, pedalling joyfully towards a certain house many miles from my lawful place of rest beside Captain Brooke's horses. I spent a convivial evening, seldom remember a better in all my puff. When I came out it was very late and I had quite a few drinks inside me—an unusual situation for me because, as you know, I am not, and never was, a drinker.

Facing a pleasant ride back through the end of the night followed by an illicit entry that offered no problem to me, I made my narrow tyres fairly sing up the road. I felt at home, for I was in Grafton country, and many a fine day's hunting had we enjoyed there from Weedon. The cool air was wonderful. I suspect that my course was serpentine, when a car came racing up astern and knocked me for six. They gently stuffed and folded me into the car and carried me to Northampton Hospital. I was in civvies. Nothing to account for to anyone. No questions asked. Just a road accident. I was shaken, and I said nothing. My thoughts were muddled. . . .

If you were not in barracks you got back to your digs by morning and all was well. My military habits had been unusual, thanks to Brooke's abilities in the saddle and his regard for my more prosaic skills with his stud. Yet although circumstances had put me outside the normal run of soldiering I'd never abandoned or ignored the rules. I'd been careful to know how far I could go, and had gone not a step farther. What should I do?

Daylight brought with it a pretty little nurse, pleasant and friendly. She produced breakfast, to which I did full justice, finishing even the marmalade jar, and only wishing that there had been coffee instead of tea. The bandages on my head and hands hardly bothered me. 'You ought to be speaking out, Trooper Marshall,' I said aloud. 'You know what you are? You are A.W.O.L., and that's a most serious crime.' Then I found myself laughing as though it were the hell of a joke, though I'm sure my injuries were superficial, and there was no hint of concussion. I rang the bell and the same pretty one came.

'Bring me my pipe and baccy, there's a dear. And tomorrow I'd rather have strong coffee than that watery tea.'

'Quite illegal,' she said, fetching my pipe. 'But as you're in a private ward and pay accordingly. . . .'

'Who pays? Not me I hope.'

'No fear, don't worry. The people who knocked you over are paying. I heard them telling Matron. You're to have everything you want.'

'That's a tall order,' I said, giving her a wink. 'There are some things can't be bought.'

'You're to have everything you want,' she repeated, flushing but pretending not to understand. 'Everything.'

'Are there no flowers?'

'Yes,' she said to my astonishment. 'But we take them out at night. They make the air heavy in the bedroom. Normally I'd bring them in a little later, after your blanket bath. But as you've asked for them. . . .' She came in with a vase of blue irises and white ones. They were lovely, clean, and delicate, and from that moment I settled in to enjoy myself. Not swinging the lead, you understand? I never pretended to be ill. I laughed at the doctor when he told me I must take things easy. The people who'd run me down were trumps. They came nearly every day and were so charming and kind. They gave me a brand-new bicycle, you never saw such a beauty, a Rudge Whitworth with mudguards shaped like roofs. They don't make bikes like that nowadays. . . . I stayed in that comfortable place for a whole fortnight.

Towards the end of that interlude (I had led a spartan life, you know, and was unused to even such simple luxuries) I became increasingly apprehensive. I obviously ought to get in touch with somebody. Brooke was abroad, so he was no use to me. Should I write to the adjutant at Weedon or the adjutant at Nottingham? No, adjutants were inhuman. That would only lead to bother. I had it! I'd write to Colonel Graham who was temporarily in command at Weedon. He was a friend of Geoffrey Brooke's, a Yorkshireman, and a foxhunter. I knew he was all right, and felt that he was kind enough to be sympathetic to anyone who got into a scrape. I got a letter off to him three days before I was due to leave hospital, telling him I would report back and would then explain my conduct. When my delightful nurse had posted it I felt more at ease about my impending return to duty.

After almost tearful goodbyes to the benefactors who had run me over and to friends on the hospital staff, I mounted my Rudge and bicycled up to Weedon, a distance of eight miles. Arrived there, I halted, sitting the bicycle with one foot down, wondering where I might find Colonel Graham at such a time. Right there by the main gates there was a civilian police station. A sergeant came out.

'Hey! Your name Marshall?'

'Yes.'

'Come inside a moment.'

When I went in, feeling perfectly friendly, he took a short

run at me, pushed me headlong into a cell, and locked the door behind me.

It made the hell of a case, this deserter apprehended by the civilian police as he hung about under the stupid noses of the military. That sergeant was determined to suck the last ounce of profit from my predicament. I was in the clink for ten days or more. But I had a group of good friends outside, people with influence, and eventually I found myself on the mat with Colonel Graham in the seat of judgement. After delivering a savage reprimand, bringing in the regiment and all the rest of the bag of tricks, he cleared the room and said, 'Now, Marshall, sit down, try to stop fidgeting, and tell me what it was all about.'

He'd already heard in evidence of my bicycle accident. I said I'd knocked about and roughed it since I left Hickling Manor, aged sixteen, and that merely to sleep between sheets and be brought decent food was a tremendous experience for me.

He was listening with obvious sympathy. Then he gave himself a shake and said, 'Being absent without leave for so long a period is a damned serious offence, as well you know. If you stop in the Army it must prejudice your whole future and make the next weeks very uncomfortable for you. You understand me?'

'Yes, sir.'

'Tell me honestly, Marshall, how much does the Army mean to you or, let's put it another way, what do you feel you have done for the Army during your—let's see—four years of service.'

I told him I'd been to South America and North America and of the pots and prizes we'd won for Britain. I told him about our Olympia wins with Alice and Harriet and Combined Training.

'Alice, I remember her well. Such poise!'

'She wouldn't be beat, she was more tiger than mare, and that was her weakness.'

'Courage a weakness?'

'She'd build up such disdain of showjumping fences, that only Captain Brooke could make her go.'

'Good Lord!'

The colonel cleared his throat, shuffled his boots with their gleaming spurs, and glared at me as much as to say, 'The next move is yours.'

'I suppose I've lost my job for Captain Brooke, sir,' I blurted out. 'I've got fourteen pounds saved. Would you think it possible I might be allowed to buy myself out of the Army?'

I'd done well to write to him for he was a gentleman, and very fair. Most of them were if you didn't push them too hard. He let me out, away, clear. I cut straight down to London to see Ambrose Preece.

I forgot to tell you. I'd written to *him* too.

6

Off to America

So it was at Weedon that I left the 16th Lancers, Weedon, only fifty-four miles from Hickling. I knew that my father, Sam, and Mitchell were at Hickling. I could imagine how disappointed my father would be with my poor showing in the cavalry, since possibly his head still swam with the dreams put there by Captain Thompson—commission, rich wife, hunters, polo. Ah well, I wished too that the Captain's forecast had been accurate. Because, let me get this straight in your mind, I never once felt the slightest twinge of jealousy for all those sparks of cavalry officers with their clubs, their money, and their friends. I admired them and liked them. If I'd been lucky enough to be inside their boots, why, I'd have played out the stakes of life much as they did, I hope. Later, in Flanders, they were to show that if they knew how to enjoy life, they also knew how to die with grace and dignity.

But no need to be morbid. . . . I took the train to London in high spirits. I had a bit of cash in my pocket, since I had not divulged my *entire* resources to Colonel Graham. I arrived in London on a Thursday and went straight to get a room in the Y.M.C.A. off Tottenham Court Road. I then searched the second-hand clothes shops in the Charing Cross and Victoria areas. I'd had plenty of time with Geoffrey Brooke to learn how a riding man should dress himself. I knew the tailors of London, and when I saw names like Sandon, Lesley & Roberts, or Huntsman, on the labels by the inner pockets, that was the time to start trying on. Had I had the

money, I'd have bought everything new, had it made for
me naturally, but I really don't know that I'd have got the
same pleasure out of the proceedings. I was very poor indeed
by Friday evening. But I actually had an invitation to stay
with friends.

Jim Dawkins, who had been in my barrackroom at
Aldershot, had come out of the Army and married a widow
who kept a little shop at Richmond. Jim, more than thirty
years my senior, had had a hard go in life, often in trouble.
Molly was five years his senior. How they laughed over my
A.W.O.L. business and my dismissal from the service, and
Molly Dawkins was thrilled by my thorough exploration of
the used-clothes market. She pressed every bit of clothing,
exclaiming at the excellence of the tweed and the whipcord,
and wherever she could find work for her needle she used it.
Meanwhile Jim and I were working away at my new-old
Maxwell riding boots, boning and polishing until they looked
nearly as good as the king's. Because the man who looks after
a boot is just as important as the man who wears it, and nearly
as important as the man who makes it.

On the Saturday night they took me to a music hall in
Richmond. We sat out, after, in a riverside beer hall with
further singing from the stout ladies and the gentlemen with
waxed moustaches who had entertained us indoors. The
Thames went sliding past like dark brown oil or, as Jim
said, like stout without much head to it. Somewhere around
midnight we ate vast plates of whitebait and then rasp-
berries and cream. I remember the gnats swimming into
the yellow glare of the gas lights and the man bouncing up
and down on his hard-looking behind as he thumped the
wilting piano. It was a bonus night in my life. Those people
had asked me to stay not because I could ride or because
they wanted anything from me, but simply because they
thought me a good sort. I had gone to them because I was
poor, and had nowhere else to go, and once with them I
found everything perfect, Jim so friendly and so gay, Molly

with her wrinkled brown skin and distinguished features
and her gorgeous London voice, the little flat above the
littler shop, the river smells, the mist clinging to the Thames
valley, and Richmond, which is still an attractive place but
which then was so perfect, so lovely.

Their shop was open from seven-thirty on the Sunday
morning to sell the papers. I got up at five o'clock, harnessed
the pony to the trap, and drove Jim to the station to fetch
the bundles. He and I sorted them, and then he went round
delivering to the big, comfortable, sleepy houses and the
long terraces while I stayed in the shop selling to whoever
came in. Jim got back about eight and put up the pony.
It was a hot morning. We let the striped curtain down across
the door in case the entering sun should soften the boiled
sweets and the chocolate. About quarter to nine, unrefusable
smells came down to us, and after setting the doorbell
of the shop we went up to eat devilled kidneys and bacon
and coffee and muffins and honey. At one o'clock (it being
Sunday) we closed the shop. There were children playing on
the grass verges of the Thames with toys we had been selling
all morning, simple toys, propellers on sticks, coloured a
strangely intriguing bluish-purple. The stick was held
vertically and a sleeve pushed up it, which sent the propeller
spiralling into the sky like a wilful and rather drunken
dragonfly. We set off rowing downstream in a gig, Jim at the
oars and Molly and I in the cushioned stern-seat. We stopped
for lunch, cold roast beef, cold venison, and cold almost
everything else, with potato salad and gallons of ale, and
strawberries and cream. When Molly had left us for a
moment Jim said to Mrs Corcoran Senior behind the bar,
'Give us two tots of your vintage, my dear,' and she produced
huge glasses of soft Irish spirit, and with it a jar of Fribourg
and Treyers' Oriental Mixture which we stuffed, gratis, into
our pipes and puffed away at as we swung on vigorously
down the placid river. Landing at a bathing place called
The Man Replete, we all put on striped costumes and swam

When we came out Jim thought that so hot an afternoon demanded Somerset draught cider. We had some of that and then the day petered out in a golden haze. I found it perfect to be with the pair of them.

Next day was Monday. I packed my bags and caught the London train. Jim drove me to the station. He had a grand little pony he called The Weazel, a mealy-muzzled thing, squirmy and hot, a bit of an animal with a leg at each corner. The mood I was in, I liked Jim and every blasted thing he owned. I wouldn't have changed The Weazel for The Tetrarch. How I laughed as the pony took a hold down the hill, with Jim hanging on as though in a trotting race!

There was not quite the usual crowd at Tattersalls because the season was ending or over. But the professionals were there, and they are the ones that matter. I, of course, noticed Mr Ambrose Preece as soon as I got in there.

'Thank you for your note from hospital,' he said, somewhat nervously, when he at last rolled up to me and caught me by the lapel of my newly-acquired tweed suit. '*Are you all right?*'

'Why yes, thank you, Mr Preece.'

'And you can still ride?'

'My goodness! Yes, why?'

'I feared you'd doctored yourself to get clear of the Army— it's been done before, you know. But you *are* clear? Good. And have a clean passport? Good. Well, my boy, there are some blood ponies coming up today, and if they're in the bracket we shall have 'em.'

He took up his stance by the ring, and for hours I watched him, quite fascinated. The auction ring to anyone who cares about such things is as passionately interesting as a race, or a love affair, or the prospect of a fortune. Mr Preece stood there absolutely immobile. He was keen on anything that was going below its market value, or anything that was real quality. He bought in two price brackets, lower and higher. And he immediately established a rapport with the

auctioneer. With any big buyer, the buyer who deals in
thousands of pounds in a morning, the auctioneer is receptive,
understanding, almost instinctive. Mr Preece when he was
beginning to bid might raise one finger by the ringside, or he
might boldly name a figure, 'One hundred and ten.' But once
the bidding was going, and he was *in*, it was impossible for
any but the auctioneer to know whether he was bidding or
not. Time and again I was surprised (and I was not by any
means a novice) to hear the auctioneer say quietly, at the
end of a tousle, 'Preece'. And the clerk booked it.

Every now and then Mr Preece would beckon George, the
charming waiter from I don't know which caravanserai round
the ring, and say, 'Mr Marshall and I are thirsty.' And
George would bring us brandy and sodas, which I could
have done without.

In the late afternoon we walked to his stables in the Fulham
Road. (The Preece brothers had been left the livery business
there, and a substantial fortune, by their father, until whose
death they had operated a horse-trading and livery business
at Neasden, and had run a pack of drag hounds to attract
their numerous clients.) Two lovely little hackneys were
harnessed tandem to a dogcart. He drove them down Fulham
Road and across Putney Bridge, then handed the ribbons to
me saying, 'Saints of India, boy! I can buy 'osses, but you
can make the darned things go. Each to his own crib.'

While I drove he took papers and pencil from his pocket
and did sums, presumably about the day's deals and their
possible outcomes. There was a discreet signpost at the
entry to Combe Warren House, where he lived with his
daughter. It was a substantial property off the Kingston
road and opposite the entry to Richmond Park. I thought at
the time it belonged to Miss Mona Dunn, a very famous
figure in the horse world who had a series of marvellous
show horses, hacks, hunters, jumpers, polo ponies, at Olympia
through the early years of this century. It was said that a lot
of Dunn money went into the backing and planning of

Olympia, the most magnificent, interesting, subtle, and attractive horse show ever produced anywhere in the world's history. In that show everything aimed at perfection, from the Master of Ceremonies, the Earl of Lonsdale in person, a great peer, a great person, and a pugilist ready to set about any bully or boor, to the stabling built to resemble the yards of earlier centuries, the boxes thatched, the grooms in scarlet woollens and cloth leggings, and a tame magpie in his wicker cage talking horsey Anglo-Irish and shouting the odds. Everybody went to Olympia from the highest to the lowest, and everybody got value for his entry money. Miss Dunn and the Preeces were good friends, and many of her horses were stabled at Combe Warren. I had never, until that day, entered the hallowed portals.

A butler came out from the house, and a groom from the stable yard. Mr Preece, at my side, was asleep. The butler gave his arm a shake.

'Bless my soul,' he said, taking off his bowler and looking around him. 'The birds are singing, must be after four-thirty. *Is* after four-thirty. This is Mr Marshall, Haliburton; Haliburton, Mr Marshall. Staying with us for a little, till he goes to Mr Godfrey in Amurrica. . . .' That was the first I had heard of it.

'Indeed, sir. Miss Preece is taking tea in the oak room sir.'

'Damn the oak room!' Mr Preece said shortly. 'I intend trotting Mr Marshall round the stables. . . . We have our share of Chinese puzzles at the moment, Howard, my boy. Yes, we have our share of Chinese trouble.' He was talking, as I was soon to learn, of problem horses, the ones the dealer finds difficulty in getting his profit on. I knew at once by the behaviour of the two grooms on duty that he was redhot where stable management was concerned. And the next day I knew he knew what was what where horse-making was concerned.

He had eight polo ponies there, all destined for Long

119

Island. One was straight off a Kilkenny farm and never backed, while the others were in varying stages of greenness. On my first morning of schooling them he took up his position with a female secretary in a Georgian teahouse that overlooked the paddocks. I could see him well as I worked, and he me.

At quarter to one he came down to me, rotund but immensely purposeful, with the walk of a hen-toed panther.

'Now put that pony up and tell 'em to move him till he's dry,' he said. 'And come back here,' gesturing towards the teahouse. 'We'll find ourselves a glass of sherry or Madeira, shall we?' And when I rejoined him he said, 'As I was saying, Howard, or wasn't I, you have, or I think you have, what's wanted in America.'

'What can that be, Mr Preece?' I asked, fascinated.

'Patience, Howard. Patience, diligence, perfectionism with horseflesh, allied to discrimination. It's bred in you, my boy. They haven't got it yet. But they'll get it ere long, and then they'll be selling *me* made 'osses.' I knew from those words exactly what he expected from me, and it was exactly what I had to give, and have always given, to the horse trade. I would get on any horse and ride him, but I was also prepared to look after him, to study his habits of sleep, action, feeding, temperament, and to cater for him accordingly. I was just made, I realised later (though never ungratefully) to work for astute people like the Preeces.

Our schooling went on for some time, and I very quickly got the feel of Combe Warren. For someone like me, who enjoyed his work and knew it backwards and adored good horses, the place was all right. To the other sort, the kind who skimped or who bullied, Combe Warren was the top of the slippery slide. Soon Ambrose told me that we, myself and eight horses, were booked to leave for America. The day before we sailed I saddled the best-looking of my splendid ponies and rode him across Richmond Park and through Richmond itself to the shop near the river. A sign

painter was up on a ladder. He had painted out F. J. Tow-
cester (Molly's first husband) and was substituting Mr and
Mrs F. J. Dawkins. We put my blood pony in the next box
to The Weazel, who looked as though he would murder him.
I said goodbye to the Dawkinses as though they were my true
parents. To me that pair of English worthies were sacred.
The one explanation I can put to their fascination for me is
that they were, in all my life, and it has been a long one,
the only people quite unconnected with horses. 'Send us a
p.c. from New York,' Molly said as I left.

It was a glowing, balmy afternoon when I rode back
across the park. A massive branch had been blown off one
of the royal oaks. I edged the pony over the grass, wondering,
as any horse trainer will, how he felt about it. Sure enough,
as we drew near the obstacle, which would be about three
foot nine inches high, I felt him grow keen and measure his
distances. I let him go at it. He took it perfectly, but banked
it, changing legs on the top. Those Irishmen! God bless
them! They never forget their origins. I think it was the last
fence he ever jumped. He grew into one of the top ponies
on the American continent, and he turned over a ton of
hard money in his career. He was four years old when
he and I banked the royal-oak branch.

Next morning I loaded my charges on the *Minnewaska* at
Tilbury, and we left for New York. It was to be the first of
several trips, and I never again travelled with so small a
consignment. No doubt they were trying me out. My trip
on the *Raphael* had taught me a few things, though.

7

Long Island

I LANDED in the United States of America in 1909 much
as I landed in France in 1914. I had my horses to worry
about. To the specialist, the earth is one. He sees to his eggs
or his pictures or his women. I noticed that America smelled
different, that the food was different, and that the horses
were different. But my first worry was to get my ponies
settled comfortably with Mr Godfrey Preece. He met us
at the docks of New York, a tall tweedy man, lean and
charming, with a squad of Negro grooms, who were to ride
the ponies home, while he and I followed in a rubber-tyred
trap drawn by a spanking bang-tailed high-stepper. The
ponies were quite unused to such traffic, and I was out in
the road more than once, and so busy I hardly knew where
I was.

At length we came to more open country, bare to my eyes,
with stout timber fences, and a sign at the corner of a lot
proclaimed:

POLO PONIES

GODFREY
PREECE

NONE BUT THE BEST

I believe that all that part, Queen's, Long Island, is now
town, and it amuses me to think of people living out their
lives in the fields where we spent so many long hours working,
teaching our different horses and ponies. I was given quarters

in the Preeces' comfortable timber house, warm in the very
sharp but delightful winter, cool in the hot summer, when
before the dawn we would all be afoot to get the best out of
the early part of the day. Then a light luncheon and siesta,
and work the horses again in the long evenings. We were not,
however, so restricted climatically as you would have
expected because Mr Preece had set up an indoor schooling
area on his own lot, and we passed much of our working time
in New York itself.

Godfrey Preece was a better man than his brother on a
horse, for he was slim and tall and had the leg for it, and
although he was a hard master and an ironbound worker,
always seeking from his employees value for money, he was
fair, kind, and professional. As for his wife, she was perfection, and they had three young children who were being
brought up to the horse as Sam, Mitchell, and I had been.
The story was that Godfrey had run away from England with
a ward in Chancery. All I knew was that the house was a
joy to be in, and I had never met a nicer person than Mrs
Preece.

The complication at first for me was that colour business.
You see, the stable work was done by Negroes, and they were
quite good. But I was accustomed to plunging in and doing
my own work on a horse's ailment if that horse was important.

'Go ahead, Howard,' Godfrey Preece always said. 'They're
good lads, else they wouldn't be here. They won't take
umbrage once they see you know what you're at.'

He was perfectly right. To them, after a few awkward
tussles I admit, I wasn't the boss, I wasn't the white man,
I was the horse master and the horse builder. Once I'd established myself there I enjoyed those stables.

In the open weather we'd usually start schooling ponies
at dawn, carry on with them after breakfast, and then, if
it was to be a New York day, set out in Godfrey's open
four-seater Ford. We'd go to Durland's Riding Academy,
a large and complicated building occupying a whole block

123

beside Central Park. You could drive a coach and six into the entrance and be carried (with coach and six) to the eleventh floor. Godfrey had his stables there, and if we were not selling he would allow me to school. Sometimes that went on all day. The rings were well kept. It was always a pleasure to work horses there. Very often, though, I would show horses to potential buyers, sometimes three or four in a morning. Then we would eat lunch, standing up at the sandwich bar, pale frothy beer and shellfish and excellent sandwiches of many kinds. The thing I liked best was strawberry shortcake. I ate my way through tons of it, and drank the coffee like mad. The others were not so abstemious. The barman slid a whole bottle of rye or Bourbon or Scotch across the counter at them, and they drank what they felt like, which seemed an awful lot to me.

I never could drink like that. I never liked the smell of it. Wine, yes; spirits, no. And as they were generous hosts and payers I had to become adept at avoiding giving offence. Many an aspidistra must have died owing to my libations, and many a carpet in New York (I regret to admit) must have suffered from a douche of gin or brandy. Whisky I could never bear, following the episode with the bookie at Trent College.

After lunch, if there was no more work to be done in New York, Godfrey would whip me off to Piping Rock or Meadowbrook to school or play polo, or perhaps back to Queen's. Then, after eating *en famille*, he would drive to New York for the night sale of horses at Van Taseel and Gurney's. It was so like an auction in England. Admittedly there were Belgians, Dutchmen, and Germans importing horses as we were doing, but in the main the horse world of New York and its environment were Anglo-Irish, or seemed so. It amused me no end to see Godfrey buy. For all that he was long and thin while his brother Ambrose was short and thick (only physically, mind you) and for all that this was New York instead of London, the procedure was exactly the same. There was Godfrey first lifting one finger and then apparently not lifting even an eyelash, yet in the end the auctioneer would say in the same flat voice, 'Preece', and his clerk would book it. We were the International Set, we horse-copers, and we worked long hours and with much worry for what profit we got. More than once he bought the danger number, three, at those night sales. If he bought more than three he'd engage other help. But he reckoned I could ride three home to Queen's quite easily. So I'd saddle one stranger in a hurry, wondering if he were cold-backed, and set off for home leading one either side. Even in daylight Long Island Bridge was a hazard for horses, with street cars on the left and the railway on the right, and the elevated crossing over the New York end. Traffic in that place was really something for any horse, and the motor cars were not then the worst of it, for although they were numerous, they went slowly, and looked out for you. No, it was the noise, the street-cars banging, crashing, belling, and the shouts. If there's one thing that upsets either horses or cattle, it is men shouting. Well, each time I got 'em home in the end and Godfrey would say to Mrs Preece in front of me as we drank a cup of tea on the veranda, 'It's Howard, darling, he's a light-handed wizard; he just charms those horses.' And she would smile her dark-lashed, secret smile.

Queen's was near Belmont Park race course. When we overflowed with horses, and we often did, Godfrey was able to hire extra boxes and stalls there at cut rates. Like his brother at the London end, he was a smart specimen. He gave value for money, and he worked the clock round. Absolutely straight in business, a buyer who pulled out his cheque book as soon as he clinched a deal, he was so artful that he often seemed positively angelic. He had built up an enviable reputation in America, and I don't have to tell you that in the horse trade reputation is nearly everything.

Among the many polo ponies standing at Belmont Park were those of my old acquaintance from Melton days, Mr

Ambrose Clark. That sportsman spent, as I have told you, the latter half of each hunting season at Warwick Lodge, Leicestershire, and most springs he'd come back to Long Island bringing with him a string of absolutely tip-top Irish ponies bought from Slocock at peak prices. When we heard that Mr Clark had shown up at Belmont with a new batch of beauties, generally in April or May, Godfrey and I used to ride over and meet him accidentally on purpose, you know what I mean? Each of us would be on a good-looking and sound Arizonan or Californian pony that I'd schooled until it went and played collected and handy in all paces and angles. (I'd had to learn how to do such schooling with Geoffrey Brooke, by gosh I had!) We would engage in a bit of stick and ball practice with the delightful millionaire. Pretty soon his Irish pony would be fighting against the bridle and hanging away from the stick. I would know what was the matter. The blood pony was green, straight off a boat, overfed, and fresh. (If you want to teach a horse, and it's important for him to learn his lessons, CUT his oats.)

A neat return back-hander, and a schooled pony coming round so smoothly after it like a gannet after a herring would be too much for Mr Clark.

'Damn it, Godfrey, How d'ye do it? Let me throw a leg over that blonde mare for a moment, and just see what you make of this one of mine.'

Our chestnut Californian had cost less than half one thousand dollars, and certainly was not in the same class as the thoroughbred Irish one, but before many days most, if not all, of the imported batch would be in our hands and replaced by sound and excellent American-bred ponies. The customer always got a well-schooled, genuine animal on which he could stop or score goals. As for the Irish ones, it took very little time for us to make them so valuable they might sell to England, South America, anywhere.

One morning a gentleman rang from his bath in the Waldorf Astoria Hotel. He asked Godfrey in a perfectly matter-of-fact voice (and why in the hell not?) how long it would take him to get into playing polo? What would it cost? Would he be able to join Piping Rock or Meadowbrook, being acquainted with members in both cases? What about clothes, sticks, boots, tack? And could Mr Preece immediately sell him ponies with lads to look after them? Also, this was the last query, could he immediately be taught to play polo? Now that was the kind of straightforward, and wholly admirable, question that you never got asked in Europe. Here was a genuine man, unashamed, ambitious, probably rich, asking genuine questions.

Could he ride? Godfrey asked. Oh yes, he could *ride*—as though that were the most ordinary of accomplishments. All Godfrey did was make an appointment for him to see some ponies at Queen's. Then he rang his contacts to inquire about the financial status of the new client. He heard that the man who rang from his bath was as sound as the gold in Fort Knox. Now let me tell you how we dealt with this paragon.

Godfrey's head man and friend of his youth was Joe Davies, who at one time had been Lord of the Manor of Shipton-under-Wychwood, Oxfordshire. Joe was one of those numerous English gentlemen who like mucking about in old clothes. I'd often see him in a pair of scruffy trousers and a singlet, mixing up the feed. (He was a great feeder.) On the other hand he could turn to being the grand seigneur, and played that part to perfection. He was fond of opera, and I would see him setting off for the Metropolitan in the full rig of those days, looking like minor royalty, or perhaps a Rothschild or a movie mogul.

Our ponies were stabled in a barn—the wooden buildings there were absolutely beautiful—well lit by numerous big windows and roof lights. The boxes were in a circle forming a schooling ring floored with coconut matting so that when we were pulling out ponies there was no clatter of any kind. We worked a lot in that ring, so that the ponies in their surrounding boxes took an intelligent interest, you may be sure, learning as they watched. When a customer was expected, all was silence and discipline. The ponies had been turned facing the ring, and put on pillar reins. As the customer came to the double doors a couple of Negro grooms, strategically placed, threw handfuls of dried peas at the high windows so that the ponies, looking up keenly, showed themselves as he entered.

The client from New York turned up five minutes early but that was not going to disturb such an organisation. He found me giving a show on one of our best ponies to Joe Davies, who was togged up half-horsey, half-City, extremely London in *ton*. I twisted and turned the lovely pony on a halfpenny, with stick and ball, professionally watched, very solemnly, by all the tethered ponies. The shrewd-looking customer was led to a ringside seat of padded leather smelling of saddle soap. I pulled pony after pony out for Joe Davies, and in his supposed role of buyer he gave a sales talk on each, asking the rock-bottom price (he thought it most reasonable), and mentioning the animal's good or bad points. Occasionally he'd mount, do a bit of fancy stickwork, and say a child could play good polo on that one. All this was mixed with a flow of criticism of us and the ponies. Finally he 'chose' half a dozen, walking in and out among them, lifting a foot here and there, measuring their withers against his own dropped chest, feeling their necks, looking in their mouths, as though he had all the time and money in the world, and did not give a damn whom he kept waiting.

'Mr Marshall!' It was the customer, who said his time was money, and he had made an appointment with Mr Preece. Where was Mr Preece? In New York, I answered truthfully. If he would step through into the office I'd fit him out with a pair of overshoes, as we'd have to take him through some mud to show him all the ponies.

'What's the matter with those ones right here in this ring.'

'Matter! Why those are the best ponies in America.'

: Winners of the Hunt Team at Madison Square Garden 1922, '23, '24. Mitchell all, 1st Whip, is second from the right and the Master, Mr. Bowman, is on the e right (*by kind permission of Mrs Catherine Dennett*). BELOW: H.R.H. The Prince of takes a liking to Mr E. Stanley Young's 'Passport II' ridden by Captain J. H. all at the Bath & West Show, Dorchester (*by kind permission of Mrs C. M. Marshall*)

'And who's he?' pointing at Joe.

'One of our regular clients,' I said, dropping my voice. 'He buys batches of polo ponies for Canada. The only bother with him is, he expects us to give them away.'

'I'll have these six, Mr Marshall,' Joe now halloaed, 'with the usual full warranty and at the following prices. . . .' He read from a piece of paper in his hand, giving the name and price of each pony.

'Cash sale?' I asked.

'I'll have to get authority from Ottawa, but when have I ever let you down?'

'It's deuced awkward, Mr Preece not being here. Hope he hasn't had an accident coming out of New York; he had an appointment with that gentleman behind you. You've picked out six of the very best, as usual, and for all I know Mr Preece intended selling them to *him*. I'm only an employee. You put me in a difficult position. Our terms as you know, are strictly cash.'

'Good grief, man!' Joe shouted. 'I've been dealing here for donkey's years and have spent several fortunes with Godfrey Preece. You can't shuffle out of a deal. Those ponies are mine.'

'Not until I hold your cheque. Do you maintain that if that little mare, Persephone, dropped dead in front of us now she'd be your loss, not ours? I have definite instructions from Mr Preece: "If anyone pays cash and the animal in your opinion suits the buyer, then sell. If he doesn't pay cash, postpone the sale till I am here." I must abide by Mr Preece's instructions, much though I regret doing so in your case.'

'Would those ponies suit me, Mr Marshall?' The voice came from the ringside, behind me.

'Have you played much polo, sir?'

'No, but I aim to learn fast.'

Soon the noise of the Preece Ford was heard outside the barn stables. Godfrey, extra tall in his slit tweed coat and brown bowler, swept in followed by Joe, pretending to be angry. Assured, suave, deep-voiced, emanating prosperity and integrity, Godfrey was full of apologies for his delayed arrival, pressure of business and so on. At last I was accorded a hearing.

'I hope I haven't done wrong, Mr Preece, but I've just accepted this gentleman's cheque for six ponies, and obviously the deal must stand. . . .'

'Which are they, Howard?' Godfrey asked. 'Let's have 'em out and line 'em up. Yes, saddle them.' The lads got busy and very soon all six were lined up, a fine show. We walked from one to the other. We legged the customer up, sitting him on one after the other, while Godfrey stood back, chin in hand, considering.

'These are six of the best,' he said when we ended the line. 'Mr Marshall here has schooled them until they are letter-perfect. For the enjoyment of any game of polo you would not find any better, but. . . .' There was a long pause. 'You told me on the telephone you were going to learn to play polo.'

'That's right.'

'Now listen, sir. I want to do business. I hope to stay doing business with you. It would be bad business to sell you six ponies when, as a beginner, you'd be far better off with two. Ponies, even the very best of them, have individual mannerisms and vices. You'll do very well indeed if you get to know two of these ponies within six months. I strongly advise you to have the chestnut mare and the little bay gelding with the star.'

So the cheque was altered and the customer went away thinking Mr Preece the grandest straightest man in the world. The two superb ponies were sent over to whichever club he had joined and within eight months they were back in our stables at Queen's, ready to earn a few more dollars. The man who had telephoned from his bath at the Waldorf had a good try at polo and was clever enough to acknowledge to himself, if not publicly, that the game was too difficult. He took up golf and may still be golfing. After all, in golf you hit a static ball. There is something about a golf ball and the open spaces you belt it into that stirs a man's blood. The same thing happens in polo, only polo is fifty times more difficult and it demands physical courage and a special kind of horsemanship. All the time I was in the U.S.A., sniffing the gathering power of the country, which was in the air like brimstone dust, I thought of the future of polo in that place of wealth and hot dry summers. Alas, it was golf, the safer, easier sport that was to catch on. Had it been the other, the country would have benefited. Not many years after my time there with Godfrey Preece there was an explosion of wonderful polo in the U.S.A., but it was confined to the millionaire group. In a country so rich as that there was no need for it to be so confined.

We were catering for people who knew what they wanted. They had no time for ill-behaved or fractious horseflesh. That was where I came in. Nearly every horse can be sorted out by long hours of silken schooling and by judicious feeding. I don't think I ever did such extended hours of schooling in any other period of my life, up and down, round and round those building lots that then were coarsish grass fields and today are the sidewalks of New York, well, so to speak.

'Quality in a horse is fifty per cent manners, and any horse can be taught manners,' Godfrey used to say. He did not miss a trick, and I cheerfully worked my year away for him because I knew that such industry was noted and appreciated. He was always ready himself to take his coat off and work like the devil. I must admit, though, that a lot of the hard graft was taken out of such a life by the coloured lads who, in my opinion, were bad feeders but very fair strappers and grooms. Godfrey had plenty of them. Some of them could ride pretty well, especially the ones from Kentucky. By and large, they were given a fair bit of responsibility. I had plenty of fun too, as well as work. Very often

I was called on to make up one side or another, and I dearly
loved a game of polo. One day we were practising with the
team the Duke of Westminster had sent out there and Godfrey
said in my hearing to Colonel Lockett, who was one of them,
'Howard Marshall and I with my two boys aged twelve and
eleven could out-play your lot using broomsticks and bi-
cycles.' One of that team was Captain George Bellville from
Papillon Hall. It gave me quite a turn to meet him there.
I always had a soft spot for his family, and in my spare time
I worked hard on his ponies, smoothing away their man-
made faults. The Captain played well that series, though the
side did badly, and I took comfort from his success. While I
was trying to help them I saw a good deal of Mr Ambrose
Clark. The horse world is an odd one. There probably was
not a much richer man than he on that Continent, nor a
much poorer one than young Howard Marshall, yet because
I sat easier on a horse than he we met almost as equals. I
had met him in Leicestershire, in London, at Papillon Hall,
and now on Long Island. I have thought since that I might
have hitched my wagon to his star, and saved him quite
a lot of worry and expense. Such thoughts never entered my
head at the time. I was green, I was happy, I was good at
my job, I believe. And it was there I learned for the first
time (perhaps from studying Godfrey's goings on) that I
could sell a horse as well as anyone.

When I first dealt on Mr Preece's behalf with Americans
I tried to talk as they did. But I soon reverted to our English
habit of clipped understatement, and I found they liked it a
lot.

'Some pony!' a prospective customer might ejaculate
after a trial or a demonstration.

'Goodish sort,' I'd agree quietly.

'Good*ish*? What's wrong with him then?'

'Why, nothing that I know of. He's useful.'

'Good*ish*, useful,' I might hear him mutter in astonishment.
But in the horse world, where those in the know mistrust

superlatives, useful is a more than useful adjective, never to be underestimated.

* * *

Godfrey, Mrs Preece, two of their boys and I were sitting after dinner on the veranda at Queen's when a horse train pulled into the Belmont Park siding at the far side of the paddocks. Fetching his racing glasses, Godfrey made out a lot of sick horses emerging. One whacking big horse got loose, jumped into our paddocks, and came galloping up towards us. We caught him with a bucket of feed, a splendid Kentucky blue-grass sort of gelding, and stowed him safely in our isolation box before going down to talk to Mr Ryan, the owner of the consignment.

'I can't move them any farther, Mr Preece,' he said. 'I must ask you as an act of kindness I'll never forget, to take them in for a while.'

After a few remarks from Godfrey such as, 'I've enough sick ones of my own to look after without taking on other people's,' they came to terms. We had empty boxes galore, and plenty of lads to lay down straw beds. Mashes, damped hay, and vinegar steam soon sorted them all out. But the big Kentucky horse hammered on his box as though he would soon have it down. *He* was not sick at all. I went into the box to have a good look. I'd seen him in a picture long ago in the night-nursery at Hickling, an overseer's horse in the cotton fields when 'darkies led a happy life, playing on the old banjo'. He was, besides, a tremendous model of a saddle horse, fit to carry Henry VIII, gout, armour, lance, and wives as well. I slipped a saddle and bridle on him, couldn't resist it, and out we sallied.

If I hadn't known a good few tricks he'd have killed me. Strong! You never saw his like. And as for automobiles, as we then called them, he could smell them a mile off, and if one came his way he'd swivel like a weathervane in a cyclone, and no bridle could stop him. And yet he had a flowing mane and tail and a smooth-as-smooth five-gaited action. Potentially, he was a jewel, and a killer.

Next evening Godfrey came home from New York with an order for a good-looking horse *up to seventeen stone* with mouth and manners. Someone in Philadelphia had been ordered by his doctor to ride every day. He had allowed Godfrey one week in which to find the right animal, and the price offered, given satisfaction, was a whopper. Godfrey, with our Kentucky blue-grass fellow in mind, had made a firm appointment on the last day of the allotted span, eleven a.m. at Durland's, and had said that Howard Marshall, the young show hack expert from London, would prove the horse's paces and capabilities.

So he quickly bought the big horse off Mr Ryan, and all of us set about him. The whole resources of the stable and establishment were poured over him, and by George! He needed it all.

If you took a stick to such an animal the battle would have been lost for ever. The only way to get some of the gas out of him was by work, work, and more work. For three days from dawn to dark we had relays of strong lads riding him. We kept him going (I did my turn at it, to learn his ways, and get the feel of him) absolutely without pause. He neither flagged nor visibly altered. His stamina was prodigious. He covered ground like a starving Russian gobbling caviare. Work never fretted him, nor repetition.

On the fourth morning, after securing a thick white cotton rope from one of the yacht yards to his neck, we rode him to the State Highway. He was made fast to a telegraph pole. At the first whiff of gasoline he pulled in every direction with all his might, severely testing both rope and pole. His eyes popped and he sweated and grunted. At length he stood leaning against the pole, nodding his great head and just grimacing slightly as they passed him going either way. Eventually he dried off, allowed himself to be whisped and rubbed. Then he was led quietly to his box, given a nice mash with plenty of salts in it, and made a fuss of. The same treatment was administered for two more days, and meanwhile I was schooling him normally, paying especial attention to his mouth. I did so much mileage with him that the blacksmith had to attend to him every day at the midday break, when I went into the house to get some food and coffee. Very soon, too soon for me, the day came when the Kentucky horse must go to Durland's Riding Academy.

I went up the road to New York with him, hitching on to a pole whenever I saw anything extra terrifying on the horizon. You could see along that straight and horrible road, with its line of crooked poles, for miles and miles. At last we walked sedately over Long Island Bridge, passed beneath the overhead railway, turned into Central Park, and so came to Durland's. There, once inside, I hove one of the deepest sighs of relief of a sometimes anxious life. Well I knew that had he, during that long and (from a horse's viewpoint) unfair journey, decided to turn tail I would not have stopped him that side of Texas, and he was the iron sort who might decide to go slap through one side of a building and out through the other wall.

He joined the Preece horses in our reserved section at Durland's, was petted and well done, fed, and put away for the night. The last I saw of him he was down, his muzzle deep in his bed of sweet, springy straw, his head gently moving from side to side, his eyes screwed tight shut.

Next morning, a beauty, I rode him straight into the park. I had a running rein buckled to my girth, passed through the ring of the bit, and back to my hands. He went well in it, changing his gaits as often as I gave the office. There was neither hitch nor argument. That horse! Had he then chosen to be sensible, among all those people and vehicles in the strangest city in the world? Had he taken a fancy to me? If so, was I the only one he would obey? Would they have me for homicide when I put a seventeen-stone invalid from Philadelphia on that volatile back? All afternoon I worked him in Durland's ground-floor arena. I used my wits and experience to help him enjoy his work as I enjoyed it—that great shoulder, the immense thrust from the hocks, the floating as though on a cloud. . . . I gave him lots of time to look around, to watch other performances, to stand about. Most important of all, I made sure that my first lesson was not forgotten and he would stand STILL, still as a horse of bronze or marble.

Our client arrived, dead on the first stroke of eleven. As I approached to welcome him I saw him run an eye over me and my quiet, serviceable English getup. We walked together, much of a height and with the same length of leg, from the reception hall to the arena seats. He was dressed for park hacking, correctly, neither horsey nor tyro. I could not make him out. After a few moments of random conversation I asked if he would like to see the Kentucky horse. He would, emphatically.

I had not far to go because I had the horse waiting just through the double doors. When I had checked everything and settled myself gently in the plate I gave his two attendant Negroes the office. They pushed open the doors.

As he walked round the arena he seemed barely to touch the tan. His neck was perfection and he went looking about him, unfettered. Nothing shows a great horse better than that. I loved him for it. Then a trot, and after that each of his remaining gaits. . . . Whoa! He stood still as a heron, right in the centre of the ring. I got off him, put my reins on the saddle, and left him there alone, looking up half sleepily at a pair of New York sparrows chattering against one of the windows.

I went through the side gate and sat down beside the prospective buyer. We discussed the horse briefly, then we went over to him, the pair of us. He arched his neck, nibbling little bits of apple I brought from my pocket. He behaved with the solemnity of an Anglican bishop. And all the time at the back of my mind was the picture of him but a few

days earlier lashed to that huge pole with his eyes fit to
bulge out and the sweat starting from him. He allowed me
to stand him beside the mounting block while the Philadelphian edged aboard. He walked the horse round me and the
block a few times, came back to it, got off, got on again. . . .
You may be sure I was watching, outwardly sphinxlike,
inwardly with the gravest trepidation. On again without a
move from the horse. A pressure of the leg, a sideways touch
of rein on neck, and they were away, all of a piece, walking
out into the wide expanses of the arena, each with growing
confidence in the other. All his gaits were then asked for,
and given. We went into the park. I waited on a bench,
admiring horse and horseman in the sunshine. Both behaved
perfectly. We came in, the three of us, and went up in the
elevator to his stable floor, where I handed him over to our
head lad to do him well and put him away.

'That saddle,' the Philadelphian said when we were
settled in the bar. 'It's yours, Mr Marshall? It fits both the
horse and me. I'd like to have it at your valuation, also the
bridle and bit.'

'These things cannot be replaced here,' I said. 'But you
may have them if you want them, and his rug and roller and
headcollar too.' I was so pleased with the horse's showing
that I almost threw in myself as well. A price of fifty pounds
for those items was soon agreed. I had also been softened,
indeed intrigued, by the expert showing of the heavy American business man. Under the original terms of the deal,
doctor's orders and so forth. I had anticipated one of those
sack-of-bran riders, legs all heels, and great, jerking mutton
fists.

We rode down in the elevator to the offices, where we
booked the rail passage and arranged for the vet's inspection
needed by law if a horse was to cross a State line. Then and
there he wrote his cheque for the equivalent of one thousand
pounds, and pocketing it with suitable thanks to him (and
more privately to God), I promised to see the horse com-

fortably entrained next morning at Pennsylvania Station, which I did.

Two weeks later I received a courteous and friendly letter enclosing a further substantial cheque coupled with the suggestion that I might 'take some friends out to dinner.' (Some dinner! I had better uses for such a sum of money. In those early days I believed in letting other people buy *me* dinner.) He wrote that I had saved his life (which was really the reverse of what I had expected to do) and he confessed that in his early days in the mid-West he had ridden all sorts of horses, and had only given up when he got heavy, believing that weight-carriers were dull conveyances. In short, as I had been privileged to observe at Durland's, he was anything but the juggins he'd originally made himself out to be.

All the same, that horse learned his stuff mainly tied to a telegraph pole and on one ride of eighteen miles along a dead-straight road. As usual when a horseman (of sorts) has pitted brains and skill against an outstandingly bold animal and got his confidence—I was sorry to see him go. At least in his case the destination was the bleat in the Horses for Sale columns of the equestrian press, 'A Good Home'.

I did not know him long but I shan't forget him, my Kentucky horse.

8

Family Interlude

WHEN the *Minnewaska* docked at Tilbury I was fussing over my charges, twelve American horses, six of them race-horses bound for Epsom, Newmarket, and Chantilly. I could sense England in the background, a mixture of smoke and grass smell, indescribable. The Customs and other authori-ties seemed peculiarly stubborn until Ambrose Preece appeared, round, rosy, prosperous, cheerful, and smoothed troubles away.

'Howard,' he said flinging both thick arms round my bony shoulders, 'Howard, how are you? Oh, I have a mare, such a mare, wait till you see her. Shan't show you her tonight. You're out of sorts. Don't argue, I see you are. How are Godfrey and Alicia? Well, never mind, let's cut on home, shall we?'

Cutting on home entailed taking the train to London Bridge where a groom waited for us with a tandem in which we spanked along the north bank of the Thames and up to Combe Warren. In the morning after our usual breakfast but without the presence of Miss Preece, who had married one of the Burbidges, the owners of Harrods, he took my arm and impelled me to the stable yard. In one of the larger boxes he introduced me to Sceptre, an extremely well put together show hack. She looked absolutely the ticket to me, but I said little. They put a saddle and bridle on her. It was raining, so we took her into the riding school, and I set about finding her paces. I had barely cantered her when I swung her back to Mr Preece and got off.

'I know, I know,' he said.

'She makes a noise.'

'But listen, Hobday has operated on her and says she'll be right as rain. It's the English air, thick as pea soup, that's bad for one like this. Otherwise we'd keep her over here, and nothing would touch her. But in the dryer, more sparkling atmosphere of New York you won't hear a whisper out of her. Otherwise she'll do, eh?'

'She might be good enough to win in any company if. . . . I don't know much about Hobdaying.'

'I'm driving you into London now, Howard. I've got business at Fulham Road and you can get a hansom up Bond Street way. I want you to do me a favour. You'll go straight to Tautz's and order a complete outfit, everything for schooling and showing. Do yourself proud. I had a word with them last time I was that way. They'll let me have the bills. You'll enjoy that.'

'I will,' I said.

'I've had a letter from Godfrey about you. You've been a good boy and we're pleased with you. Generally with blokes of your kind there's trouble with women and trouble with drink. With you, so far, nothing. But Godfrey tells me your home affairs are on your nerves. So cut along up there for a day or two, and go first class.'

'I will,' I said. 'That's very handsome of you.'

Father met me at Melton Station. He was alone at Hickling. My mother had moved to Hoveringham, between Nottingham and Newark-on-Trent. Perhaps he would have felt her absence less if she had gone farther away. It was as though a goad had been planted in him. He was both wounded and infuriated. She had taken all that belonged to her, a lot of the furniture and the younger children. It was a relief to learn that Mitchell was coming over for dinner.

He had been riding show jumpers for Mr George Van de Poole, who kept a stable at Cassington Hall, and worked a good deal with and for 'Banker' Loewenstein. I was astonished by my brother, for in my mind he was still a youth, yet here was a tall, slashing, handsome man. He had been in Belgium for some time.

'I learned a lot in Brussels,' he said. 'They're the lads to get a horse up over an extra high fence. They tend to be long-legged, and don't ride with too short a leather nor an exaggerated forward seat, but are always balanced and can give a shift of weight at any split second. From Brussels Mr Van de Poole and I took sixteen horses, all toppers, to St Petersburg. We went by sea through the Baltic and, when we were off-loading, Paddy, our groom, slipped on the icy deck and fell between ship and quay. When I got down to him his head was under water and there was a strong current knocking the ice blocks against each other and the pair of us. We were saved by the Scots captain, who in an instant had a rope and a light lowered to us. Paddy had on Mr Van de Poole's huge top coat with a fur lining that trapped the air. Otherwise he'd have gone under. The horses were all for sale. Those Russkies were hard buyers. Many times I had to ride the lot over six-foot fences before breakfast. But in the end every one of them was sold, and the prices were really something. . . . Now tell me about America, How.'

'These last years you boys have knocked round the world, haven't you,' our father said. 'More than I ever did. I had to *work* for my living. . . .'

It was true, the food did taste better, fresher, up there. The ceilings in both dining- and drawing-room were lower than I remembered. All the warmer in winter, though.

'Your mother never should have married,' he told us. 'Pass the port, Howard. When her sister, your aunt, married Lawyer Elborne, their mama said, "That's one marriage in the family, and may it be the last." Well she knew that your mother and I already had an understanding, and I was always in a hurry in those days. I see you still like the walnuts, Howard.'

'How's the tree?'

'Strong and healthy. Home Field's good for trees.'

'And the cattle?'

'Don't do much with cattle this last ten month. The horse trade's thin too. But war's coming with the Germans. Oh, I know you'll say it'll kill hunting, but think of the Army trade, Howard.'

'Yes, Father.'

'I've got horses to see in Derbyshire tomorrow. If you could drive with me to Widmerpool it would be a help. I shall be back at Widmerpool day after tomorrow. Hope you can stop a bit. I've plenty for you to do.'

'I'll have to take tomorrow's night express to London. I'll drive you to Widmerpool and then take the trap on, if you agree, to pay my respects to Mother.'

'As you please. Take some port and circulate it.'

'No thanks,' I said, passing the decanter.

'What d'ye mean, no thanks? Not turning pussy-foot are you?'

'I take a drink, but not often.'

'Tell your mother that. She may approve. Cigar?'

'Thanks.' I took one.

'That's better,' he said. Like many hard-living men he was generous by nature, and always glad to have others indulge with him. 'Let's see, ten o'clock. Like a look round the stables, lads? Come on then.'

'I'm interested in America, Howard,' Mitchell said to me. 'If I find my way out there can you fix me up temporarily with Godfrey Preece, schooling? You can, honestly? That's fine. I'd best be off then. Thank you, Father; so long, Howard.'

In the stables it was more like old times, not a straw out of place, and everything sweet and clean. I thought the standard of horse a bit lowered, but possibly my own standard had risen, and memory always plays tricks. There was nothing I could buy from my father for Godfrey in Long Island, but he listened carefully when I told him of our trade, particularly in blood polo ponies, and what we would pay for them. When we had been the rounds he went to his study, and I went alone upstairs. They had put me in the main spare bedroom with its fourposter. I walked along the back landing to 'the boys' bedroom' over the coach house. It was used as a store room. There were no beds in it. Walnuts and hard William pears were laid out in rows on the white-wood floor. A mouse slid into a hole in the wainscoting. I walked back to the spare bedroom, opening each door as I went. My father's bedroom was as bare as the room of a campaigning officer, and looked as though it were seldom used. His small dressing room next door was much as before, with the boot jack and long line of riding and hunting boots, the wardrobes full of solidly-built coats and breeches. He must have come up very late to bed that night, but he was doing justice to a huge, old-fashioned breakfast at eight o'clock when I joined him.

'Is the road to the turnpike still gated?' I asked.

'It is. Got your running shoes on? That skewbald mare is a shifter. When you've dropped me at Widmerpool you'll have a look to the stock at Curate's Goss, won't you? There are thirty-eight bullocks in the reed field and a hundred and fifty-three ewes, the south side. Fill the cake tubs. The bin's by the gate of the lane. Bennett should have the water to them by then, just check on the troughs. I'm expecting a little mare over from Saxelby this afternoon or evening. If you're here when the fellow comes give him this.' He pulled out his watch chain and took a sovereign from the case at the end. 'If you have to leave before, ask Bennett to do the necessary. She's a nicish mare, and will sell.'

He seemed to go into a patch of gloom, and sat with his hand on his coffee cup staring at the empty end of the mahogany that he and I remembered crowded.

After the usual scene in the yard, the mare pawing and snorting, the groom holding her back, he walked her off. Then along the road we spanked, the high land of Hickling

Standard on our left and Parson's Thorns, that beautiful little black covert, tight as a bottle, set in the side of the hill, and below it as perfect a bit of hunting vale as you could see this side of heaven. A mile and a half to the right along the turnpike and we dropped down to the little station.

'It's goodbye then.'

'Yes, Father.'

'Here she comes, dead on time. Don't go knocking that nice mare up now, Howard. There's a hoof pick under the seat. Don't get her home hot—surely I needn't emphasise. And you won't forget the ewes and the bullocks? Watch for a ewe on her back; there's thunder about. Goodbye then.'

Curate's Gorse is a big covert and a beauty. No sign of neglect there. I did not see a fox, but I could smell them everywhere, and the jays had been chattering as I drove down the lane and hitched the mare. The bullocks looked magnificent. It was easy to get stock to *do* there. The ewes were a lot of old girls, broken-mouthed. Either they were a batch he'd bought cheap on spec, or he was thinking of getting out of sheep.

As my father had told me, the house at Hoveringham was pleasant and substantial. I drove straight into the carriage yard and a boy took the mare and promised to rub her down and get her a feed. I left when I'd seen her stale. Mother was in the garden with, wonder of wonders, old W. Key, still a walking (or snoozing) advertisement for herb beer. It looked like the same barrow, too. That was a good start, and Mother was friendly, almost affectionate, but when she asked after Father and I said he was lonely she gave a snort and became huffy. She said she was thankful to be away from Hickling, and then I felt we were not getting on. I ate lunch with them, she and a governess from Derby and three of the youngest children. As at Hickling, the food was extra good, and I asked in consequence what had become of Mrs Murgatroyd.

'She's here, in the kitchen.'

And when I went to her, there she sat at the scrubbed

Dublin Horse Show. Constance, Duchess of Westminster, J. H. Marshall and 'Philipino', winner of the class for five year olds bred in Ireland (*by kind permission of Mrs C. M. Marshall*)

J. H. Marshall on 'The Sheik' at Olympia in 1927
(*by kind permission of Lady Mary Grosvenor*)

Lord Hindlip's daughter, the Hon. Diana Allsopp, on the chestnut mare entered
Balmanno Cup (*by kind permission of Mrs C. M. Marshall*)

deal table, and she was eating jugged hare just like the rest of us, but she'd put a yellow mountain of mustard on the edge of the plate and, as in the old days, was conveying neat mustard to her mouth on the point of her knife. *There* I had a welcome! She flung her arms around me and I hugged and kissed her and she cried in a hiccuping kind of way. She had not a single grey hair, and looked just the same. When I told her so she said, just as she always had done, 'Cooking seems to suit me then,' and gave her highest neigh of a laugh. 'I'll never truly like it here, not like Hickling, Mr Howard,' she said. 'You mustn't forget me, now, when you come home from America with a fortune and take over from Mr Marshall at Hickling. I'll come and cook for you and your lady, no matter who else in the world wants me to.'

That was a pleasant picture. But I did not see how I was going to get rich with Godfrey. Hard work and low pay was the motto there.

I had forgotten what it meant to me, that landscape of strongly fenced pastures, tight coverts, numerous brooks and vistas of canal, the narrow roads with their wide verges, the huge stacks of hay and corn.

That night, leaving a thank-you note for my father on his desk piled with unpaid bills, I caught the London express, and in the morning I was there for breakfast with Jim and Molly, grilled kidneys and watercress over the shop. I had managed to get a Hickling Stilton for them from Miss Munks, Mrs Doubleday's grand-daughter. They still kept red cows and a proper old-fashioned dairy in their little farm by Home Field.

The shop was now only the nucleus of Jim and Molly's business. They had a tea-garden running down to the Thames, and a share in the hotel alongside the garden. They owned two houseboats on the river, and rented them to Army officers.

'What's got into Jim?' I asked Molly as I helped with the washing up.

'Everything he touches turns to gold. And he'll hardly do anything bar work. He says it exciting. It's not like the Jim I married, somehow.'

'How's The Weazel?'

'Oh, he's sold,' Molly said with a giggle. 'Jim takes the papers round in a motor now.'

'Good grief!'

'And it's always breaking down, and you know the hills we have in Richmond. I don't think it's safe. But he won't listen, and it's true we've increased the round no end since he took to motor delivery.'

'Cachet, that's what it is,' Jim explained incomprehensibly. 'I've got this de Dion Bouton you see, How, for delivering. And then I've got a big Minerva. We hire him out, with shover. Weddings and such like. Soon as I find another going reasonable, a fine big comfy one, I'll have two, and another shover part time.'

I looked after the shop that morning while Jim went on his rounds in the French car, which shook as though it had the palsy. The shop had not greatly changed, except that there were two metal tubs holding ice-cream provided by Mr Luigi, the Italian down the street. I had a good many children and fresh-faced nannies as customers. After lunch Jim drove me across Richmond Park to Combe Warren. The branch I had jumped on the star polo pony had long since been cleared, but the remembrance of my rides across the park made me feel superior toward the de Dion Bouton. Haliburton came instantly out to take my bags when we drew up under the portico, and I could see that *he* was impressed.

My Tautz clothes had been delivered from London, and were excellent. Sceptre's wind was not yet what I would call clear, though it had improved. The mare had muscled up well, and taken a splendid bloom. Her mane and tail were perfection, and she had developed a sense of theatre. A show hack has to be an actress. . . . Those Preeces were artists with horses.

146

At the back of the stable block in the poultry houses Ambrose had 'stabled' a collection of fighting cocks which he had procured with difficulty in Yorkshire. I was to deliver them in New York to Mr Chipchase, who was Mr Judge Moore's manager of show hackneys. Then there was a kennel of dogs, chiefly foxhounds and Jack Russell terriers. In the horse line I had no fewer than twenty-five polo ponies and thirty enormous Percherons. Then there was an assignment of Jersey cows and heifers, and three Jersey bulls. I enjoyed that trip. There was plenty to do, and the Percherons proved to be delightful companions, considerate and genial.

9

Show Hacks of New York

'WE'VE put you in the annexe with Mitchell,' Mrs Preece said to me when, after seeing to all my charges, I finally hove up at Queen's, a tired man. 'Mrs Cafferty is going to look after the pair of you.'

Mitchell, if you please, had taken a berth on the *Berengaria*, and arriving long before me, had just made himself known to Godfrey Preece and was schooling polo ponies. My preoccupation was with Sceptre, but by and large Mitchell and I were together more than we were apart. I found him an interesting companion. He was wonderfully good on any horse, and all horses went extra well for him; but he did not take the profound delight in making and teaching a horse that I did. He would always prefer putting an animal over fences to sorting out its mental processes and getting it to understand what it was doing. We lived together very happily, though, up at dawn, working horses, back for breakfast and a shower, more work, then into New York to do more riding. We took some tosses, too, as many of Godfrey's American horses were completely green, and he was always saying to us, 'Get a move on, now. Time's money.'

Mitchell was very keen on one particular Californian pony called Blondie, a mealy chestnut, good-looking and hot as they come. Although Mitchell was long-legged and rode fairly long, he never looked big on her somehow. She was a regular *multum in parvo*. When the Brooklyn Show came round we set off from Queen's with a regular string of hopefuls most of which were to be ridden in the ring by the two Marshalls. Soon after crossing 59th Street Bridge, Blondie, terrified by the traffic and always a bit of an ass, decided that she was a rabbit and, ignoring Mitchell's remonstrances both verbal and physical, dived into the subway entrance and took him down and down the steps. Finally they plunged into the open door of a train. Then Mitchell got off her and she agreed to be led back upstairs and into the daylight. When she reached the air she gave one great sniff of pure pleasure. We all went on to the Show, and he won nearly four hundred dollars on her in the touch-and-out jumping, for she was fast as well as bold. On the way home from the Show one of the saddle horses in our lot fell at the mouth of the bridge, throwing the lad who rode him. The horse picked himself up and set off over the bridge at full stretch, with all of us galloping after, Mitchell and myself in the van, dodging through the cars and trucks. We caught him at the other side, and nobody was killed.

The time came when Mr Preece had built up a number of horses he thought would sell in England. We could see that he felt one of us brothers should go home with the horses, but it was difficult for him to send me, since I was working on Sceptre, and the National Show at Madison Square was not very distant. Mitchell began to get restive.

'If he asks me to go back to England, I'll refuse,' he said one night after supper.

'On what grounds?' I asked.

'On the grounds I want to stay in this country. I like it. I don't mean to go home for another fifty years or so, if then. But don't mistake me, this job isn't my kind of job. It's too near the town. I don't get any sport, I don't get any shooting, and I don't get any hunting. We're too much in the horse trade here for my liking. I aim to get into the hunting world. So if Godfrey tells me to go home with those nags, I'll just tell him no, and then see what he does.'

149

'He'll fire you.'

'So what? You like the work here. It suits you to take a horse and smooth away at him until he's perfect. It's the hunting and shooting I miss. I've always had 'em you know. There are a hundred and six hunts in this country, and I'm quite sure I can be of use to at least one of them.'

A few days later I heard shouting behind the stables. It was Godfrey setting about Mitchell who, without being impolite, was giving as good as he got.

'I reckon I can earn twice the money for half the work I do here,' I heard him say. There were a great many coloured lads about, as usual, and they were listening too, you may be sure.

'You call it work, sitting on your arse on a nice pony that's fed and done and mucked out by the lads!'

'Yes I do, and I call it boring. Howard *likes* it, or so he tells me, but I was brought up in the country and this is too much on the edge of a town for me. I want some fresh air. And it's to be American fresh air at that. I don't see why I should go blowing my savings on getting across the Atlantic and then go crawling straight back again in charge of some old nags.'

'You self-important young rooster. The sooner you clear away from here and start living on your fresh air, the better we'll all be pleased. Pack your grip and get out.'

Mitchell came into the annexe, all smiles. 'He's a fair bloke,' he said, referring to Godfrey Preece. 'He's given me the week's money, which was more than I reckoned on, and I've learned the hell of a lot about polo and polo ponies from him. I reckon that's going to stand me in good stead.'

'You always did have millionaire ideas.'

'Well, so long, Howard. If I need a loan I'll always have you to touch.'

'Where are you going?'

'New York. So long, old boy.'

Godfrey was quiet with me for a couple of days. We were

schooling together at Belmont when he said, 'You missing that brother of yours? Must be lonely in the annexe without him. Reckon you should come back into the house with us. Interesting young fellow. He may do well. Wonderful on a horse. Hear he's good with a gun too.'

'With a gun, Mr Preece?'

'Sure, a shotgun. I hear he's been trapshooting in New York and cleared quite a tidy sum from it.'

'What about that batch of horses you wanted him to take to England?'

'They must wait till after the National. Then you'll take 'em, unless you go sour on us next.'

I must tell you that at that time Godfrey Preece had been showing and winning in America with a hackneyfied, head-strong sort, a high-actioned animal whose tail had been nicked, so that he carried it stood up on end and (not having much brush to it) it looked thoroughly ludicrous to me, if not to the local judges. The nicking, as then carried out, meant standing a horse in his box with his tail tied for quite a time to a beam or a ringbolt overhead. It was barbarous and nonsensical.

Dr Garnier was the name of this animal, and at that time (1913) in that immense and wealthy land, he was regarded as the *ne plus ultra* in park hacks. He was the champion.

On my visits to Combe Warren Ambrose and I had dis-cussed the anomaly of the American hack. Surely a hack is meant to be the utmost in smoothness, beauty, comfort, and convenience, whereas the Dr Garnier sort were in every way harsh rides. So we introduced the other form of hack. an English thoroughbred of the highest quality and the straightest action in its trot, and a smoother-than-silk balanced canter behind the bridle. The mare could slide on in her gallop, pull up with hardly a touch, steady to the most springy walk imaginable, and keep that going if you dropped her reins to her neck. And when you asked her to halt she stood absolutely still with head up, ears pricked, lifting and dropping her bit as much as to say in a soft, deep voice, 'Look at me, darlings, and listen to this perfectly gorgeous jingle-jangle.' I was once showing a hack like that at Olympia when Miss Tallulah Bankhead swam up alongside with a couple of noblemen in tow, and when she began half-croaking, half-crooning in her celebrated way and looking at my mount with her enormous eyes, I thought to myself, *You* would have made a show hack.

How superb English hacks were! You'd find a class of them in Olympia standing in a gleaming line of perfection, all mouthing their bits, and making the most lovely music, like spinets and dwarf silver cymbals.

Sceptre, for of course I am talking about her, had a bang tail down to just below the hocks washed with Lux the night before the show, dried, bandaged, and finally shaken out. It swung from side to side in rhythm with her paces and as a complement to her trimly plaited mane, the extreme of femininity, and her shining coat. When I rolled up at Madison Square in my new Tautz clothes, Peal boots, and the rest in the Open Hack classes on that sensation of a mare, we were the means of ousting the Dr Garniers from the American ring for all time.

As for me, I was having kittens with every stride she took. For if once a horse is touched in the wind I never stop worrying. Ambrose Preece was entirely right. She never made a sound in the American air. And you may be sure I had kept absolutely mum everywhere, particularly in Godfrey Preece's stables, about her former failing and the Hobday operation.

One of the first to come up and help me drink the champagne in the silver cup was Mitchell, looking both horsey and prosperous. He had got himself hitched into the entourage of Mr O'Malley Knott, an extremely rich sportsman. Mitchell was schooling his magnificent horses and hunting them with Mr Oakleigh Thorne's Harriers at Millbrook, N.Y. Mr A. H. Higginson also had his pack of English foxhounds at Millbrook then. The country was eighteen miles long and twenty-three across, a grass country with a nice bit of woodland (for a shooting man like Mitchell), and little plough; and the obstacles were post-and-rails, snake fences, and fairly massive stone walls. Mitchell was obviously happy. He told me, in front of the chi-chi show-gentry standing round me and the cup, that he was thoroughly enjoying hunting, and digging *woodchuck* with the Sealyham pack of Ned Carle, the huntsman.

10

War

On August 6, 1914, my dear old horse-carrier, the *Minnewaska*, was ambling to New York, and was getting near. The weather was perfection, the sea flat, when we were stopped by a warship flying the White Ensign. She came alongside and, without fuss or ill-humour, took from us our Captain and his First, Second, and Third Officers. The Fourth was left in charge, though he too was a naval reservist. Pretty generous of the Royal Navy. We went on, and docked up the Hudson. Eleven grooms were waiting to take eleven of my ponies, special ones destined for the American team. The remaining twenty-two I entrained and took over the ferry from New Jersey, where they had been advertised in a sale. Within a fortnight every single one of them had gone and, with a pocketful of cheques, I was free to get over to Queen's.

Godfrey Preece was busier than ever. 'Howard,' he said, 'you fit and well? Fine. I've booked a contract. Five hundred horses for the French Government, no less. You and I leave for the south tomorrow in the Ford.'

I pulled a newspaper from my pocket and showed him the headlines: GERMANS TO INVADE. ENGLAND UN-PREPARED. KITCHENER CLAIMS 'EVERY ENG-LISHMAN'.

'I came to say goodbye to you both and the children, and to settle up and pack my things. My father must be all alone and smothered in horses and worries. I must get back to him, and then join up, though quite how I do that, I don't know.'

'What about Mitchell?' he asked. 'He feel the same way? He said he'd stop in America for fifty years.'

'I telephoned Millbrook. Mitchell left for England three days after war was declared.'

Hurrying into New York, I searched 66th Street for an address the Fourth Officer of the *Minnewaska* had given me. It proved to be a somewhat battered club where sailors of many races hung out.

'Take your gear aboard,' he said when, by the grace of God, I found him. 'We sail at eleven, the morning after tomorrow.' I went straight aboard and stayed there, fearful that I might get shanghaied or otherwise left behind—you know the feeling? As soon as we were at sea the young man promoted to be Captain sent for me. 'Now then, Howard, shall I charge you twenty-eight pound for a passage or shall I pay you three bob a day as a deck hand?'

There was a friend. I gratefully accepted the three shilling offer, always being of saving turn of mind, and I genuinely tried to do a bit of work every day under the bo'sun's instructions, though to be frank I was never good at any work that did not concern horses.

Tilbury Docks were so bunged up with shipping we had to anchor off. I got my bags, landed by tender, and from St Pancras, sadly recalling my first arrival there with the stallion, I sent a wire to my father and caught the first express to Melton Mowbray.

I was walking to the exit of Melton station followed by a heavily laden porter when I collided with the O.C. the Permanent Remount Depot, Captain 'Egham' Harris, 11th Hussars. He was catching the same train to go two miles up the line to his own house.

'Marshall, by all that's holy,' he cried, blocking my passage most resolutely. 'Guard!'

'Yessir?'

'Don't hold the train for me. I'll catch the next one. . . . Now young Marshall, you're just my man. Here's my quandary. I've got two hundred remount men enlisted and travelling to Woolwich tomorrow to draw their kit and then over to France. They're first-class men on the job, all from good stables. But they're wild as hawks. I must find somebody to take charge of them. You're the very man.'

'I'm just back this minute from America and haven't been home for years. My father should be outside in the trap, waiting for me.'

'He is. I'm coming with you and the three of us will settle things right away. If I know Sam Marshall he's not going to interfere when you have this chance.'

He was sitting in the trap behind the skewbald mare. They both looked older, and the trap was less well turned out than it would have been a few years earlier. His voice was deeper and stronger than either of ours, though, and I saw he was glad to have me home. We talked it all over until finally, tired and dispirited, I said I would leave it to my father to decide.

'Now then, Howard,' he said, 'you'll not forgive yourself or me if this war ends by Christmas and you haven't even had a go. Also it seems to me, and Captain Harris swears it is, a good opening for you. You'll be away on a tearing scent and right on his brush, leading two hundred good blokes down to London.'

It was his choice once more, and so I only had one night with him in a house echoing with emptiness. He had remembered my liking for walnuts, and put a bag of them with my bits of luggage for the London trip. We drank a cherry brandy in the hall before he drove me to Melton.

Our detachment formed up at the Bell and I headed it as the town band led us to the station. The crowd yelled its faith in us, bandy-legged crew that we were, and pressed gifts on us. Most of the gifts were made of glass with corks in them. I had a few minutes alone with my father at the station and then I poked myself away from the others in a first-class carriage. At Leicester a small man came up the train to find me, asked if I had anything to read, and gave me the *Sporting Life*. 'Make me your adjutant, Mr Marshall,' he suggested. 'I'll do you proud. I was three years at Chantilly and can *parlez-vous* a treat.' He gave me to understand that things were hectic farther down the train. Bottles were sailing from the windows, all empties. When we reached St Pancras and the doors were opened my detachment literally fell out, though most of them got to their feet and walked about shaking hands with everyone. The would-be adjutant stood beside me waving in the breeze; a black bottle poked out of his greatcoat pocket and a cheroot stuck out of his mouth.

A police superintendent walked up and asked me coolly, 'You the gentleman in charge of this little lot?'

'I'm supposed to be, I regret to say, until I can report them in at Woolwich.'

'If I were you, sir, I'd take that cab to Charing Cross, then a train to Woolwich and make your own number there. I have a dozen 'buses round the corner. I'll very soon have those jokers packed into them and on their way.'

Deeply grateful, I left my wild charges in his capable hands. They all arrived safely, for which, unjustly, I got credit with the authorities.

At Woolwich they threw kit at us and just about everything else besides. They didn't like us, but they couldn't get the better of us. Most of our Melton lot had, like myself, had a fair taste of Army life and methods, and each of us had forgotten more about horses than anybody at Woolwich would be likely to know. In a surprisingly short time we seemed to have made ourselves comfortable and had acquired or assumed a kind of discipline. There happened to be a tent-pegging competition and, picking myself out a handy polo pony sort that would go a good straight gallop, I won the thing without difficulty. This cemented my position as leader of the contingent, and I was entered as a warrant officer, pay, status, and all the trimmings. What a laugh! My stablemen were in favour of the appointment. They believed that under me they would continue to have an easy time. How did I feel about them? On the whole I loved them. They belonged to the horse world, and when I compared being with the two hundred to my life as a recruit in Aldershot I understood just how civilised and interesting they were.

'Sergeant Major!'

'Sir?'

'You and your Melton Mowbray intake leave tomorrow at ten o'clock for Euston, Holyhead, and Dublin, where you will gather one thousand remounts, load them in two ships, and sail for France. Report your arrival to Major Corrandine at the Remount Centre, Dublin.'

'Sir.' A smart salute and about turn. Me a sergeant major!

We did not have a Melton send-off on our way to Euston (far from it, they were really glad to see the backs of us) nor yet at grim Holyhead, but when my lads landed in Dublin their joy was touching to see. I suppose about the half of them were Irish, and anyone who has to do with horses is conditioned to find Ireland wonderful. Their joy was so exuberant, however, that many of them were soon in cells or confined to barracks while I, with the remainder, coped with trainloads of remounts coming in from up and down the country. We worked under such pressure that I came to hate the names of the several excellent brands of stout and Irish whisky then popular. I could not think how the men got the money to get so drunk, but I suppose many of them had come into the forces bringing their savings with them. The remount officer at Melton had been right when he described them as a first-rate batch so far as their work was concerned. Sober, or half-sober, they were grand.

When we had loaded all the horses and, a more difficult task, ourselves, we set sail for Europe and the Kaiser's war. Our two ships steamed down the West coast of England, took a severe hammering in a near-gale across the mouth of the Bristol Channel, rounded Land's End, and crossed overnight to Le Havre.

All our thousand horses went comfortably into the dye-works shed at Le Havre, a building with which I was to become familiar. The roofs were supported on strong up-rights and to each post we secured a horse. They were bedded in sawdust. While we were settling the horses in and feeding and watering were going on, a quiet voice behind me asked, 'All right for forage, Sergeant Major?'

'Never seen so much forage in my life,' I answered without looking round.

'That's wonderful news. Many of these horses are in for bad times. We must give 'em all the comfort we can.'

Intrigued by that unmilitary remark, I turned to face a rather small, smooth-skinned, white-haired officer. He was extremely well turned out in a uniform I failed to place regimentally. His brown artillery boots glinted with depth on depth of polish.

'Major Mayne,' he introduced himself. 'I have orders to set up No. 2 Remount Depot here with the help of yourself and your men. Can you tell me a little about them?'

'Keep them off the grog, sir, and a better lot you'll never find. Not one of us but has been with horses all his life, or nearly so.'

'And mules?' he asked.

'Well, I imagine a mule is just a cross between a horse and a donkey.'

'What sacrilege! A mule is a mule, a law unto himself. You must have the right touch with him or he will do nothing. If you start to pull 'em about they'll pull back. As Colonel Deauney, the great expert on mules in India, used to say, "You can't seduce a mule but you can entice him." If you have any problems with mules, Mr Marshall, do not hesitate to ask my advice.'

'Thank you, sir.'

A few days later Jack Conway the steeplechase jockey,

who was my right hand in those Le Havre days and marvellous company as well, came limping off a ship holding one thigh. 'Its full of ruddy mules,' he said. 'And there's the devil in the lot of them. Jim Rafferty and me went down to the deck among them and they set about the pair of us.'

Major Mayne was sitting in his dog-cart at the other end of the quay.

'Hold on a minute, Jack. I'll ask the old man.'

'Come into the dye shed,' the Major said. He walked down the lines of horses till he came to an oldish grey gelding, all but white. 'Saddle him up,' he said. 'Have all the mules let out on deck and the gangway there, and I'll tell you what to do.'

I rode out in front of the mules on the white animal and steadily down the gangway, cup-cupping them like a batch of young hounds. They pricked their ears at my gentle calls, then looked at the white horse, and followed him. We led them like that in a long tail right through the docks and across the city to our lines on the dunes where we lived under canvas for the first weeks. True, I had Jack Conway and a few others of the rustler type, well-mounted and carrying hunting whips, to act as collies to my West Country shepherd act. (Am I right in thinking that in the West Country the shepherd precedes his sheep, and elsewhere he follows them?) Anyway, all mules liked that white horse. I took good care to keep him in the remounts with us.

Major A. B. Mayne was of a certain age, as the French say, a re-enlisted stalwart. He had left the service of the Queen in India to take up a private post with the Maharaja of Patiala whom he served for twenty years until, with the outbreak of hostilities, he volunteered for soldiering in France. Lord Kitchener had known him in India, and Kitchener helped him get command of our remount depot. It may be fashionable at the moment to decry Kitchener, but everything I ever heard about him showed him to have a lot of brain and flair. The Mayne appointment was a clever one.

No other man that I can think of would have set his stamp so thoroughly and with so little apparent endeavour on that extraordinary establishment. It all seemed so make-shift, so temporary, men, horses, supplies running through us like a turbulent river. Somehow the Major contrived to father us as though we were part of a country estate. He was a good delegator and organiser and he possessed a calm so deep and steady that sometimes it seemed like laziness. His voice was very quiet and he disliked shouting. Even there on the quays among the dockers he had only to appear on any chaotic scene—and there were many such—for order to come and silence.

He soon impressed his personality (if anyone so urbane could be said to do anything so public) on the docks of Le Havre. His rather stout figure, spectacles under white hair, a mixture of friendliness and dignity, was familiar in the warehouses and along the miles of quays. When one of our ships came in he would drive down in his dog-cart, which was turned out to perfection, like his boots and his clothes. (His soldier servant, Woodford, one of our Melton intake, had been valet to a premier duke.) Two well-matched ponies, greys, drew the dog-cart, and while Major Mayne was sitting up there behind the whip he never used, we knew there was a brain in the docks and that any problem would be logically tackled. Yet had you met him away from the unit you would have thought him a fussy, slightly self-indulgent Anglo-Indian, a man who preferred letting time pass to using it.

Major Mayne brought us luck too. One morning at the usual conference he said, 'We'll have every horse out of the dye-works shed today. Do it in normal exercise time. Put every man on to it, there's no ship coming in. When the horses are all shifted to the lines, get into the sheds with wagons. I want every bit of bedding cleared from the shed by tonight, and if the weather stays dry we'll burn it tomor-row. There's a French unit moving into the shed at ten o'clock tomorrow to spray with disinfectant and then fumigate. So tomorrow, if we don't have a ship to off-load or load, I want you to have a thorough day on the horses, feet, clippers, delousing, everything, and we'll have a C.O.'s stables at some time in the late afternoon to be fixed later.'

What had prompted him to give that order I do not know. Possibly he had seen a horse with lice on him. At any rate it was some time before the shed could be fumigated because the very night we cleared the horses there was a huge explosion in the docks and most of the roof of our thousand-horse stabling was blown off. It was the first day that the shed had been empty in months. He soon got it repaired by the French, who were good at that kind of job. As well as holding such a number of horses, the dye-works shed was our chief forage store, and no end of that came across Channel because every time they loaded horses for France they put three days' food aboard with them, in case there should be a delay in docking our end. There was very seldom any delay. We did our horses well.

The major liked to keep a number of good chargers over our allotted or recorded strength. This was a reasonable precaution. He had lived long in the East among great people, both white and coloured, of honour and finesse, people to whom the power to give and receive favours was part of life. It was surprising how frequently high-ranking officers appeared to lose their favourite chargers through enemy action. And it was pleasant that, through our own commanding officer's prescience and husbandry, we always had a few good'ns, generally schooled to a fairly high pitch by myself and Conway, that we could let them have without formality. Major Mayne enjoyed doing such favours, and keeping staff officers happy.

General Lock-Elliot used to come down from G.H.Q. occasionally. He knew his stuff, and we all liked him. But it was through one of his visits that I came temporarily unstuck. Major Mayne had sent for me and asked me to show our quality batch to the General. 'Be very particular, please,' the Major said. 'Manners rather than looks, Mr Marshall, manners rather than looks, or even performance. None of your cold-backed ones. Nothing seems more humorous to a muddy private soldier than a staff officer grovelling in the slime and his horse galloping away.'

'I want a good-looking bay horse up to some weight. It's a special case,' the general said. 'It's for H.M. Nothing we have up there suits him. Why, here's one might do.'

By H.M. he meant the monarch, King George V, who was going round the trenches and staying at General French's headquarters. Knowing that the King was not a horseman, I was worried by the request. Scenting trouble, I tried to hedge.

'We've really nothing here I could recommend, sir,' I said. 'It would be wiser to put His Majesty up on something that's already in or near the line and used to shells and mortars and whizz-bangs and barbed wire and all the rest. That's a nice young Irish horse—jumps like a stag as a matter of fact, don't he, Jack?'

'Don't he just!' said Jack. 'But Mr Marshall's right, sir. The bay's only rising five, and he's too much horse for doddering round the front.'

'If you wish to take him, take him,' I said. 'But put Captain Browne on him or one of your other amateur jocks up there as aides. I haven't truly got anything here I would recommend for your purpose, bar plugs.'

'Let me have him out a second,' the General said. He had a nice ride on the bay. 'Just the horse,' he said. 'A gentleman. I'll take him.'

Two days later Major Mayne sent for me. His face was very long and sad. The King, it transpired, had had a nasty fall, and was hurt. He had gone riding round the troops on the bay, which had maybe been given too many oats by their grooms up there. Anyway he had tucked himself up and put in a couple, and the King had gone for a sail. He had come down mighty hard, and there had to be an operation.

I was under a cloud with the Major for what seemed an age, even though Jack Conway stuck by me like a true friend, and insisted that I'd done everything but chain that bay 'oss to his box to prevent the General taking it away.

Not long after, Major Mayne sent me off on the train with a detachment of horses and mules for the Somme area. Up there I was temporarily in command of a transport company. It was early in the year 1915. The Battle of the Somme was still a long way off, but things were unpleasant. It seemed no place for men, horses, or mules. The reactions of all three to such foul conditions of danger and hardship were inspiring. But how could God allow such suffering, and why?

When I returned to Le Havre Major Mayne told me my commission had been in the Gazette. I was a second lieutenant. He had put me up for promotion before 'that unfortunate accident'. I sat down at once in my billet and wrote to my father and then, after thinking a little, wrote another letter, to my mother.

We got rum ones, men as well as horses, at our depot. Take Mr Davis for example.

He'd been a trainer in India, pre-war, I understand. There he had known Kitchener, Major Mayne (when he was with the Maharaja of Patiala), and General Sir Pertab Singh, the distinguished Indian cavalry leader. Pertab Singh was attached to General French's staff. He wrote from G.H.Q. to Davis, saying, 'Please buy and bring out to me the two best thoroughbred hunters you can find in Ireland. You know the sort I like. Sixteen hands, quality, good and reliable jumpers even in cold blood, and with comfortable paces.'

Davis thought this just the job. He went to Dublin, got hold of two beauties, shipped them to London, and went to see his old chum, Lord Kitchener, at the War House. . . . Now Davis was a civilian. The doctors wouldn't pass him, and anyway he was pretty long in the tooth and had had all sorts of tropical diseases. He asked Lord Kitchener, as an act of friendship, to get him enlisted in some supernumerary capacity so that he could take the horses to their mutual friend, Sir Pertab Singh. Kitchener's reaction was, in my opinion, rather bright.

'Enlist?' he said. 'Not on your Nelly! You'd only get into trouble, might even get yourself killed.' (This was the chap, mark you, who'd been calling for 'Every Englishman' when I was in America in August 1914.) 'Go to Moss Bros and buy a khaki suit with plain brass buttons and a uniform cap without a badge—you'll find they're quite accustomed to selling such clothing. The horses and their destination will be your pass, but I'll give you a chit here and now that will get you as far as A. B. Mayne. You remember Mayne, Patiala's *homme de confiance*? Well, he's now commanding No. 2 Remount Depot, Le Havre. Ship direct from Southampton to Le Havre. Mayne will put you up there, he's well installed, and will tell you how to get the nags up to Pertab. I'll write you a note for Mayne. . . .'

As soon as Davis arrived Major Mayne asked me to take especial care of him. 'He's the nicest little fellow in the world, and he looks *so* seedy.'

'I wish I could keep this pair of 'osses here a fortnight or so,' poor little Davis said to me. 'They've lost a surprising amount of condition with all that shenanaging about since they left the Derry paddocks. I wouldn't like Sir Pertab to see them as they are now. He's all-fired particular.'

'Quite right too,' I said, wondering what sort of all-fired price Davis was charging the old boy for them. 'The great thing is that you are here. This is Liberty Hall and you're to have everything for which you have a fancy. Give your teeth a good gallop. You'll eat no horsemeat here. Stay as long as you like, and don't worry about your two horses. We'll build them up for you.'

'The trouble is, I'm b—— ill,' he said. 'It's one of those damned awkward illnesses. In confidence, I can drink no alc. without running into the most b—— awful trouble, no, not even a glass of wine.'

'Make yourself at home in the Mess. There's lashings of tea and coffee and that sort of muck if you don't feel like anything stronger. But you mustn't let the boys take you out to try to make you spend your money in the cafés, of which there are thousands.'

Being a clean-living bloke myself, I was always warning people in those days. But you know what war is? It hots people up and the devil takes his share. 'The boys' were too persuasive for him, and when the horses were ready to be entrained for G.H.Q., Davis was ill. He had a disease that needed something called a catheter. He had not got one, and we could not get hold of one.

'I could cure myself,' he kept repeating. 'If I could only get my hands on one.'

'Jack, Jack Conway, and I will take you to hospital.'

'I shouldn't have touched their b—— brandy. Though it was good while it lasted.'

'That's the spirit. We'll just take you to hospital and get you fixed up. Here's Jack with the trap now.' It wasn't exactly a trap. It was a two-mule light waggon with made-up springs on it and a kind of Cape hood. It went extra well over the *pavé* of Le Havre behind his pet pair of brindled mules, the silkiest and most disdainful of smooth steppers. I tell you, mules are really something when they are good, and really something else when they are bad.

Crossing the dock area at speed, we came to No. 6 Hospital, where the orderly behind the reception desk asked me for poor Davis's name, rank and number, also his unit or regiment. (Kitchener's dodge of the dummy uniform from Moss Bros worked well, you see.)

I drew Jack Conway back from the desk and whispered, 'This situation stinks. We're running straight into trouble bringing a civilian into this red tape abattoir. Major Mayne won't like it. We must go extra carefully.'

166

'Why don't we just buy him his cafeteria, or whatever he calls it, in a *pharmacie*? He says he can use it on himself, and he seems fairly reliable.'

'He might kill himself and he has friends in high places. It would be awkward for Major Mayne. . . . No, let's try the Frogs' hospital. I know where it is.'

'*They*'ll kill him,' said Jack.

'Not them. Another time,' I said to the orderly. 'Clear the docks and straight up the *grande rue* to the top of the town,' I told Jack as he put his mules in motion.

At the French hospital they received Davis with open arms, and did not give a damn whether he was a civilian or a zebra. We left him there explaining, loud and slow, in English what his trouble was. They seemed to be in control.

Pleased with our good deed, Jack and I stood each other a pint of champagne in a small place we knew, and then set off for our depot. On the way the cart's rims got stuck in the tramlines. There was a tram following us, and it ran slap into the back, overturning the cart and crushing it. The pole broke free and both mules went off like a pair of fairies, but Jack, who after all could sit a horse that at Becher's Brook came down and then got up again, had the skill to leap out on to their backs, like one of those Romans in *Ben Hur*. Meanwhile I had caught them up, for that night I could run like a hare. We each rode a brindled mule home, the pole scraping the sets behind us. Nothing was said about the lost wagon. Exigencies of the service. That man Conway was a good sort. By Jove he was! I thought that jump he had done the neatest thing I ever saw, and in all that infernal noise too. The tram driver, I bet he went to bed a happy man that night!

The next thing was to get Mr Davis's horses up to G.H.Q., which might not have been as easy as it sounds, because even in that war there was a good deal of security around such places. However, as Lord Kitchener had pointed out to Davis, horses are a wonderful passport, and of course we both knew as well as the Kaiser where G.H.Q. was. By now we had worked on that pair of thoroughbreds until they were in peak let-down condition (if you get my meaning, plenty of bloom, yet no oomph) and were about six times better schooled than when they arrived. I looked at a map. We entrained the horses to the nearest station, and then we simply hacked on there, eager to see how the other half lived. Major Mayne had sent a signal to say we were coming.

I was surprised by the spartan conditions the General Staff lived in, monastic-looking bedrooms, simple table, and the faces round it were long and sombre, I can assure you. Of course the officers were on the whole exquisitely turned out. I don't think I ever saw better examples of Peal and Maxwell boots, and there were some decent horses in the establishment (including the one from my depot that had sent the King up into the firmament). There were none better, though, than poor old Davis's pair. Sir Pertab Singh had left a message. He was doing an inspection, but would see me when he got back in the evening.

I took Jack along with me, and introduced him with a sketch of his achievements in the steeplechasing world. Sir Pertab, because he ate different food, had got his own quarters. He invited us to spend the night. He behaved as though we were both commissioned (Jack was still a sergeant), and he did us really proud. Jack and I dined with him, plenty to drink and the most delicious food, piles of lean rice and little spiced and curried dabs of stuff on top. The pair of us were later shown to adjoining bedrooms.

We gave him a bit of a show on his new horses the next morning, and he said something I've always remembered. He said to me, 'Mr Marshall, you ride as though you do not have stirrups, as though you do not need stirrups, and never will need them. And you also ride as though you do not have hands—at least I am sure the horse does not feel any hands impeding him.' Could anything be nicer than that? Jack, having been a jockey (and he was one again after the war), and a good one, rode a lot shorter. I never held with the short brigade. I reckon it's clumsy, ugly, and nothing gained anywhere. I know Sloan brought it over and Donoghue, bless him, copied. But if skirts go up and down, up and down, why not leathers and legs and feet, even jockeys' feet. The horses would enjoy it every time the feet went down, that I know for certain, and as the horse does all the work I'm for giving him what he wants.

Sir Pertab Singh then got up on each of them and went through their paces and over a few obstacles in the easiest and most polished manner imaginable. He was a little, elderly gentleman, and he rode with a Turkish (or Russian) cigarette smouldering between two fingers. His staff car, a Rolls Royce with an incredibly elegant, bearded and turbaned chauffeur, was waiting to take us to our train, but he insisted before we left on our joining him for a farewell drink and when we did, do you know what he gave each of us? A gold cigarette case. There was also a package to take to Davis, to whom he sent tender messages.

'I am ready to die for the King-Emperor,' he said as the sun came through the windows and the champagne bubbles tickled our noses. 'Until I do so I wish to ride thoroughbred horses such as you have brought me. I hope to meet my end charging the enemy. It is what is called a death wish.'

He was killed in what I believe was the last full-scale cavalry charge of that war, at any rate so far as our Army was concerned. It was at Neuve Chapelle. I suppose he took one of that nice pair of horses with him. Personally, if a man must charge the enemy I am in favour of him doing it on a motor bicycle or in a tank.

*   *   *

About mid-1916 I was given the command of No. 20 Auxiliary Horse Company, and I said goodbye with the deepest regret to Major Mayne. I had learned from him, and I think from my father too, that in our job the horses had to come first, and then the men, and last of all oneself. And I had learned a thousand other things as well. Often when I had met the Major merely in the course of duty I felt that I had drunk from his calm, balanced wisdom as though from a spring. I only want to emphasise what kind of a man he was. I know that there were some who thought him a sybarite. But I understand that the Buddha did not despise creature comforts. For the rest of a long, long life I was to remember Major A. B. Mayne, and thank God that our ways had crossed, and that he was so patient with me, the Major I mean, not God. . . . As well as taking over the A.H.C. I undertook on behalf of the Deputy Director of Remounts to accept every artillery horse that was unfit for service, to give a replacement out of my company, and to endeavour to make the rejects fit for work again. It was a wearing job, and on the whole it was an unhappy time for me. The wastage in horses was frightful. I used to wake in my tent or billet with the taste of death in my mouth and the smell of corruption or pus about me. However, there were simple rewards.

Frequently I would get a reject that I could cure quite easily of whatever caused him to misbehave or miss work. Not seldom it was something as simple to put right as a saddle gall, an aching tooth, or an ill-fitting shoe. Then I would get attached to the patient, and conjure excuses to prevent him going back too soon to the mud and the shells.

One of the serious ailments common on the Western Front was a kind of opthalmia that clouded a horse's eye and made him blind, or nearly blind, rather similar to New-Forest eye in a cow. Hundreds, thousands perhaps, of good animals were destroyed because they had caught this disease, and were sold as meat to the French. My friend Scott-Nimmo the vet fixed me up some eye-ointment, and I managed to cure a fair number with it, some of them quickly.

I had a pleasant and hardy pair of Irish draught-horses to pull my company water-cart, a mare and a gelding. They did me well through all the cold, the mud, the flies, the dust, the blood, the guns, and they seemed so intelligent that I would not have been surprised if they had been able to write their names, which were Molly and Dick.

Poor Molly caught the damned opthalmia in both eyes, but as she was always under my observation and I had plenty of Scott-Nimmo's ointment, I had hopes of curing her. She was happy in her work because Dick could see for both and they only worked as a pair.

Whenever I got the chance I used to turn my working horses loose to graze a bit (if there was any grass) and to forget their harness. I had turned out Dick and Molly above our camp, on a little hill behind Mont St Eloi. They were nibbling at whatever fragile grass remained among the diggings of the disused trenches. The gelding found his way over the trenches and semi-bogs and through the horribly rusted barbed wire to some better grass on the other side. He whinnied back to the mare. She went to his call, but stood on the edge of the first trench, half unwilling, half unable because of her eye trouble, to get across to him. He kept whinnying, and then he came all the way back, still talking to her. At last he was beside her again, and he pushed her legs one by one with his soft nose, gently guiding her down into the trench, and along it, and up over the other side, and through the bog and the entanglements, and so, finally, to the precious green grass.

When he had got her there I sat for a long, long time on the upturned canister (I expect it had held poison gas), wondering if I would ever again see anything so touching, so noble, no matter how long I lived.

*　　*　　*

In 1916 my father died, alone and unhappy. Very soon after his death Sam, who had been wounded in France, was invalided out. But he could not save or arrest the dispersal of Hickling, the house and the land, to pay off creditors. It was my father that mattered to me. Of course I loved Hickling, but I loved him more, and I miss him today, when I have far outlived him. He was only fifty-six, and I wonder if he understood how deeply he would be missed by many, especially me.

*　*　*

That year in the square of Arras there was a casting parade of artillery horses. Colonel F. S. Kennedy-Shaw, Deputy Divisional Inspector of Remounts, and a few others were there to look them over. As we moved down the line I noticed a bay mare standing only fourteen hands three inches and aged about six. Overshadowed by two immense Shires, she looked pathetic but game. I read the label attached to her headcollar:

DANGEROUS

UNRIDEABLE

RECOMMEND DESTRUCTION

Her death sentence was signed by a colonel of artillery.

Corporal Wren followed me, according to my instructions, with a hunting saddle and bridle over one arm.

'See if you can put that lot on her,' I whispered to him, pointing at the mare. 'Gently now. Take your time over it.'

Presently he came along with her. She led quietly. There and then I got on her and started off over the cobbles of that grey and historic place in the drizzle that so often falls in the Pas de Calais. At that time only the odd building had been demolished by the war. The cafés were open. Soon I was cantering back, her shoes hitting sparks.

As I dismounted I hissed at Wren, 'We don't go without this one. Get it?'

'Yessir.'

I tore the label off her headcollar and shoved it, crumpled, into my pocket. Then I began to pick our first twenty-five horses. We had a lead horse with a breast collar and a strad stick across his backside so that the traces did not gall him.

From the strad a ten-fathom boat rope went back to another steady horse with breeching and a strad stick in front. By keeping the rope taut and attaching horses on either side of it, two men could take on twenty-five horses or more.

'It's the big 'uns we want,' Colonel Kennedy-Shaw said. 'Runts like that mare you rode, Mr. Marshall, should go to the abattoir to make soup for the French.'

I made no reply, but catching Corporal Wren's eye, I gave him a brides-in-the-bath look. And when I got back to our lines near Mont St Eloi I found her picketed with the crowd and looking happy with a nice bit of sweet hay and oats in her poor tummy. Good bloke, Wren, you could trust him with your sweetheart.

From that day I rode her in my work and she got fit immediately as those horses do that are always keen and eager to please you. She *was* keen, to the point of being hot, and a little beyond, but there was no vice in her, not a hint. It was not long before I thought to find what sort of a lep she had in her, and when I had tried her the once I sent for that wily Caledonian sportsman, Jock Scott-Nimmo, the horse vet.

'Howard, you're a genius,' he said when he had watched her disdainfully sail a triple bar and the paddock gates and then do the same in reverse order. 'She's no racehorse of course, but she's a top-class fizzer of a jumping mare. A flipping flea. I doubt there's a mare in France to beat her over a course. We keep her right under our hats. Agreed? No more showing off on her, now.'

So, when one of my farriers who came from Newmarket went home on a leave unexpectedly accelerated by me, he carried specimen shoes, and he brought back jumping shoes into which studs could be screwed as required. He travelled back to France with some of the Irish Division. They were returning from a freshener period in God's country, and were immensely proud of the horses they had found over there. As soon as they had settled into their quarters at Hazebrouck, near Dunkirk, it was announced in Orders that they were holding a jumping competition open to all comers. They put up a course to stagger the boldest. I entered the mare. She was a completely unknown quantity, and as for me, I was just a show hack, foxhunting, remount sort of chap, by no means a jumping enthusiast.

On the day, the mare and I and Major Duckett, Provost Marshal of our Corps and a good fellow, travelled together in a veterinary ambulance provided by Jock S.-N. When we got to the ground we unboxed the pony, led her around for a little, looking enviously at the big horses, then popped her in again and went to the unofficial betting office run by God only knows what Samaritan (Ireland for ever!). We bought every ticket we could get, on the mare.

Four of us had clear rounds out of twenty-eight starters. Then it rained so terribly that the jump-off had to be postponed. I stabled her in her nice comfortable ambulance, washed out her mouth with sugared water, rustled straw under her until she staled, and then and only then went to get yet more money on. Duckett was busy on his own, doing just the same thing. They were raising the fences, and the general view was that my mare, though a great one, was too gassy and too small, and that the wet going would flummox so free a jumper. I knew differently. The answer lay in my pocket—the Newmarket screw studs.

We were last to go. Our three opponents did well until the final obstacle, a wall of ammunition boxes filled with sand and topped with a layer of emergency-ration boxes. The approach was downhill, and there was no grass left. It was like jumping off a glacis. They each of them slid bang into it. Meanwhile I had her pacing about smoothly in her plain snaffle and standing martingale, moving her little head about freely, looking everyone in the eye, and getting thoroughly used to her non-slip studs. She gave me a copy-book ride. She stood miles back on the slope before the wall, and looking down I saw the ration boxes unscathed far below me.

So the gunners' cast-off was the clear winner. Major

Duckett and I took a couple of bottles of Veuve Clicquot (was it only two?) with us and the mare for the ride home in the ambulance. Our pockets absolutely *bulged* with valid paper money. . . . The little beauty!

* * *

That same year the Battle of the Somme raged, and one way and another I saw too much of it. But the moment I remember is when I was moving rearwards with a column of horse-drawn limbers and we passed one of those more swagger motor ambulances. The driver, stretcher-bearers, and lady nurse stopped me. It was getting dark, but we were only a mile or so outside the first Field Hospital. I agreed to carry their wounded there. And when I opened the front door of the ambulance, there was my brother Mitchell, dressed as a captain in the 4th Hussars, his face chalk-white and streaked with blood. He looked ghastly, absolutely drained of energy and of life.

'Why are you standing up?' I snarled at him with the swift reaction of anger when one sees a loved one hurt.

'You'd be standing if you'd had half your arse shot away,' he answered, and then he passed right out. I got a quarter of a bottle of good brandy between his poor, muddy lips, and we carried him into hospital stinking of the spirit. His hands were colder than ice.

It must have been ten days or a fortnight later that I next saw him. He was in bed, but looking tons better, and about to be shipped home on sick leave. I put my foot in it twice, first by saying that I thought my brandy had saved his life and then by hoping his wound would not affect his riding. His life had been saved by C. V. Smith, not by any old brandy, he declared, and as for riding again, once the stitches were removed he'd outride me on any horse any old day over any country I cared to name, and he would suggest a little bet on it too. He did me good.

* * *

175

My dear old Company was being wound up in 1919. I had got pretty fond of it, I can tell you. Thanks to Major Mayne (how I keep harking back to that Anglo-Indian personality!) I had learned how an officer should father and befriend his flock, and I felt the break-up almost as though my own fingers were being torn off. Some of us went to the Army of the Rhine, some went home to be demobbed. There were sales in the French markets to dispose of the majority of our horses. Early on I filled in all the applications and other bumf necessary to take four Army horses home to England. There they would have to be publicly auctioned, but at least one would have a chance—so I reasoned—to buy them not too dearly. My four horses included, you may be sure, the little mare, the gunners' reject.

When I was ordered down to Étaples to take over a somewhat indeterminate command there, I popped my four horses into a veterinary ambulance and travelled with them. The motto in the Army in those dissolution days had to be. What you have, hold, before someone pinches it. I was not going to let those horses out of my sight.

From Étaples I entered the mare for the Concours Hippique at Le Touquet in a jumping contest open to soldiers and civilians of all nationalities bar the Germans.

When I was saddling up the mare in her usual (horse-ambulance) box and seeing to the studding of her shoes, who should appear to watch but General Gill, the Director of Remounts, and that same Colonel Kennedy-Shaw, his deputy. I scented trouble, though my conscience was not far off being clear, but they seemed *pleased* that one of their clan was having a go. They stared at my wonderful pony.

'Can that be the little rat of a thing you insisted on saving from the knacker three years ago at Arras, Marshall?'

'None other. But I doubt if you'll call her a rat when you've seen her at work. If you fancy a flutter, sir,' I turned to the General, 'It'll be an uncommon good'n that sees her off today. If I were you I'd put my shirt on her.'

My first ride was on a chestnut gelding that had won a race or two. It belonged to my dangerous friend, Scott-Nimmo, one of those never-a-dull-moment fellows.

It was a winding, trappy course with stiff timber, particularly where you jumped into a wood, turned left, and jumped out over a drop and a spread. The chestnut was clear until then and going a strong hunting pace (it was judged on a time-and-faults basis), but leaving the wood he hit that fence a crasher and flopped into the ditch. We stayed together in the flesh, but his mind was elsewhere and we finished wobbling. He even made a mess of the bank, which was a genuine Irish one, and not a nasty Continental excrescence. Two, perhaps three, of the French horses had clear rounds. But all were on the heavy and slow side, and my mare could *fly*. She jumped the course without any semblance of a fault and we won by a mile on time. It was one of the easiest rides of my life. All I did was sit and soothe.

When General Weygand came off the dais to present the cup I saw General Gill and Colonel Kennedy-Shaw behind him, both delighted. (Up the Remounts! What?) Weygand stood dead in front of the mare, who faced him slightly pigeon-toed, giving him her four-square look.

'You have a wonderful mare here,' he said in creditable English. 'I understand she was in a gun team. How lucky the Boches did not kill her.'

'How lucky the gunners did not kill her, *mon général*,' I answered, glancing again at Kennedy-Shaw.

General Weygand was in trousers with an ugly stripe down them. Otherwise his cavalry uniform and his képi suited him to a T. Brigadier Etienne Gerard had been one of my boyhood heroes, and in Weygand's open yet shrewd expression, his bold eye, his highly-strung hands, I saw Sir Arthur Conan Doyle's hussar officer so plainly that I found myself peering at the General's ears, to see if he had had one cut off.

But both ears were there.

The Jumping Mare

A TELEGRAM from Corporal Wren sent me hurrying to
catch the first boat for England. He had got to Southampton
with the jumping mare and two others, and they were
leaving for London where all three would come under the
hammer almost on arrival. After the mare had won so
convincingly at Le Touquet I had pulled out every known
stop to get her and my other horses away from France.
Danger had come from a not altogether unexpected quarter.
Scott-Nimmo pinched the best of them (bar the mare) off me,
saying the gelding had ringworm and must stay for treatment.
I did not let him get away with it easily, but the Scots
conjurer had me properly. That good horse just disappeared.

Arrived in London, I took a room at the Grosvenor Hotel
and fitted myself out in an old suit, cap, and muffler borrowed
from the floor-waiter. In that disguise I mooched into Aldridges in St Martin's Lane an hour or so before the sale began.
Wren nearly jumped out of his skin when I sidled up to him.
He had done well, and things looked hopeful. The three
horses were filthy. Prices, Wren said, had been ludicrously
low the previous day, and nobody had shown interest in our
three. He had them coming up early, when bids were likely
to be mean. The mare was first of the three.

I bought her for seventeen guineas. The others I bought
for nineteen and twenty-one guineas respectively. I paid
cash. No name given and none asked. My next move was
to put all three safely away at Melton.

The mare carried me from the City to St Pancras Station, Corporal Wren following us, riding and leading.

'You must have been asleep,' a porter said, looking me up and down. I suppose he wondered what such a seedy-looking customer was doing with three horses and a smart n.c.o. 'We're on strike, all railwaymen. It began an hour ago and we're only here to take incoming traffic.'

'Here's a rum do,' I said to Corporal Wren. 'While we've been away fighting the war for them, all these perishers think of is striking for higher wages. Now what?' What indeed? Ambrose Preece had gone from the scene, probably to America, or I could have stabled them in his place in Fulham Road or ridden them out to Combe Warren. 'Hold this 'oss,' I said sharply to the corporal, flinging him her rein. A train had just arrived, packed to bursting, and in the crowd hurrying down the platform I had spotted George Miles, who had drifted into No. 2 Remount Depot from Milan, and who now owned, so I had been told, a livery stable at the Marble Arch.

'George!' I cried, taking him firmly by the arm. 'George, how marvellous to see you!'

'I was hoping you wouldn't,' he answered, almost nastily. 'I saw you get off that horse, and knew what you'd be after.'

'I'm not short of the ready; the reason for these rags is that I've just been buying at Aldridges,' I said with a wink.

'I know, I know,' he said testily. 'You want to put those three nags up. All right then, don't let's waste time. . . . I don't know where my next forage is coming from. You may bring them to my yard, *but only for one night.*'

Again we set off across London, along Euston Road, down Baker Street, and right-handed from the junction with Oxford Street. George's place proved to be in a mews behind what is now the Cumberland Hotel. With some difficulty we got all three put away in one box, and scrounged hay and oats for them.

Then I took that dear fellow, Corporal Wren, to a glowing, panelled London pub. We ate oysters and eels, steak, kidney

and mushroom pudding, and jam roly-poly. We drank
sound English beer, full of good barley and hops and natural
sugar. Out in the street I hailed a hansom. The driver took
us to a yard along towards Notting Hill, where I bought a
sack of Scots oats and half a dozen trusses of hay to be
delivered at George's place the following morning. We drove
on to the Grosvenor where Corporal Wren slept on my
sofa and where I returned the waiter's useful clothes. After a
tremendous English breakfast in the pillared dining-room I
said a temporary goodbye to Wren, whom I would shortly
be rejoining in France. My horses had behaved themselves
in their cramped quarters, but it was a matter of urgency
to get them out of there.

Poking round the yard I came upon an elderly dog-cart that
had been left outdoors like some rusted bit of farm machinery.
I also found some disreputable harness to go with it.

'George,' I said. 'Is that old cart scrap, the one behind your
muck-heap?'

'It's yours if you can make use of it. But I don't know how
far it would take you.'

'If I can only get one of those three horses to go in harness,
I might be able to lead the other two up the road to Melton.
Once we got clear of London I could keep the dog-cart going.
There must still be wheelwrights and blacksmiths in England.'

'It hasn't been on the road for ten years. But take it, take
it. I'll ask Johnny to grease it up for you and give you any
help you need this morning.'

We greased its hubs, checked the tyres and shafts and
reinforced the floorboards, and when we had worked on the
harness with neatsfoot oil and saddle soap and a stitch here
and there we loaded four trusses of hay in the back and the
sack of oats in front. Johnny and I then wheeled the cart
backwards round the Marble Arch and stood it with the
shafts propped, at the end of the Hyde Park riding track.

Now came the crux of the matter. I chose the gelding we
called Elder Statesman as being the steadiest of the three.

After lungeing him and then long-reining him through the traffic and on the grass, I tackled him in the shafts. By the grace of God, he went.

Tucking a long line from the headcollars of the other two under my arm, I drove out of the Park and struck a course northwards up the Edgware Road. The pair behind came on fairly well, partly I think because the instinct of the jumping mare was always to forge ahead. As they came they nibbled at the hay in the back of the dog-cart. In Finchley and Barnet the streets seemed horribly narrow and the double-decked tramcars swung out over us as they screeched and grunted round the bends.

About tea-time I got to Hatfield, and asked at The Comet if they could put up three horses and one man. Not a hope for the horses. I drove up the road some way, and turned them loose in a field where there was a pond and a stack of hay. It was a frosty September evening. They rolled, then drank at the pond. I pulled them out a good supply of hay, shut the gate, and went back to the hotel for the night.

It was a hellish start in the morning. First I had to get cold harness on to a horse quite unused to it; then, once he was harnessed, get him to lead out of a wet field slightly uphill on to the road. Elder Statesman hated the feel of his collar, and kept backing away from it rather than going into it. I propped the field gate open, thinking he might go with a rush. That was what he finally did, pulling the reins through my numbed hands and darting out on to the road. Meanwhile my led pair were still in the field, and walking quietly away. The shaft horse came to a stop, nibbling the grass on the verge. I could only hope he'd stay until I had the others. I shut the gate behind them and by good luck he stood. I caught his reins. We made a reasonable start, all together, until the led horses stopped, pulling the leading line away from me. Another stop. Then I moved off, rattling in the tin the few oats I had used to catch them. Gradually we worked up a steady rhythm and I kept them jogging on all day, not daring to stop, until we hove up at Sandy Gilmour's farm near St Neots in Bedfordshire. Sandy had been in France with me under Major Mayne and with him the horses had their one comfortable night of the whole journey.

We went on next morning, the weather getting harder and colder. Frost and ice slowed us. When we got snow on the road we went better. It took us three more days, each with its difficulties, to reach Dick Black's place at Frisby-on-the-Reach, where the horses were to winter out. I had nearly lost all three when we struck a patch of black ice near Huntingdon. Both led horses went down at once, and how the shaft horse kept his feet I don't know. Fortunately no leg damage, but the mare cut her head on the back of the cart as she struggled up. The wound bled into her eyes and made her, for once, reluctant to get on. Dick drove me to Melton station after breakfast. I had no heart to look at Hickling now that there were no Marshalls there. The country round Melton and the Black family's cheerful talk of the cubhunting wrung my heart and made me feel very much on my own, a jackal howling outside the walls. There had been nothing my father did, whether buying or selling horses or general farming, that I could not do. I had believed since my mother left Hickling that sooner or later I would take over and run the place with him and for him, and go hunting with him, the pair of us as equals and friends, father and son. Why could he not have waited for me?

Hickling had gone in the War, and so had Richmond. Combe Warren, at one side of the park, was empty. It had always seemed possible that Ambrose Preece would retire or move elsewhere, but I would have bet a hundred pounds to a shilling that the end of the War would find Jim Dawkins owning quite a slice of Richmond. What had he done, though, but got himself into the Army again. In September 1917, when I was in England on short leave, I had gone to see them. The shop front still declared, Mr and Mrs F. J. Dawkins, Newsagents and Tobacconists, Sweets and

Toys, Minerals and Ice Cream. But Molly, poor dear, was all in black, Jim had got himself killed on June 7th of that year in Lord Haig's attack on the Messines-Wytschaete ridge. He was a sergeant in the Machine Gun Corps when he copped it. Molly produced the Military Medal he'd won at Mametz Wood the year before. All through the War the shop and its corollaries had made money, especially the car-hire business and the tea garden. After Jim's death Molly married again, very rightly I think. Her third husband was a builder in Herne Bay, and before she went down there to live she sold off all Jim's strange developments in Richmond. Many's the time I think of him, and wish he were here.

* * *

When I had wound up my unit in France I was appointed to command a horse transport company at Colchester, and very soon I was able to get the jumping mare down from Melton. I sold the other two horses up there. Elder Statesman went for a really good price to a friend near Market Harborough who hunted him and then raced him locally with some success. The horse's name was changed and he ran in the 1921 National, but came down at The Chair and damaged a tendon. A good sort. He got us out of London that time, anyway. The other gelding I let go to the Hickling baker for a hundred pounds. He drew the cart for donkey's years, never sick nor sorry. I should have got two hundred pounds for him, but deals at a distance are always tricky, and sentiment came into it. As for the mare, I took her on the strength as my own charger under the Army order that allowed one horse per officer if that horse did military duties. She had been named—badly, I fear—Little Lady.

Soon motor lorries took over our garrison transport at Colchester. I presented myself at the War Office.

'A trustworthy and experienced officer is needed to wind up a horse transport company at Crowborough, Captain Marshall.'

'Sounds a bit of all right.'

'It should last you eighteen months. Take over everything you can see, but double-check all indents. Then your best plan might be to have an all-consuming conflagration in the office.'

Crowborough, which is in Sussex, was hardly my idea of a sporting place, being largely devoted to golf, but we were exceptionally well housed in modern huts, and there was hunting with two packs. My own installation was not bad. I arrived from Colchester with three private horses, a Lawton gig (you never could fault a Lawton), and a civilian groom, Larry Mulligan, known to his friends as Mulligatawny. He had been one of the civilian drivers dismissed from the Colchester unit by the C.O. whom I replaced, and a thundering good groom he became under me. (I had learned a lot with and from Geoffrey Brooke.) As for the work side of the card, I had fifty waggons, a hundred horses (pairs), and twelve spare horses. We carried rations and stores to the Signals unit in Maresfield Park, the big house of the locality, and we served many other units in and around Crowborough.

I had just settled in when Mitchell turned up to stay. They had operated on his backside and he had finished the War on active service, but not on a horse. He had been undergoing various courses of physiotherapy and osteopathy. His admirers in America were clamouring for his return. My set-up was just right for him. I was infinitely pleased to see him and had plenty for him to ride. Starting gradually, he worked himself into full fettle.

He laughed when he first saw the jumping mare. 'Your feet must touch the ground,' he said. But like all of them he changed his tune when he saw her fly. 'When you crossed that triple I felt the wind of her passage on my face. And you say they were for putting her down? If you do nothing else worth while in your life, How, you did something when you taught her to jump.'

'I didn't teach her,' I answered truthfully. 'She taught me.'
There are some horses, rare enough, that flatter the rider
over fences, and others, good though they sometimes are, that
do the opposite. She was a flatterer. So workmanlike was
she in any practice we gave her that I entered her for three
major events at the coming Olympia. She was a hard one to
feed for indoor jumping of that sort, as she was naturally
hot, and a good doer. We took her there in great shape,
though perhaps just a shade too full of herself.

She was astonished, not overawed, by the indoor arena,
the flunkeys, the clothes, the music, the smells of women and
flowers. When our turn came in the first event she flew round
without fault until the last, where she touched off a lathe
with her off hind. (In those days they had two-foot lathes
set along the top of an obstacle to prove whether or no
there had been a touch.) She did exactly the same in her
next two events, although on time we were among the best.
There had been clear rounds, for after all we were competing in the highest class in the world. We did not get
into the money, but she was a favourite with that knowledgeable crowd, and even Lord Lonsdale (in the centre of
the ring as always) accorded her more than polite applause.
Her smallness, her dash, the way she looked intently to see
what other massive obstacle lay ahead, and just flicked one
ear—she was fascinating.

And when I'd ridden out through the double doors for the
third time a foreign officer approached us in the collecting
ring. He was Count von Rosen, senior member of the team
competing for Sweden. Touching my mare with one gloved
forefinger, he uttered that beautiful phrase.

'How much?'

'One thousand pounds.' I held up my index finger. 'One.'
(Nothing confuses a foreigner more than guineas.) I signalled
to my civilian groom and muttered to him, 'Just hang on a
bit, Tawny. It's on the cards those people mean business.
They're simmering. I'll stay on her till they boil.'

Another Swedish officer had joined Count von Rosen. They did some reckoning with a gold pencil in a crocodile-bound notebook. Presently he came back at me.

'Eight 'underd, ten.'

'That will do me,' I said, thinking that indeed it would, for a mare I had bought for seventeen pounds and had won a packet on in France.

He made one stipulation. Nothing about a vet. Merely that I was to take her to the East India Docks with the Swedish horses and see her safely on the ship for Gothenberg. Then I was to return to the De Vere Hotel, Kensington, where they were staying.

You may think I was greedy in the price I asked. Well, a gunner friend of mine, Squeaker Morrison, had an invitation to take his good horse Carintho to jump in Rome, and some Eyeties had bid eight hundred pounds for the horse.

'Did you win anything down there then?' I asked when he had got back to London and was telling me of the offer.

'Not a thing. He was terrible, right off form.'

'And you didn't clinch! You'd easily have bought two others just as good as Carintho for that money.'

Squeaker shrugged his houlders. He liked the game, and usually was fond of having a deal. I was mystified, and made up my mind I would behave differently should I ever be lucky enough to be in his situation.

When the Swedish string left Olympia I squeezed myself and the mare safely in among them. At the top of Haymarket (that was the route we took) our cavalcade was held up and I managed to hail a prowling taxi. He pulled his flag down and tailed us to dockland. The keen mare gave me something to think about when, in the East End, the urchins threw orange peel and other missiles at us all. She tucked herself into her box on the ship happily enough.

In Kensington I was given my cheque and a warm welcome by the compatriots of that celebrated horseman, Gustavus Adolphus. Von Rosen, I learned, was Master of the Horse to the King of Sweden, so the jumping mare was going up in the world, as she deserved. He insisted on taking me to the farewell dinner given for the foreign competitors by the Earl of Lonsdale.

It was a splendid affair in the Pillar Hall, most perfectly organised, like everything in which his lordship had a hand. He was more of a miracle than a man and of course he never forgot a face. When the speeches had broken covert he had me on my feet, playfully accusing me of gatecrashing. Me gatecrashing! I went hot and cold. That's one misdemeanour I am incapable of committing. Nobody was ever better than Lord Lonsdale at being either rude or charming. When he was playful with you it was like being in a small cage with a big panther, I should think. What the deuce did he want me to say? Did he know I'd sold my mare? There was little he didn't know.

I told them my breast pocket was securely buttoned and pinned as well. I declared that the slip of paper with a Swedish signature in that pocket gave me as much of a glow as did the company of all those equestrian geniuses from foreign lands, and as did his lordship's presence and his princely hospitality. The end of the dinner was almost rowdy. Lord Lonsdale came through the noise, obviously making straight for me. I thought I was in for the dickens of a wigging.

'I have not seen you since your father's death,' he said gently. 'We all miss him. We breed few men now of the stamp of Sam Marshall of Hickling. . . . If that mare had been a hand higher I'd have bought her myself. A very taking mare. By the way, you wanted to sell her? I thought so, or you would not be Sam's son. But I told Rosen he'd have to go high to get her.'

My room in the Kensington Palace Hotel seemed a lonely place when eventually I got back to it, though I had made one of the best sales of my life, had immensely enjoyed the whole day, and was happy about the mare's destination.

12

Beacon

With the mare gone to Sweden and Mitchell to the Fairfield
and Winchester Hunt at Greenwich, Connecticut, I began to
think it time I rode a few races. I put out horse-probing feelers
which soon brought me into contact with my friend Geo.
Hone of Ross-on-Wye.

'I've a blood horse here I bought for thirty pounds in
Leicester Repository,' Geo. said on the telephone. 'He has
the W brand on his near hindquarter. He rides like one
that's been in training, and he won't go ten yards down any
street for me, though he might for you. He loathes traffic.
On the other side of the balance sheet he's a liver chestnut
with one front star and no other white on him and he's
clean in wind and limb and a corking free mover. If
you're interested, Howard, I'd let *you* have him for fifty
pound.'

'What do you think I'm made of, money?' was my
answer. But I went down there and after a look and a ride
I was interested. I felt that the chestnut was a horse of
character, and one that knew perhaps too much of racing,
but was still fresh enough to recover. He was nine. I went
home from Ross-on-Wye with three horses. The second was
a nice mare, polo-pony bred, aged only five and afterwards
brilliant, and the third was a black thoroughbred that Geo.
had picked out at an Army sale.

'Take him and send me something for him if and when you
can, old boy,' he said. 'He's more often lame than sound,

but he warms up, jumps really well, and could be a better proposition than the chestnut.'

I went to work on all three. The mare was too easy. After one hunt on her I had sold her to a Mrs Bullock, a sister of the Wilmott brothers, joint masters of the Weston (Somerset) Harriers. She stabled a few hunters at the White Hart in Lewes, and hunted regularly with the South Down. Through doing her a good turn, I met trouble. We were chatting one day by the covertside.

'Shall you be out tomorrow?' I asked, knowing that the Meet was at Maresfield Park, very near my camp.

'I'd give anything to hunt. But I've two lame horses in the stable, and won't have a mount.'

'I can't hunt tomorrow,' I said. 'Official duties. But I'll send you a horse over to the Park if you like. It's only a step from my camp, and I've got at least one would carry you well and could do with a short day.'

'What an angel you are! I'd simply adore it.'

Colonel Mordaunt, O.C. Maresfield Park, was hunting from his H.Q.'s portico. He soon got into conversation with Mrs Bullock. 'I see you have a new horse.'

'Alas, no,' replied the lady. 'It's one Captain Marshall has most kindly lent me. Such a charming man, and so wonderful on a horse.'

As luck would have it (and it was lucky for me) I took it into my head the very next day to call on Colonel Mordaunt. The cubhunting was nearly over. As November approaches, most foxhunters, and hunt secretaries in particular, begin to wonder about subscriptions for the coming season. I knew that Maresfield Park had formed a hunting club as a cheap way of keeping in with both local packs. I supposed that as I did all their transport and also could assist them in many ways to enjoy their hunting, they would welcome me as an additional member. But as soon as I met the colonel I knew something was up. The atmosphere was glacial.

'We *have* formed a hunting club. We most certainly can

not include you. You are not in the Corps of Signals, nor are you a member of this Mess.'

And they say foxhunters hang together! thought I. What's bitten you, *mon colonel*? Never mind, I'll soon know. I won't give you the satisfaction of being asked. And next time I find you in the hunting field I'll lead you over the most ghastly, gruesome, yawning places and break your little neck for you.

Colonel Mordaunt's first hostile move came immediately after breakfast the very next morning in the shape of an odd-looking bloke who said he was veterinary officer at Maresfield Park, and that he must examine all my horses. I took a long time lighting my pipe, the most important of the day.

'You can't see 'em all at once except on a Sunday afternoon when they have a bit of kip,' I said. 'Otherwise at any time of any day seventy-five per cent of 'em are out hauling.'

'Don't come the barrackroom lawyer with me, Captain Marshall. And as a major in the R.A.V.C. I'm entitled to a salute from you.'

'Not in a British warm with badges removed and wearing a bowler hat, you're not. I've nothing to hide. Quite the contrary. We're proud of our unit, which is never idle. If you must examine my horses, you'll have to fit in with our work schedules, that's all.' I knew I could take care of a hundred such vets and their so-called examinations. Colonel Mordaunt had as good as lost the first round. The next hostile move was a chit from the War Office.

'Please state in writing before Thursday next why you are allowing civilians to ride and hunt Government horses. . . .'

'In reply to your so-and-so dated such-and-such,' was my response, 'no civilian, repeat NO CIVILIAN, has ridden any Government horse in my charge. I am at a loss to understand your completely unfounded and insulting communication and demand an immediate investigation and apology. I have the honour to be. . . . etc., etc.'

And cursing all mean and nasty people who would begrudge a good-looking woman a day's foxhunting, of all things, I said nothing to anyone, but took silent measures to defend myself. They included a trip to London and back.

A further *billet-doux* was not delayed.

'A Board of Officers has been convened to inspect the horses of your company on the. . . .'

I was ready for them. My position was eased from observation of Major Mayne's methods at Le Havre. The way to stay clear of *angst* in those depots was always privately to be a bit over the establishment with your horses, and always officially to have exactly the right number. It is the old, the age-old, strategy of Reserves. So I moved the little chestnut horse that Mrs Bullock had hunted, moved him at night in an ambulance, to a discreet and pleasant hiding place in Seaford. Meanwhile on the Monday I had bought at Tattersalls another chestnut. A touch on the hindquarter with the broad arrow over the one he originally had, and hogging his mane, made him a goodish substitute. I stood him in my private stables under Mulligatawny alongside the two thoroughbreds. Needless to say, I coached Tawny until he was word-perfect in relation to the 'origins' of the little chestnut. Tawny enjoyed that sort of caper. . . . I really looked forward to the Board, especially when I learned that Colonel Mordaunt was its chairman. I dressed up to meet them, with extra lustre (if possible) on boots, spurs, and Sam Browne. The camp, tidy as a Quaker carnival, looked a picture—we really were a good unit, a credit to the Army.

It was not hard to see what they were looking for. They skipped all bar the chestnuts and I had taken good care to have none of that colour, and of the size Mordaunt sought.

'Have you no other horses here?' he asked when they had been through every shed.

'Just my three private ones.'

'May we see them now?'

'Certainly. This way, gentlemen. Morning, Mulligan.'

'Morning, sir.' Tawny was hard at work on the tack and dressed very much more than usual *en civile*, I mean without Army boots or shirt or muffler, or even issue braces. He hardly bothered to glance at us, as though such an intrusion of hard-faced officers was a normality.

'Those two blood horses I'm qualifying for point-to-pointing,' I explained. 'I bought them from my friend Major G. Hone of Ross-on-Wye. And this little fellow here I bought in Colchester Market at the disposal sale by Messrs Sexton & Blake of Colchester Horse Transport Company.' (I knew they could never trap me on *that* sale.)

Colonel Mordaunt's face proclaimed him beat. They left at once. I did not forgive him, and did not cease to regard his unit as potentially hostile. Soon I thought it safe to send the chestnut back to Tattersalls. He was not my sort of horse. I had paid thirty guineas for him with a mane, and he fetched forty-seven without one, so apparently his stay with us at Crowborough had done him good, as it had me.

* * *

We called the liver chestnut I had bought from Geo. Hone by the good name of Beacon. (I cannot recall how we arrived at it unless it derived from the Beacon Hotel at Crowborough.) The other one was Hadlow Down.

As Geo. had indicated, Beacon was really dodgy in traffic, skittery and dangerous. I reckoned that in his youth he had been raced and that possibly his horse box had been in an accident. As soon as I rode him I learned that he had a peculiar hatred for horse boxes. The very first one we met on the main road he pirouetted, then reared, and put me down dangerously. After that I decided to send him back to school. I got Tawny to mash and mash him until he was in a more flabby condition. Meanwhile I mouthed him and fiddled about and tried to get him to go in harness. He was just too old and crabbed to do that, so I got out the long reins, and for two or three *months*, yes, as long as that, I drove him on foot for at least an hour every day except Sundays, when I went to church and he had a rest. When I finally backed him and rode him he was a different horse, vastly improved in mouth, carriage, and appearance. And since most of my long-reining had been done on the public roads, he had become absolutely traffic-proof. To cure him of the obsessive hatred for horse-boxes I borrowed or hired (I cannot remember which, but knowing me, it was probably borrowed) an elderly veterinary ambulance, and we fed him and stabled him in it for some time, then put two of our draught-horses to it and took him for rides. Anyone less experienced would have imagined, I think, that he had an entirely renewed animal in Beacon. I knew differently. I knew that somewhere in his mind there was a scar caused by mistreatment in his youth, possibly in training or hurdling or steeplechasing. Why, you may think, did I not do the same with Beacon (lash him to a telegraph pole while the traffic passed) as I had done with the Kentucky Horse? The answer is that horses alter cases. Had I treated Beacon in that way he would have been useless from then on. I don't know how I knew it, but I knew it.

When I took him cubhunting, and later hunting, he was, if not a star, very good indeed, and I always enjoyed him, he was such a nice horse.

I had got Beacon for forty pounds (Geo. Hone had *asked* fifty pounds, you may remember) and had turned him, I was sure, into a valuable property and a potential winner. Hadlow Down, for all that there was more rake and steeplechasing potential to him, was a problem. He was a genuine enough horse and did his best, but he was always stiff and pottery in the morning, and it is worrying riding anything you suspect of unsoundness. On the other hand, as George had said, he warmed up fairly quickly, and, hunting, he could on occasion be spectacular.

One day out with the Eridge on Beacon I was riding with a Mr Neilson who then lived near Crowborough but soon migrated to the Ledbury country. (I remember meeting him many years later when he was showing at Olympia a lovely docked middleweight by Watershed named The Brook, and was winning with him.) Well, he and I were on our own. We were sitting our horses quietly at the bottom of a big wood near Crowgate when the hounds came out beside us on a good line. They had been hunting well in the thickets for quite a time, perhaps forty minutes. We had not seen their fox emerge. They went for fifteen minutes as hard as they could lick to a long, sloping bank, where they marked.

'He never went in,' said an old hedger who was standing watching us, hook in hand. 'He be for'ard through yonder gap.'

Neilson was a cracking good fellow to hounds. He and I had come fast and straight across a bit of stiffly enclosed country without opening a gate or pausing to hesitate, and absolutely on our own with hounds. We were, as you can imagine, well hotted up. In my excitement I capped and spoke hounds on to the line, and they went handsomely away. They soon ran into another big wood, and proceeded to hunt their fox about it with a noble cry. We galloped round the wood to the far side, then heard them behind us, and decided to go in search.

We were splashing along a deep and sticky ride when, turning a corner, we came face to face with the Master, Lord Abergavenny, with his huntsman. The field was jammed in behind them. His lordship had been watching us from an eminence during our exciting hunt, and he was looking for us and for trouble.

'Ah, you are the *gentlemen* who've been hunting my hounds.' Pause. 'Thank you kindly for hunting my hounds.' Pause. 'What do you *mean* by hunting my hounds?' Then his soliloquy became more insulting, and it was prolonged. His words reverberated in the stuffy ride, among the horses' steam.

I had been trained like every self-respecting foxhunter

never, NEVER, to answer the Master back, and never to mind what he said to me in the hunting field. But on this occasion I made the mistake of opening my silly mouth. 'Very sorry, my lord, very sorry indeed. I'd waited over five years to see hounds run like that again. . . .'

'Blighter says he waited five years, pity he didn't wait fifty,' Lord Abergavenny observed to the field, who raised an embarrassed titter.

'I'll get on back now to camp,' I was stupid enough to add. 'And I won't come out with you again until I hear from the secretary that you've been good enough to forgive my lapse.' I turned to look at Neilson behind me, but he, wily fellow, had slipped off.

'Damned glad to hear it,' his lordship said, slapping his thigh. 'Deuced glad to hear it. Indeed, Mister, that's about the best and gladdest news since the Armistice. DON'T come again.'

Those beggars could make you feel small! And it cost me dear because I could no longer hunt with the Eridge, and had to do all my qualifying of both horses with the South Down, whereas Neilson, after staying away for a week, went out again, watched his Ps and Qs, and Lord Abergavenny treated him in the most open and friendly fashion. That's foxhunting. You're bound to sail a bit near the wind at times, particularly if you're seeking to sell bold horses. There's an art in shedding the blame and keeping the favour of the all-powerful man (or woman) who provides the sport.

*   *   *

About that time the Rashleighs came to stay in Crowborough. I had seen a good bit of him during the War, but he was now a civilian. A Cornishman who claimed to be descended from a surviving hidalgo of the Armada, he was spectacularly handsome, with an olive skin and black hair. His wife, a kinswoman of Lord Jersey, dearly loved a deal in horseflesh and went extra well to hounds.

I sold Beacon to her for two hundred and fifty pounds on the understanding that he was to be qualified, then raced in point to points, and that I was to ride him. When he was qualified she sent him to be trained by 'Stoker' Cannon at Clifton Head. Cannon was in a position to run trials with horses from Herbert ('Barty') Bride's stables (then going very strong), and he seemed to have the knack of cleverly pulling out a horse and winning with him at Gatwick or some such place at about ten to one. When I saw how well Beacon was doing I also sent Hadlow Down to Cannon. He soon diagnosed the black horse's almost chronic unsoundness as rheumatism in the shoulders and arms. What was even better, he dealt with the trouble (don't ask me how, he wouldn't tell me, for trainers hold by their secrets) and Hadlow became in an instant rather an asset.

Cannon advised us to run Beacon in the Open Race at the Eridge Point-to-Point on Easter Monday, and before that to give him a pipe-opener at the West Kent fixture. Hadlow was to go hunter-'chasing, and was entered as an unknown quantity for the Artillery Meeting at Sandown Park. Stoker Cannon had taken to both animals, and he was both interesting and helpful.

My first ride on Beacon the racehorse was exciting from start to finish, and it certainly confirmed the horse's form on the gallops.

I had a puncture on my way to the meeting. It was before the days of spare wheels. I got there only by scrounging a lift, and I arrived barely with time to declare my horse and weigh out. I had not walked the course. Worse still, we were the first race on the card, there were no hoof prints to follow, and the course was a twister. As we rode down to the start I kept asking the starter to explain which way we were supposed to go. But he was having trouble with his cob, which was fresh and frothy, and could not help me. One of my opponents was the redoubtable Captain Leveson-Gower. I heard him say to two or three others riding near him as he cast a knowing eye over Beacon, 'Best let that bloke make the running, for the nag looks a corker. Let him beat himself going the longest way round.'

I made up my mind to disappoint them, but when the flag fell, try as I would, I could not keep my fellow back with them. He was away in a flash, flicked over the first two fences, and galloped strongly uphill. I expected to see the next flags at the top. Absolutely nothing! Looking back, I saw the field away to my left, having done a sharp turn at the foot of the slope. I gradually overtook them, and Beacon, catching hold of his bit, threaded his way through them. We'd lost thirty lengths, and had pulled them back. Now, seeing my way clearly for home, I settled down to ride like a feather and nurse him there. I heard them closing on me, or at least one of them, and that confounded Leveson Gower just passed me before the post.

'Well,' Cannon said. 'That's what might be called a promising start. I'd a tenner on each way,' (there had been twelve runners) 'so it isn't all loss, and at least we know what to do. This will be our programme between now and the Eridge. . . .'

We gave Beacon a gallop on Clifton Downs very early one morning with Midas, one of Bride's star selling-platers. Beacon pulled up six lengths ahead after one mile.

'He could be a great horse,' Cannon said. 'For he stays and his jumping's impeccable. He's got a lot of brain and character, but there's a kink somewhere. . . . This time just let him run his own race. Steady him when you won't fret him. You're going to win. Barty and I are each putting one hundred pounds on him.'

That time there was no nonsense. I walked the course and was properly organised. There was a big field and a good favourite. Despite the horse's sensational showing at the West Kent we were down in the ten to one lot, and both Bride and Cannon got bets of one thousand pounds to one hundred pounds.

'How much d'you want on?' Cannon asked.

'Twenty pounds,' I answered. 'But there's a hell of a lot of them to beat.'

'He'll beat 'em like rotten eggs. Just watch yourself and sit tight. I know you can do it.'

Riding down to the start we passed the local chemist at Crowborough. He was standing under a kind of wigwam, making a book.

'What price mine?' I called over to him while Beacon fretted and sidled under me.

'Tens.'

'Lay me one hundred pounds to ten pounds, then,' I said.

'You're on, Captain Marshall.'

The rider of the favourite, just in front of me, screwed round in the plate, ran an eye over Beacon, and asked, 'D'you think that fellow'd lay the same again against your nag?'

'Don't know,' I answered, doubting if the chemist would be able to shell out two wins of one hundred pounds on one race. At that moment a dapper little Jewish gentleman, very tweedy, stepped in front of Beacon. I'd seen him looking from me and my mount to the amateur bookie.

'That was quick work, Captain,' he said, laying a light hand on Beacon's shoulder. I can see that small hand now, the nails pink and shining, the black hairs on the back of it, the white-gold signet ring. 'Do you really fancy him, honestly now?'

'Yes I do,' said I. 'But if you want a substantial bet take my advice and don't do it there.'

'Not likely,' he said. 'No half measures. If I may say so, I like the looks of both of you, the horse and the man.'

'Hope we don't let you down,' I said. 'Good luck to you.'

He'd taken my mind off the start, and I was grateful.

If anybody knew that course he would confirm that a section of it went through a hopfield. That afternoon the sun glinted fiercely through gaps in the high poles and festooning vegetation. Beacon had started well and was in the lead and right as rain when we came to the track through the hops. It was like galloping down an arterial road after dark, with shafts of light darting into your eyes and blinding you. He kept dodging and changing leg, peeping about, and reaching with his head. Once he all but managed to run out at an opening. This slowed him of course, and a number passed me. We went over the water at the end of the hop-field and Beacon, usually so bold and fluent, propped even at that, the easiest of obstacles. After the water the stand and enclosures were on our left. Beacon obviously of a mind to go in and rest, hung toward the rail and got himself farther astern. I could only sit still on him and keep muttering, 'Go on, go on! Get on!' At least I had the strength of mind not to use my whip. We looked a beaten combination. Barty Bride lowered his glasses in disgust.

'I thought you said that beggar could ride,' he said to Cannon (so Cannon told me later).

'Don't worry. That horse might still travel and catch 'em,' Cannon answered. But as he admitted afterwards, he was cursing himself for not putting a more experienced jockey on so good a horse.

Lagging more and more up the hill, Beacon suddenly took notice again. It seemed that I felt strength exude from his body to my lower leg, up through my chest, and right to the ends of my fingers. Now he was concentrating on the horses in front. He was beginning to hate them, to go after them, getting keener with every uphill stride. There was a well-made black fence at the top. One of those in front fell a somersault over it with a crash like doom and a flicker of steel as a plate reflected the sun. Beacon went at that fence like a lion, landing yards and yards beyond. He was now passing horse after horse. A corner flag loomed. He shot round it, grazing my knee. He was now looking for his fences in the most greedy manner, and I knew that, depending al-ways on those confounded hops, nothing in the race could live with us. He kept up his gallop to the hopfield, took the lead in it, galloped on and propelled himself in an ecstasy of speed over the water. He bore away from the stand and, straight as a gun, accelerated to the winning post, which he fully understood because he pulled up immediately of his own free will. We were twelve lengths ahead of the next one.

Major and Mrs Rashleigh waylaid me at the entry to the weighing tent.

'Oh by Jove, well done!' he cried.

'What a patient race you rode!' Mrs Rashleigh said. 'Quite outstanding.'

'Nothing of the sort,' I answered. 'I died a thousand deaths because, for almost half the distance, he wouldn't go a yard. Had he not suddenly taken it into his queer head to win we'd *still* be out there in the country.'

'Quite right, quite true, Marshall,' the voice of the great one, the M.F.H., the Steward, Lord Abergavenny in fact, chipped in from behind my shoulder. 'I kept the glasses on you after the hopfield first time round and I saw the chestnut change from slug to racehorse. It bears out my contention that horses win races on willpower and brain even more than on constitution and conformation. Congratulations, my boy.' My somewhat sour answer to the lady's gush had pleased him. 'I liked the way you rode him, nice and long and easy. . . . We meet again, eh? . . . Nothing a man hates more than to see a stranger from outside the country lifting his hounds and tearing over his pet farmers' fields and fences. Understandable? No hard feelings though, either side. We have a likely bye-day on Thursday, near you. Cripples' Gorse. Sir Edwin always has a fox and it's usually a flyer. Ring the kennels that morning about eight. If we're hunting I'll be delighted to see you out.'

'I should just think he'll be delighted,' Mrs Rashleigh said. ' "Nice and long and easy" indeed! I believe he had a jolly good bet on Beacon and won a packet. . . . Didn't he, darling?' She addressed herself to her horse in that undignified way some women do. Horses don't care for it.

The horse-coper's mentality is unstable. True I had bought Beacon for forty pounds. Then I had virtually remade him (I had enjoyed the performance and its success, mind you) and had sold him with certain conditions for two hundred and fifty pounds. The thought came that now he was worth a good deal more than that, and I might have done better to hold on and sell *when* he had won a race for me. But my preference, then as now, was, when you get a reasonable deal, take it. In those days, too, there were masses of horses crying out to be bought and sold.

When I emerged from the dressing tent after Beacon's good win I ran straight into the smiling little man who had cheered me up before the start. He now smiled even more warmly as he handed me an engraved card.

'Here's my address, Captain Marshall. Before you come to see me let me know. If you don't I shall be in touch with you. I've a house down here, and often get to these holiday meetings, but thanks to you, today was one of the best I ever had in these parts.' As his short, broad back receded into the crowd I read his card:

J. HYAMS
High Class London Clothier
RACING SILKS AND SADDLERY
PADDOCK SHEETS, ETC., ETC.
Wilton Street, S.W.1.

Two weeks later I went by appointment to his shop. There he was, astride a Persian rug under shaded lights like a sultan, but surrounded by clothes and saddlery rather than women, hookahs, and eunuchs—a pretty good exchange in my opinion. 'I've a little present for you,' those were his delightful opening words. 'Don't take offence, I trust you not to. You see my friends and I had a good bet on Beacon, and we won. . . .' The sum made me reel. I would not think it fair to him to repeat it.

'You mean to say you had *that* kind of bet on a green jockey and an unproved horse in a provincial point-to-point?'

'Not exactly,' he answered quietly. 'I sounded Barty and Stoker, and I happened to know each of them had a hundred quid on your horse. Then I liked the cut of his jib and I noticed that you sat him easy and looked at home, and he with you. Then, though screwed-up for the start, you backed yourself with that chemist bloke. When I spoke to you I noticed that you naturally checked the horse and did it so smoothly that he stopped fretting. I weighed you against the favourite and one other, and decided to make you the bet of the week. As for having a bet of that size on such a race, when you're betting it's the bet that matters, when you're racing it's the race. If you've money to lose there's always someone, thank goodness, ready to take it off you. . . . Now then.'

He pressed a bell. Men entered carrying a complete London outfit for those days—morning coat, tails, dinner jacket, three suits, shirts, collars, socks, cuff-links, studs, a town overcoat, a tweed overcoat, an opera cloak with heavy scarlet-silk lining. The clothes had been half-finished to his order and visual measurements. He asked me to step into a fitting-room with his head cutter to see what alterations were needed. When I emerged he was still there.

'Here's something I hope will surprise you,' he said, handing me a grey squirrel fur coat. 'Give that to your girl. You must have one.'

These doings happened on a Friday. I was to go back for more fittings on the Monday afternoon. That morning I bought at Tattersalls an exceptional three-quarter-bred brown hunter mare. And when the kind Mr Hyams enquired if I had 'cashed in on the squirrel coat', I answered with enthusiasm that I had. (I'd sold it for one hundred and eighty-three pounds and had got the mare for one hundred and fifty pounds.)

Mr Hyams moved later to Piccadilly, where I believe he prospered for many years. His presents have lived on with me, since I am always in working or country clothes, and my town ones seldom wear out. When I put on a Hyams' coat it always brings the donor to mind as well as Beacon, Stoker Cannon, the Spanish brigand and his wife, the Crowborough chemist who cheerfully stumped up my one hundred pounds, the way we beat the favourite, and the bye-day of Lord Abergavenny. I never in all my life put on an ounce of flesh, and when only a month or so ago the daughter of an old friend got married in Sherborne Abbey my Hyams' morning coat fitted me, if anything, rather better than on that Monday morning in Wilton Street more than fifty years ago. The morning coat above its gayer pair of trousers and its paler waistcoat—good old Hyams!— nearly made me burst out laughing in that solemn building. It reminded me of the time I lifted Lord Abergavenny's hounds, of the fifteen minutes Neilson and I enjoyed alone, a pure thing. And then that steaming ride, and all the fishfaces behind the infuriated peer in his scarlet coat splashed with clay. Goodness, what venom! In retrospect I believe I enjoy the wigging even more than the memory of those fifteen minutes across country with Neilson and Beacon. That's queer, isn't it?

* * *

Hadlow Down's turn to race was postponed for three weeks because of the late and foggy spring. Eventually the day came. Both Sandown Park and Hadlow were looking well. We thought we were in with rather more than a good chance, but feared the favourite Prestissima, a well-proved 'chasing mare trained by Major Powell and ridden by Colonel Nicholls. The Artillery Gold Cup was won by Colonel Gibbons on Caradoc.

Cannon had entirely cured Hadlow Down's unsoundness. He swore by the horse and he had made him twice as good as when I bought him. All the same, I never reckoned him in the same class as Beacon. However, we seemed to go smoothly

for most of the three miles we were due to cover. I began to
think I had underestimated the horse. He strode out in the
lead over those fences along the railway side. Rounding the
station turn, I took a pull to give him a breather going up
the hill. I was not entirely happy about him. Nearing the
fence at the top, the last but one, we were mending our pace.
Someone appeared to be coming up behind with a great
head of steam. Hadlow went into that fence still in the lead
and really travelling, and I don't think he rose a single inch.
We measured our joint lengths in a tremendous smash—
talk about the thunderous collapse of the giant of the forest—
from which neither of us could soon rise.

A figure in uniform filled my vision. He wore a blue peaked
cap and he held a glass under my nose. There was a taste of
blood in my mouth.

'Don't try to move please, sir. Drink this if you can.'

I complied, and went completely out. When I came to I
was in the jockeys' room wearing my own blue town suit. My
hands, all bandaged, lay in my lap. The pain, especially in
my fingers, was quite something.

'For God's sake somebody, take these ruddy bandages
off,' I had time to say, and then I passed out again.

When I came to I was a little stronger, or perhaps I was
more accustomed to my helpless situation, and to the pain.
I sat looking at my poor hands. Several fingers were obviously
broken. I must have dived into the ground with both hands
outstretched before turning over on my neck and shoulders,
which had been flayed.

'How are we now?' the valet asked.

'Damned awful. Did I dress myself, and if not, how did I
get into this kit?'

'We have the knack of decanting injured jockeys into their
suits,' he said. 'You weren't any trouble. I should sit quiet
as long as you can bear it. The doc's seen you and says you're
a concussion case, multiple bruising, and some bones gone
in the hands. Would you like a brandy?'

'Brandy and soda without ice. . . . Have you seen anything of Cannon?' I asked when he brought my drink.

'No.'

'I've got to get myself back to Crowborough. I'll have to catch a train from here to Victoria. Then across to Waterloo in a cab, then a train to Crowborough. I'll have to send a wire to my man to meet me at the station with the gig. . . .' The valet was busy, and could not stand listening to such drivel.

Captain Frank Forester came in, helping his son Henry who had taken a heavy fall at the same fence with Devil to Pay in a later race. Young Forester seemed to have broken an arm or a shoulder. I envied him his solicitous M.F.H. of a father. I sank into oblivion again.

I regained consciousness gasping for air, and staggered out of that stuffy place. I didn't know where to put my bandaged hands, which felt worse hanging free. The crowd was moving against me from the paddock to the course. People must have thought I was tight. I could not steer straight and my knees kept buckling. Someone probably helped me into the telegraph office. I had pound notes in my right hand and a pencil in my left. What was I there for? Ah yes, a telegram to Mulligatawny. I wrote it out slowly and handed it over the counter. The clerk read it through, then looked at me.

'You sent approximately the same telegram to the same address ten minutes ago.'

'Never mind. Two telegrams are better than one.'

My next flicker of memory is of sitting in a first-class carriage at Esher Station. It had a long table down the middle and Captain Forester sat opposite me, across the table. I remember nothing more until I was getting out of the train at Crowborough, helped most kindly by a Mr Ross, a rubber broker in the City, who commuted from Crowborough. He and Tawny between them hoisted me into the gig. As we climbed to the heath ground some two miles from the station I revived in the clean country air.

They helped me to bed in my own room and the M.O. had a go at me with sedatives, pillows, dressings, thermometer, stethoscope, and long starings into my eyes. I said I'd be all right for the night, which was naturally what they wanted to hear. They all went, and did not come back. I thought of the sick animals I'd nursed. I seemed to get stiffer and weaker. My pillows slipped and I sagged lower and lower in the bed. I sprawled, glaring at the electric bulb, for I could not reach the switch any more easily than I could the bell. I made up my mind they would find me stone-dead in the morning (and serve them right!) but in that I exaggerated.

At six o'clock Percy Briggs my batman came as usual with a cup of tea. No earlier. The English must have their sleep. Extraordinary people! Wait till you hear his opening words:

'I nearly didn't come, sir. Thought you might want a lie-in, like.' There was a pause. 'You have a decent night, sir?'

'No.'

'What made you send two telegrams to Tawny, sir?'

'I've no idea.'

'I see, sir. Drink up your cup of tea. It'll do you good.'

What had happened to Stoker Cannon at Sandown? I got him on the telephone and asked him why he hadn't bothered to come to the dressing room. He replied that he'd never seen a more crashing fall and had made up his mind that the horse and I were write-offs. He reminded me that he had other runners, and that race meetings were his business. When he did get to the dressing room I had disappeared and he was told that Captain Frank Forester was looking after me. I thought it a poor explanation, and said so, which did not bother him. How was the horse? He would take a lot of nursing, Cannon said, and certainly would not run again that year. And I must not forget that I was riding Beacon in less than three weeks. Would I be fit? I said I would.

*   *   *

206

'What's the matter with Beacon?' I asked Cannon as one of his lads led our horse into the paddock at Ringmer, a bona-fide hunt meeting. The pair of us were standing in the middle, swaddled in coats, near Colonel Gibbon, whose Caradoc was running in our race, and vastly workmanlike the pair of them looked.

'Matter? What d'you mean?' Cannon answered quickly.

'He looks pinched and cold, anything but his usual bright self. He's half-bored, half-apprehensive. Something's wrong. When and how did you bring him here? Did he eat up last night? Has he staled this morning?' I listened to Cannon's answers. 'He doesn't mean to race today,' I said. 'He won't go a yard. And as for me, I'm far from fully recovered after the Sandown smash. So if you've got your usual hefty bet and it's on us, I'd hedge.'

He took a swift look into my face and then at the horse and then at the bookies' stands. Strangely enough Beacon had been made favourite, and Caradoc was at the most unlikely price of six to one, extraordinary odds for a horse of his quality and reputation, in such a field.

'All right,' Cannon said. 'You know the horse, and maybe he does look peaky. As for you, can you do the ride? You can. Then I'd just take him round easy and steady and concentrate on bringing him right at every fence. Nurse him, and remember you'll both of you live to run again and win a pot.' He slid away, and did not come back. But soon I noticed from the paddock that the odds were swiftly changing. From the shouts, Beacon was going right out, while Caradoc's price was shortening. I saw Colonel Gibbon straighten his back and listen. Then he strode over to me.

'What the devil's up?' he said. 'Five minutes ago I could get sixes mine, but I was a bit nervous of you. Now somebody seems to know better than me, and I can't even get a bet on.'

'All I know is that we don't fancy ours today against Caradoc.'

'Damn and blast!' He went back to his horse.

Soon we were off, with Caradoc in front, majestic, and Beacon going sleepily, nearer last than first, and that was how they finished.

'Now then,' said a very cheerful Cannon when we'd checked round the horse to see that he was clean as well as sound, 'He's entered for the United Hunts at Lingfield in four weeks' time. I'll produce him there jumping out of his skin. We'll get a price, after today's showing, and we'll have a corking good win.'

He was as good as his word. Beacon was a picture of vigour in the paddock and kicking his heels over his head. Just as well. He really had something to beat, a good favourite, Friar Tuck, a class three-mile 'chaser. Friar Tuck was evens and Beacon, even when Cannon had got his bets in, started at ten to one.

They went all the way jumping each fence as though tied together, and on the run-in Beacon just stuck his long neck in front and kept it there with what appeared to be nonchalant ease. I was a spectator, grounded by the doctor, who feared that one of my ribs broken in the fall with Hadlow Down was threatening a lung. So it was a profitable but a sad day for me. Mr K. Goode had the ride, and nobody could have ridden a better race.

Soon after that most impressive win Mrs Rashleigh sent Beacon to continue his training with Mr James Broom in Cambridgeshire, and as though our destinies were linked, the horse was to leave Stoker Cannon's place on the day I was to hand over my unit at Crowborough to motor transport and personally to report at Woolwich for demobilisation.

I did not know what to make of my second attempt at being a soldier except that it left me with a good taste in my mouth. I had become fond of the Army, the blessed thing, and consequently had done my best for it, for the men under me, and for my horses. As though to round off my experience of Woolwich I again won the tent-pegging there and the following day Tawny and I left the Army (not that he was in

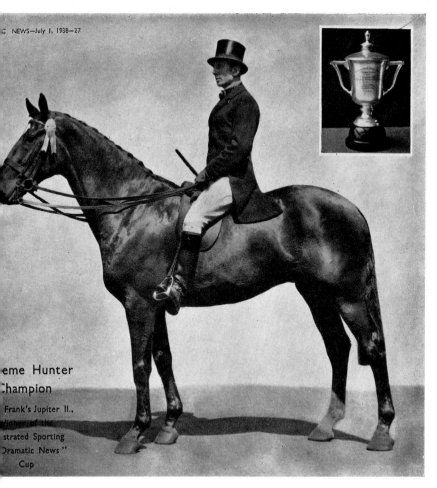

eme Hunter
Champion
Frank's Jupiter II.,
inner of the
strated Sporting
Dramatic News"
Cup

The Roman-nosed Champion Hunter, 'Jupiter II', J. H. Marshall up
(*Illustrated Sporting and Dramatic News*)

'One of the best in Leicestershire', Mr Harry Beeby of Melton Mowbray
(*by kind permission of George Beeby Esq.*)

Captain Frank Forester, M.F.H., out with the Quorn on 'Christmas Daisy'
(*by kind permission of Mrs A. M. Bailward*)

it, he'd been a civilian for years, and I'd told him that without the assistance of His Majesty's Government I had small hope of maintaining myself, let alone a groom and a string of three plus a racehorse in training). What he also knew was that before I found myself a berth I would find him one. We were both as cheerful as the sun poking through an April shower when Tawny brought the Lawton gig to the steps of the Mess with two of our horses harnessed in tandem. Our luggage was carefully placed in the back of the gig. We balanced the seat. I got in and kept the horses showing themselves until Tawny appeared from the stables, riding the third one. Nobody much was watching, nobody cared, but we left gaily, and properly turned out. We rattled through Greenwich, Bermondsey, Southwark, over Westminster Bridge, up Horse Guards' Parade and Constitution Hill to Hyde Park Corner, along the south edge of the Park to Kensington High Street and the Blyth Road entrance of Olympia. The show was on, and I had enough friends there to be sure of finding accommodation for man and beast.

As I drove in with such panache as could be drawn from a tired team an Army friend, Major H. A. (Tommy) Graves, later Lord Graves, a racing enthusiast and a bookmaker, spotted us and thought it a practical joke to tell Horace Smith that I'd been out driving his horses into the ground and had just come in. Tawny and I were putting the horses away in the semi-dark outside boxes when Horace, nicest though not the calmest of men, came rushing round shouting, 'What the hell! What the hell!' Then Tommy appeared and we all went off to have a drink, and it was good to be at Olympia.

*   *   *

I spent most of that scorching summer with my brother Sam near Market Harborough, and contrived to keep myself and Tawny by horse-trading. If the market was sticky there were masses of horses still about, and they could be picked up and turned over cheap. Also I cashed in on Hadlow Down. I rode him morning and evening, stabled him through the hot days and turned him out nights. I fetched him right back to normality, and it was something of a feat because the fall at Sandown Park had affected him severely. Ernest Stokes bought him for Lord Burghersh.

Hadlow did a good season's hunting with his new owner. Then he won two point-to-points and was going well in his third at the Grafton meeting when he fell at the last fence and broke his back. He had given me one of the worst pulverisers of a long life, but I know he had turned into a really sound horse. He was unlucky. Any horse can slip up going hard into the last under pressure, and but for his accident I believe Hadlow Down would have won important races.

Meanwhile what of Beacon? Mrs Rashleigh wrote to me that summer saying they proposed to run him in the early autumn at Bungay, and hoped I would take the ride.

'On the going brickhard as it is now,' I answered, 'I advise you never to run a free-mover like him. It's the tundra.'

'Do change your mind,' she wrote. 'When you've seen Beacon I know you will.'

So I borrowed a car and drove over to Broom's fine establishment. Beacon had a leg in antiphlogistine, swollen and full of heat.

'He can't run unless that leg comes down mighty quick,' the trainer said.

'How on earth did it happen?' I asked.

'It didn't "happen". He always had it.'

'That's not true. He was a hundred per cent when I bought him off Geo. Hone, and all the time I had him, hunted him, and raced him. He passed the most stringent vetting when Mrs Rashleigh bought him. There never was a better set of tendons. Something's happened to him here, this summer, on the hard.' That started it. How tedious those arguments are! I knew Beacon had arrived there sound. They were out to convince themselves, and everyone else, that he arrived with a leg. 'Anyway, you'll never run him at Bungay,' I said. 'You need four sound legs and a stone in hand before taking on such opposition as may turn up there from Newmarket and other pools of talent.' But run him they did, at the September meeting, in a two-mile 'chase.

A smart two-miler from Newmarket, Kincaid, was in it. Those two joined battle and galloped together as hard as they could lick, raising clouds of dust at every fence and puffs at every footfall until two fences out, Beacon landed on three legs, and was pulled up hopping lame.

He walked in, hopelessly broken down, as nice a blood horse as ever you would see. That was the end of him, the very end. And *that* is steeplechasing. Any enthusiasm I had for it ebbed as I looked at that poor, doomed, gallant animal. Hadlow Down and Beacon had taught me a lesson, and it cost them their lives.

13

Beeby's Circus

TAWNY and I travelled down to London late that September, unboxed our three blood hunters at St Pancras, and rode them straight out to Hampton Court. The horses were going to Colonel 'Vinegar' Fortescue, a well-known gambler, whom I'd first met at Le Havre and then on the Somme. He was staying with his Belgian wife at The Mitre, hard by the Bridge, then one of the finest pubs in England. I think the best things in it were the pea soup, which had to be tasted to be believed, and the cucumber sandwiches we ate on the riverside lawn at teatime Is there any more subtle food than a perfect English cucumber sandwich?

'Vin' might be, certainly was, incredibly fast in the casinos of Europe, but, Lord Almighty! he was slow about buying a horse. I went riding interminably with the pair of them, usually up the towpath. The Thames Valley's misty and individual beauty was then unmarred at Hampton Court and Kingston. Great trees, their leaves just turning and dropping, drowsed in the soft distances, punts slid languidly on a brown-green river surface shimmering with reflections of willows and mown grass and comfortable houses. On the third afternoon, when all three horses had passed the vet and had proved themselves over the show fences in a dealer's yard, we were riding back to The Mitre when Vin asked in his sharpest voice, 'What about water?'

'All three have been well tried and would take the Whissendine,' I answered. 'You can't expect them to jump the Thames.'

'Not jump it, no,' he agreed. 'But it's a fair test. Come on, darling.' With that he legged his horse to the steepish bank, and although, loudly remonstrating (remember the horses were still mine, not his) I followed and tried to snatch his rein, within seconds he was immersed, and then riding the horse as it swam strongly for the far bank, under the walls of the Palace. My animal immediately followed. There is a weir above there, and the river is wide, not much less than a hundred yards I would think. I lost my cap and my stick and I was furiously angry, not only because of the unwarranted risk to my valuable horses, but also because of my saddlery and the damage to my clothes. When Vin and I landed almost simultaneously on the sloped causeway at the other side I had taken a stern grip on my temper. Two constables were waiting for us in any event, and quite a crowd of onlookers. Then and only then did I hear the yelling from the far bank.

That damned Belgian woman was flogging her mare on the brink of the river. The mare, an upstanding thoroughbred with tons of bone and quality, by Balthazar out of Selinaba, was probably the best of my three, but very few women riding side-saddle would have got any horse down that bank and into the drink. She was going absolutely berserk though, swearing in French and her whip arm rising and falling; we could hear the cracks from our side and see the mare wince. Leaving Vin to deal with the police, I galloped my animal up, over the bridge, and down the towpath. I caught her raised whip arm, wrenched the leather-bound whangee from her hand, and threw it in the river. At the same time I caught her rein and led the mare, sobbing with fury and fear, away from the bank.

'Bloody coward, rotten horse,' Mrs Fortescue kept repeating. I said nothing. All three of us met Tawny in the stable yard. His eyes were on stalks.

'Ah, that was very interesting,' Vin pronounced with satisfaction. 'Now for a bath, a drink, and change for dinner. Belinda and I are dining out, Howard. I'll drop a cheque in your room for the two non-refusers. Shan't take the mare. She's yellow.'

Again I kept silent, not trusting myself to speak. I went off to have a bath myself, leaving Tawny to cope with all the sodden tack, to say nothing of two half-drowned horses and one lathered one. I ate dinner alone, the pea soup helping to restore my equanimity, and then sent the waiter to fetch Tawny to the bar. We settled beside the fire.

'We've had a pretty fair summer,' I said to him. 'Picking up horses here and there and selling them off grass. But now the cubhunting's begun, winter's coming on, and any horse trader has to operate from a secure base with his forage and oats in store and his warm stables. Those things I haven't got. All I've got is you, and the one good mare. I can sell the mare any time. I feel responsible for you.'

'No call to feel like that, Captain M.'

'As I see it we have two alternatives. I feel sure I can get jobs for both of us either in London, in establishments like those of Horace Smith or 'Odol' Haynes, or in Leicestershire, say at Melton with Harry Beeby. You say: which is it to be?'

'Leicestershire,' he said at once. 'Let's 'ave some 'unting while we're at it.'

I bought him another pint, and went to the office to telephone Mr Beeby. He answered immediately. Like most dealers, he was quick and at ease on the telephone.

'I'll book a room for you at the Bell,' he said. 'Get here just as soon as you can. Yes, bring the mare. I'll give you a price on her or you can sell her out, as you please. We're full up with horses, and there's too few can ride 'em. You're employed. Yes, all expenses paid. As for your Mulligan, is he your stamp, a maker and improver?'

'He's a first-class groom.'

'I'm ready to start him in the yard, and see he gets a fair crack of the whip. If he don't like that, why, we'll find him a fit job in the area. Fair enough?'

I went out to the horses, putting my hand under the rugs to see that none of the three was sweating or shivering. As I stood in the quiet stable with its three night-lights making the horses' eyes look melting, I wondered why I was so glad that I appeared to have shed the responsibility for Tawny, when we had become attached to each other, more like friends than master and servant. Was that how my father had felt, that same relief, when he pitched me out of Hickling?

Next morning, I went to Coutts to cash Vin's cheque, and right there in the bank I heard General Lort Phillips tell some fellow officer he was looking for a blood mare that would do both him and his wife and from which they could breed after two or three seasons' hunting. Within a matter of minutes I'd all but effected a sale. We got in his car outside, drove to Hampton Court in it, and Tawny brought out the mare, absolutely blooming. I said he could have her on trial if he sent a horsebox over from Camberley that afternoon. Vin and Mrs Fortescue came riding into the yard while this was going on, but they didn't know the general. That night Tawny and I got off the train in Melton. Mr Beeby, worn out after a long day, much of it in the saddle, had gone to bed. Porton, his manager, told me to clock in at the Bell and led Tawny off to his quarters, warning him that work began at five-fifteen every morning and unpunctuality was not tolerated. Nothing like that would worry Tawny. He was a tiger for work. I had many a groom after him, but never one that worked such hours so cheerfully.

When I woke at the Bell, some time around seven I suppose, I might have been in the cavalry. From the streets outside came the splendid noise of string after string being led out at exercise. Beeby, after all, was only one of several dealers in the place, and he never had fewer than a hundred

hunters in condition until the end of the season drew near,
when the numbers would tail off. He employed two skilled
men merely for clipping out. His main yard was still through
the archway opposite the church, but of course with so many
horses on his books he had them tucked in all over the place.
In my young days they used to say the town could put up a
cavalry division and not notice it. For a youngster like me,
brought up in the saddle and in the hunting field, to live
in Melton was like living in a club. I was always running
into people I'd known in Hickling or during the War, and
then I had the Dick Blacks and other farming friends in the
neighbourhood. As for my work, it was pleasure. I'd first
ridden Beeby horses when I was fourteen. Now I had more
responsibility. I was the head nagsman when not hunting
and the leading demonstrator, apart from Mr Beeby himself,
in the hunting field. My quarters at the Bell were delightful,
and I was able to make them more so with various bits
and pieces saved for me from Hickling by Sam and my
sisters. With three top-class inns and many others functioning
in one small town, competition kept the food, quarters, and
service, to a high standard. Had I been a drinking man the
temptations would have been overwhelming. Hospitality
was freely offered, and there were parties every night of the
week. My first and most pressing need was for clothes and
more clothes, especially breeches and boots, for with the
Quorn's opening meet on the first Monday of November I
found myself hunting six days a week, and two or three horses
a day. However, I was in funds after my prosperous sales
of the summer, and if not up to top London standards, the
tailors and breeches cutters in Melton were good.

Let me describe one of my hunting days with the Beeby
circus in some detail, in an attempt to give the flavour of
them all. It was with the Quorn, from Lowesby.

'Jump in the car, Howard my boy,' Mr Beeby said. 'Our
nags are on, and you're riding a stranger, first horse. He
belongs to the Hon. Mrs Wansborough-Slaughter, you

know the ones, near Harboro'? And he's hot they say. If you knock anyone down, choose an enemy, ha!'

'Am I to school him or sell him?'

'Why, sell. He's not a lady's horse, not by any means. But if you could work out a market for him, my boy, we've got a dozen would suit Mrs Slaughter, fine handsome woman that she is. Looks well, don't she, when (like the hart) she's heated in the chase. . . . Jezebel Jinks comes to mind as a good lady's mare, or Tarrant Gunville, or Miss Baker, there's a lovely mare, once you've sorted her mouth out. Just give a show now with the Slaughter horse, and I'm warning you, he's *a soldier's type.*'

Fresh, strong, and full of himself, he was a bright bay standing sixteen hands two inches, aged five. There was an obstinate bump to his forehead and a steely sparkle in his little eye. As I raised a gloved hand to feel his neck he flinched. When I gently moved the bit about in his mouth he resisted. I had Mrs Slaughter's groom walk him about at the meet, and as hounds moved off he brought him to a bank, where I got lightly on him, just felt his mouth, and trotted after the receding tail-enders. When they stopped at the first draw, Lowesby Wood, I hopped him over a low bit of timber and, unseen by authority, slow-cantered him round to the south side of the wood where I trotted—he had a velvety trot—up and down in the shelter of a high hedgerow. Presently the hunt gate clicked and a whipper-in appeared in the take-it-or-leave-it, cocky way those customers have. He chose his observation post and he and his horse stood there as though set in wax.

Not wanting to get in bad with the hunt servants, I took my youngster off round the field, now walking him, now jogging. We were closing again on the man in scarlet when he let out a halloa that made my horse stand straight on end. Hounds were out in a flash, their fox close in front of them, a royal sight, but one I did not have time to enjoy. A charge of some four hundred pent-up horses and riders engulfed us.

They were all making—racing would be a better word for their behaviour—for a low bridge under the railway which the fox had crossed followed by the hounds.

As for my 'soldier's horse', he was off full pelt, and he took some holding. I kept an iron hold on his nearside, not liking the look of that low, dark tunnel under the railway. He plunged away to the off each time I held him evenly, so I gave him a few things to remember on that side. He swung to the nearside, and I got a short hold with my left hand behind my left knee and with an offside reminder with my spur behind his girth I at last had him turned in a safer direction and sent him into his bridle clear of the rest of them and along the edge of the railway, slightly uphill. That blessed slope gave me a chance to win some control and at the top a rustic opened a gate leading into an eighty-acre field. Round that field I went, asking my mount for no favours, just reasonable co-operation. By the time we returned to the gate, where the kind fellow still stood emitting country noises, we were getting to be a sort of wary combination.

I'd expected the hunt to flash on leaving Sludge Hall on its left for Botany Bay fox covert, but they were stationary, a couple of fields the other side of the railway. We agreed, the rustic and I, that our fox had been headed by a ploughman, and keeping our eyes open we soon saw him creeping back over the railway, his belly fur stroking the clinker. He crossed one hundred yards up the line from us.

'Keep quite still,' I hissed to my frenzied companion, 'I'll put Wilson on. Don't make a sound.'

I jogged a little way down the fence to see the exact line Charlie followed, taking the chance to try my horse over a nice set of rails with an open ditch. By Jove, he could jump! He enjoyed it. Then, seeing that our fox had stolen away alongside a thick hedge and was well clear, I returned to the gateway and, lifting my hat to the full extent of my arm and standing in the stirrups, let go as clear and loud a halloa as I could manufacture. I was answered at once by a toot-toot

and Wilson, the pack clustering round him, came bustling
back to the bridge. Watching them, I became aware of a
nice-looking hunter with an empty side-saddle that was
careering about on the other side of the railway. I remembered seeing a side-saddle lady go into the railway tunnel,
but had not seen her emerge.

After an inexplicable delay in the tunnel Wilson emerged
with the pack and came fast to me. I could feel my horse
shivering with nerves as they approached. I led Wilson to the
gateway and showed him the hedgerow down which his fox
had travelled. Then I positioned myself to take on the ditch
and the rail we had previously tried. Hounds gave tongue
in a banshee cry and streaked down the line of the hedgerow.
Out of the corner of my eye I watched the field gallop towards
me, the familiar figure of Mr Beeby, well mounted as usual,
in the van. His raking black horse was between two fast-
galloping greys, on the one side Mr Aloysius Bird, an American enthusiast, and on the other pretty little Mrs Wardell,
Sir Daniel Cooper's daughter, bright and flushed on her
Crackerjack, one of the finest hunters in England.

Commending myself to the god of battles, I gave my horse
the office and with a snort he went at that obstacle as though
it were cheese and he a hungry mouse. We floated it, and
heard behind us the crash as the first-flighters came on in a
row. Wilson and the odd hound were jumping out of the
big grass field by a holly tree in the corner. I could not
steer him. He carved his way on, took the natural fence with
its wide ditches at its highest part, and flew it. He came more
to hand crossing the ridge and furrow beyond. Just before
the next, a stake-and-bound topping a vertical bank, Mr
Bird passed me. I never in my life saw a horse stand farther
back than that grey did. He reached for it, and just scraped
over. His rider was still getting back into his proper place
when we were halfway across the next pasture. To ride out a
hunt alongside a pair such as that was the greatest possible
help. The fox set his mask north for Ashby Pastures, a big

covert. But it must have been well stopped, for they raced him through it and through Cream Gorse, less than a mile beyond. He then took a nice line, left-handed as though for Rearsby. They pulled him down in the open just short of Brooksby Spinney.

I dismounted to rest his back and stretch my legs, his rein hanging loosely on my arm. We had been in front with the American for thirty minutes, and were the cleanest pair there as the others crowded past, excited and happy. Mr Beeby came up.

'Let Mulligan take that nag home, Howard,' he said. 'He's done more than enough for today, and from all I saw of the pair of you he'll be a ton the better for it. We'll give him ditto with knobs on with the Belvoir on Wednesday. You get on Mulligan's grey now and see what you make of him. Ballykilty's his moniker and he's straight from the bogs of West Cork. He jumps well, but likes to trot into his fences. Keep him awake if you can. . . .'

After dining at the Bell I strolled round in my slippers to get Mr Beeby's instructions. There was a sharp frost. You could smell the smoke in the air and the pavement rang underfoot. Life was good at that moment, with every day bar Sunday a hunting day, and Sundays in Melton so peaceful and sleepy.

'Come in, come in.' He settled me with a glass in my hand before the fire. 'That bay of Mrs Slaughter's jumps a bit of timber too, don't he? You remember a goodish rail when you'd fetched us all back?'

'The first fence.'

'That's it. Queer. Wilson had gone through the gate. Yet someone had jumped the rail before you. Who was that?' (He'd observed the double set of marks.)

'I did a rehearsal to keep warm.'

'You did well. A lot of them were taken with the bay, including Mr Bird. Now he *could* ride that 'oss, and he's a grand payer. . . . But did you not know Lady Victoria lay dead under the bridge. Yes, she was late at the meet and was last through on a fresh horse that got scared by the dark and the echo, reared, and crushed her skull against the brickwork. Well, we had goodish luck and a run from it while Lady Bullock, one of the best, met her end. That's hunting for you. Now, Howard, I'm laying on three 'osses for you tomorrow, Captain, that's the big roan, Guy Mannering, and the wall-eyed Pinkerton.'

That was my life. Take a horse, keep him balanced, and when in view of all conceal his faults, display his virtues, flick him over this and that, change horses. Trade was fast and good, and everybody seemed pleased, including Mr Beeby.

*   *   *

There were occasions when I had a dual role in the hunting field, to sell the horses I rode and to act as guide and tutor to some novice. One such was a young German lady by the name of Beit. She was quiet, had very good manners, and rode well. She hunted with us over a longish period, and when she went back to Germany Beeby said, 'I'm disappointed in you, Howard. A pleasant young woman and rich enough by all accounts to build five or six battle cruisers, leastwise her old man is. She was always saying how good-hearted you were, and how well you looked after her. . . . I should have thought you'd have hung up your hat.'

'I'm not the marrying sort. I never have any money, for one thing.'

'But in her case the money was *there*, you dumb-bell!'

'You didn't marry for money.'

'But look, Howard, just reflect a minute: a rich young wife like that and you could make yourself comfortable in some handy place like Stapleford Lodge, or Hickling Manor if you preferred, with a really good string of hunters and tons of polo ponies. Think of the good you could do your poor old friend Beeby then, and the times we'd have together. . . .

But what can I do? I can't rope you up with them. You let
the turbine engines go as well.' By turbine engines he referred
to a Miss Parsons whom I had also shepherded with the
Quorn and the Belvoir. She was an attractive young lady
who ran into trouble later when she bought Branches Park,
near Newmarket. One of her stable lads struck her, and she
died. It was an accident. He got off.

Harry Beeby himself, the hard dealer with the warm
heart, was always a source of joy to me. When he was
away buying horses, the place, even the hunting, seemed
only half as good. Do you know what his hobby was?
Carpentry.

One absolutely filthy morning with rain falling in sheets
and the country so flooded we couldn't hunt, Beeby said
at the morning conference in his box of an office, 'We'll jog
on a string up to Wild's Lodge, and have a good school.
Let's see now, who shall we take?' He ran off the names of a
dozen horses, or their descriptions. He should have been a
king, he had such a memory for names. Neither of us
complained to his face, but both Algie Porton and I thought
the schooling plan monstrous. Inside the yard we were
dry and warm while the wind howled round Melton and
the rainwater drains were choked with surfeit.

'To hell with that!' Algie said. 'Ride those out to school
up there in such weather and come back dirty and maybe
cut about, and all that tack to clean, just when the lads could
be having a hard-earned easy!' He thought for a moment.
'Howard, there's a partition was kicked down this morning.
Box No. 6. Take a handful of five-inch nails and a four-
pound hammer. Get along there and see what you can do.
Make plenty of noise, mind.'

I no sooner started hammering than I saw Beeby dart
from his office.

'What's that noise? What's up in there?' he cried to Porton.

'Partition kicked down. Howard's having a go.'

'Partition? Howard!' He came bustling in, and after a

disparaging snort at my preliminaries sent me to fetch his box of tools. Much later he emerged. 'What's the time?'

'Nearly two-thirty, guvnor.'

'Well, no use going schooling now. Soon be dark.' He was probably glad enough to let his men and horses rest. Neither suffered from lack of work in his yard. Tawny, as I had anticipated, after a stormy first week had shaken down and was coming to be regarded as the best man in the place. He was getting plenty of rough-riding and plenty of hunting too.

The man who enjoyed his hunting most of us all was Beeby himself. He was a man who had the gift of enthusiasm, the kind who could be happy even on a blank day. Many was the good day I had with him on the cattle-feeding land from Melton to Market Harborough. Across those wolds you'd get a bit of the Cottesmore country and then the Fernie with its selection of true oxers, strong ash rails to keep the cattle out of the deep ditches either side of the fence. The ash goes hard as iron. You'd hear your horse's feet knock on it as he landed over.

One day he and I were out with the Belvoir and they'd run us into Cottesmore terrain. Lord Robert Manners was hunting hounds. We'd had a bit of a burster when they checked, feathering, before a great big bullfinch, thick and dark as the Black Forest with a yawning ditch either side and an extra stout lot of oxers.

'That'll stop us, Beeby,' the huntsman observed to the first man up, closely watching his hounds. All of a sudden a current went through them and they seemed to be drawn through that awesome fence as a silk handkerchief is drawn through one's fingers.

Beeby shook his horse to attention and sent him at it. As they took off he dropped his reins and crossed his arms in front of his face and eyes to protect them against the thorns that could cut like razors. Clatter on the near oxer, swish, crash, crackle, clatter on the far oxer. They had vanished, and might be in another world for all we could see. But Beeby called from the other side.

'Will it, my lord? Will it?'

* * *

I saw him once have the queerest, slowest fall.

It happened at the end of a long run with the Quorn. We were going along the hillside above Gaddesby Hall. Beeby had sent his horse at a decent fence that ran down-hill. It was a question of landing across a steep slope, and he seemed to twist the horse uphill before he had properly landed. The horse's front feet slid away from him on a cowpat, and while his head was uphill, his other end half-turned and slid down, and he buckled over in the oddest way imaginable. Beeby went elsewhere, over his mount's shoulder, and as he departed took the bridle with him. Once clear, he went rolling on down the slope.

That horse, it's true, was blown, and should not have been asked the question, but you know how it is at the end of a good run, you go ahead, and have regrets afterwards. He lay on his belly, and when he got up he just could not remember where to put his legs; he had too many of them one second and too few the next. Beeby got to his feet, plastered over with with mud and dung. He looked at the bridle hanging from his hand and then at the big valuable horse swaying there, his forelegs well apart, his head hanging, giving pathetic little coughs as he fought for his breath.

'Well, my little fellow, where's you and me bin to then?' Beeby asked. He patted him on the neck, and gently began to replace the bridle.

People have differing reactions when they take a fall, and those differences are interesting to the professional observer.

Another foxhunting man who when he had to take a toss took it well was the Prince of Wales, who in those days kept a fair number of blood horses at Craven Lodge. He was out with us regularly, nearly always accompanied only by his

ln't see her for nine years and then I married her'. Captain Marshall's wedding to Miss Muriel Bates (*by kind permission of Mrs Catherine A. Dennett*)

Marshall on Mr G. Cornick's 'Smoky', aged 4, on which he won the Handy Hunter Class at Dorchester 1950 (*by kind permission of Mrs C. M. Marshall*)

Major (later General Sir Richard) McCreery black cap, about to win the Military Hunters' Steeplechase

aide, Major 'Fruity' Metcalfe, and he treated his hunting seriously. By that I don't mean that he was sad about it, or was not friendly and good company if you happened to be beside or near him. But he shunned the social side of it, and disliked more than anything being shut in the crowd. He had stolen off with Major Metcalfe one afternoon and the pair of them joined Mr Beeby, Algie Porton, and myself. We were on the edge of Lorne Wood, sitting our horses waiting, listening, watching, in silence while hounds bustled their fox about inside. We were in a likely position for a good start should he break covert. The field were held back round the corner of the lane by Major A. E. Burnaby, a strict field master. In front of us was a drop fence into a field of swedes. The fox darted out into the field; then, though we did not see it, as swiftly doubled back into the wood.

H.R.H. jumped slap into those swedes. Brrrrr! went his horse's feet, slipping and sliding him right in among the hounds. At that moment Major Burnaby came galloping round the corner of the lane.

'*Hold hard, you*! You double-dyed bounder!' he roared. Then he saw whom he thus addressed, and qualified his justifiable anger in the weakest possible manner. 'Oh I say, sir, ripping, ripping!' His field, crowding behind him, afraid of being left at the start, laughed heartily, and the Prince of Wales, looking solemn, apologised as he rode out of the swedes. Of course, jumping into that field almost on top of hounds was an error of judgement. What keen youngster does not make such mistakes from time to time. Major Burnaby withdrew the field again, giving us a fourpenny look, but as we were with the Prince he let us be. We waited again in silence. A burst of hound music would approach, then dwindle into the distance. It began to rain gently. Water dripped from our hatbrims.

'Well, Beeby, I think I'm for home,' the Prince said. 'It doesn't seem likely they'll push him from this fastness to-night.'

'Don't you do anything so daft, sir,' Beeby answered at once. 'They're sticking to him. You stick to them. In the end he'll go, and he'll go fast and straight.'

In another quarter of an hour out he came stealing, the same dog fox, and all five of us quiet as poachers, our breath hanging round our wet faces. We let him well away.

'What did I ruddy well tell you, sir?' Beeby hissed at the Prince. 'Now you'll probably gallop after him all the way to Ranksborough and get home to bed envying not a commoner in the land.' He let out his screeching halloa.

Welsh was hunting hounds. He jumped out of the wood, skating on the roots as the Prince had done. 'Which way, Mr Beeby, where'd he go?' Toot, toot, the horn. Hounds bunched, then launched themselves into an avenue of scent and screamed away. We followed, the five of us.

* * *

By mid-January our wonderful trade in horses was easing up, and I was grounded through lack of mounts more often than I liked. At that time the Quorn had their second meet at Willoughby Lodge, a mile south of Widmerpool. It was a raw, cold-scenting day, with too harsh an east wind to promise sport. Welsh drew the near coverts blank, Green Hill and Flint Hill, and then as I saw hounds crossing the Nottingham-Melton and Leicester-Newark roads I knew they were going to draw our old covert, Curate's Gorse. Now Curate's has the railway just west of it, and although it sits on a west-dropping slope, we never thought it a good draw in east wind. Well, he drew carefully through it three times without a whimper, then lifted them and hacked on to Parson's Thorns, where they at once stirred a fox that ran to Holme Pierrepont, nearly in Nottingham, and we had a good afternoon hunt, too. But the Curate's Gorse business stuck in my gullet. I knew that England had changed and cheapened, and it hurt me as it did many others. But the changes, the lessening of standards, in that unimpressive clump of trees and undergrowth just below the Melton-Nottingham turnpike, hurt me more than anything. I think it was the next Saturday the Belvoir met at Eaton Grange. We spent much of the earlier part of the day in the woodlands along Harby Hill, Brock Hill, Hazeltongue Lodge, Holwell Mouth, and Bleak Hill. We had our second horses when in the afternoon the south-west wind abated and grew suddenly warmer. It felt like business when they went to draw Clawson Thorns. They had a fox afoot in no time and after a ringing hunt, in which we twice crossed the canal and twice the Smite, he tried to take refuge in Sherbrooke's. At least I was spared seeing that covert drawn blank. He was pushed through it. We jumped the Smite yet again and leaving Hickling slightly on our right we galloped across what had once been my father's fields and fences, up and over Hickling Standard and killed him on the slope from Kinoulton as he struggled to reach Kinoulton Gorse. It had been a fast hunt. Not many were up at the finish, and the field was straggled all over the place. I turned my horse away from the rest of them and lit my pipe as I walked him down the Kinoulton-Hickling road, that being the direct route for Melton. Not a field, not a ditch of that strong vale that I did not know by heart. I thought of my old man in his high-crowned hats with his ducks and his horses and his sometimes extravagant ways. And of course I reflected bitterly on my own situation. I longed for my father; for the flagged kitchen with its sizzling joints of beef; for the velvet gloom of the hall, with its sounds of life elsewhere, on either side of the green baize door; for the chilly boys' bedroom over the coach-house, even for my brothers' teasing and bullying.

'What's wrong, Howard?' Mr Beeby asked. He had cantered up behind me on the grass verge. (I knew quite well why he was on the verge. He rode a well-known hunter he had sold to Lord Ivor Churchill. Lord Ivor, ill in London, had asked us to keep his string, and especially this one, his favourite, fit pending his recovery. It was the best hunter, a star, and the most awful hack in the Midlands. It would dodge and prop all the way along a flat road and was fully capable of falling down and breaking its knees. Lord Ivor always had it led or boxed to the meet.) 'I've seldom seen you go better, Howard,' Mr Beeby went on. 'But when we get back you must have some Gregory's Powder, you must really. You look ill, my friend, green in fact.'

I wanted to tell him about the turmoil of bitterness that was in me. Instead I blurted out uncouthly, 'I think I'll go south and work in the Blackmore Vale for a time. That man Stanley Young seems to get hold of good horses. There could surely be a lot of trade between the West Country and the Melton area.'

'Take your time about it,' he said in a serious voice. 'Ah, we're in Hickling. 'Tis that has turned you, I see. Well, whatever happens, this grand old hunting country will be good enough for me. You're your own master. I wish you'd stay. Sleep on it. And meanwhile. . . . You never rode this 'oss, did you? *Such a hunter!* Just let me change with you.' He looked with approval at the nice little horse I was on. It was one of his own, of course, and had been bought for two hundred guineas in the Eglinton country, and sold that day to Mr and Mrs Farmer, a delightful American couple well known in the Shires, for three hundred and fifty. He had carried me well, and was still full of go. So was Lord Ivor's quad, but as his stud groom said to me once about that particular animal, 'He could cross any country in England with the best, but if you set him to jog down the Mall from Admiralty Arch to Buck House he wouldn't know whether he was jogging on his feet, his nose, or his knees.'

I pushed my horse up alongside Lord Ivor's horror, adjusted my leathers to Mr Beeby's length, and slid to the ground on the off side. He lightly swung himself from one saddle to the other, gave a feel at his new mount's mouth, and, with a wink and a touch of his leg, he left me.

'Well, good-night, Howard. Eight miles to Melton,' he called over his shoulder.

'I'm feeling low, I'm very depressed,' I said to Lord Ivor's hunter. 'But nothing on earth would induce me to ride *you* on this or any other road.'

We started to walk, me leading, he stumbling over his toes, and then we had company. It was an American lady, Mrs Perkins, on one of her hunters from Maryland, a pretty brown mare, absolutely cooked, hardly fit to go another step.

'Slide off,' I called to her, hurrying to release her small foot and help her down. I loosened the girths and pulled the mare on the wide grass verge ridged with cattle steppings. Several cars had now appeared with grooms in them, looking for their employers. Mrs Perkins said her own man had taken home her first horse two hours earlier.

'I'll soon get you a lift to Melton in one of those cars,' I said. 'Come back immediately in your own car with your groom. Make sure that he brings a bottle of Day, Son & Hewitt's pick-me-up for your mare, as well as a rug and roller, and *two* sets of kneecaps.'

In half an hour the lady was back in her car with her tough-looking groom. We gave the mare her drench. She was reviving quickly. The kneecaps were buckled on both horses and I put the groom up on Lord Ivor's mighty hunter. He wasn't an American, and he wasn't a local either, or he'd have known that horse's reputation.

'Just drop your ridden horse at Mr Beeby's yard,' I told the groom as I settled myself in Mrs Perkins's car and drew the fur rug over my knees.

When I'd changed out of my hunting clothes I strolled round to Beeby's. Mr Vincent, the stud groom, came popping out.

'I thought those were your fairy footsteps on the sets,' he said. 'Now clear off, Captain Marshall. We don't want any trouble round here.'

'What d'you mean, trouble?'

'That bloke of Mrs Perkins that brought in Lord Ivor's gelding. I don't know how many times he tumbled with him. He's got a sore leg and a sore nose and a split boot, and he's very, very angry with you. I should go straight back to the Bell and enjoy your dinner and keep off the streets tonight.'

I did enjoy my dinner and while doing so decided to finish out the season and then try to work again on my own. I liked everything about my life under Beeby except for these aspects of it: we were too near Hickling for my peace of mind, and I did not get any selling to do. I was surprised how much I seemed to miss that, the financial side of horse dealing.

* * *

Before I leave Mr Harry Beeby I must tell you about his poker lesson.

He never did much showing, but he made an annual trip to London when Olympia was on. All his usual and potential clients were there, and if you're in business it's unwise to let people forget your face and voice.

I was riding many show hacks and hunters when they gave him his poker lesson. Tring Show was held in the middle of the Olympia session, and a few of us riders would occasionally dodge a class or two at the major show in order to pick up a prize at the smaller one. That evening I got back rather late from Tring. They told me at the Olympia doors that Mr Beeby was looking for me everywhere. I found him in the stables.

'Howard my lad. I'm due at Mrs Whitburn's do in Portland Place. Take these numbers and ride my two jumpers, will you. They'll be on soon. No bother?'

'I've just come through Portland Place in a cab,' I said, 'and the awning and red carpet are out at Mrs Whitburn's. Royalty expected, shouldn't be surprised.'

'Don't rub it in. I must change, I suppose.' He left, muttering that such entertainments were not for him.

Although we knew Mrs Whitburn quite well at Melton, it seemed a different matter when, as a hostess, she was queening it in her London mansion.

The doors flew open. A competitor came out. I remembered that in a matter of minutes I'd be in the ring on one of Beeby's jumpers. Through the entrance I could see some of the obstacles. It didn't look to be a straight jumping event, but one for 'handy hunters'. I slipped round the corner to the competitors' box to watch one go. He was a poor entrant, and he was eliminated before the last test, a big park gate whose posts were let into the ground. The gate was supposed (had I but known) to be opened by the competitor and then latched behind him. I was tired, however, after an extra long day with little time for food, and I wasn't concentrating. I merely made a mental note that the gate *looked* on the high side, but no doubt, thought I, that was an optical illusion.The rest of the course was a bit of jam. I hurried back to the stables.

My first mount was a nice sort of lady's horse, well put together and with manners. In I went, enjoying myself, popped into the lane, turned along it, popped out left-handed and over a treble, straight back in over two small fences, right turn and out through a rail which had to be lowered and then put back, over two hurdles, turn and thread my way quietly through them. The little horse was easy, and we had done very well. Now there was only the park gate to contend with. I took him back to the very end of the ring. The gate was in the middle distance. It struck me from there too. Whew! What a whopper to be set in a handy-hunter course! It would have been outsize in a puissance. I set Beeby's horse at it for all he was worth, and as we picked up speed I half-saw, half-sensed the house rising to us, heard the growing rumble of intense interest. He met the top rail with his arms above the knees, and turned the most fantastic aerial somersault. Any time I remember that normally happy Olympia arena I think of the angry rattle of those massive posts in their sockets. Nothing had given an inch, not even the top rail of the gate, and the pair of us just lay there. I was lifted, rather than helped, to my feet while Lord Lonsdale came crab-wise over from his chairman's position in the centre of the ring. It was said he never left that place from the start to the finish of Olympia, except to give his luncheon and dinner parties in the Pillar Hall. Anyway, there he was, looking into my face, shaking me roughly by one of my aching shoulders and asking if I'd been laying bets outside the ring. I don't know what I answered. The audience was on its feet, and there was a good deal of laughter, and some applause. Nothing like an unexpected and crashing fall to please them. The horse ambulance came in and demonstrated how to pick one up and take it out. I was half-supported, half-carried after it.

'Are you all right? Are you *sure* you're all right?' they kept asking me as they always do, and I kept insisting, as one always does, that I was *perfectly* all right. The truth was that I couldn't even see properly. Everything was going round and round.

Several other horses were sent in, to give me a bit of time to recover after my spill, and then the double doors were opened and Mr Beeby's second number was called. I hadn't a chance. As soon as I saw him I knew *my* number was up. His name eludes me. He was a well-known great big resolute bay horse, hard-mouthed and hot. It was all I could do to sit on him. The whole glittering interior, all scarlets and hot-house flowers, was spinning round me. I couldn't focus. As for him, he caught hold of his bit and, settling into a very strong canter, he jumped anything that came his way. He turned at the far end and steamed on back, clearing another obstacle and then, with ease, the park gate. As he did that he landed me first between his ears and then in an untidy and flaccid bundle on the ground. The double doors swung open as though for a normal exit. He just sailed out through them, leaving me all alone in there, the most public aloneness of my life. The crowd, normally so mannerly, seemed to be standing up and roaring as, once more, I was pulled to my feet on a pair of sagging legs. My hat was picked up for me. I bowed to his bewildered lordship who was glaring now at me, now at the (sacrosanct) clock. As I rolled and staggered unassisted out through the doors the noise of people continued, though whether it was applause or laughter I could not tell. It sounded friendly. A fat lot of good that was going to do me with Beeby.

When I'd been to the stables and Mr Vincent, busy treating my winded first ride with vinegar steam, had asked me angrily whether I'd been drunk or mad, I had a bath, changed, and waited for Beeby in the Exhibitors' Club. I ordered coffee, but that made me sick, so I sat and dozed in a leather-covered armchair. About three a.m. I heard the Beeby voice at the entry to the smoking-room. I rose to make some sort of explanation.

'Sit down, Howard, sit down, man,' he said at once. I saw he had an enormous and fragrant cigar and that he was flushed, positively radiant. 'Sit down, I say, and put your feet up. I've heard all about it. Whatever you did, you couldn't have drawn more attention to two good horses. The bigger one's sold three times over already. As for me,' he added triumphantly, 'they were so kind as to teach me how to play poker, and I won two hundred pounds.'

He was, and always had been, an extra good poker player.

14

Passport

STANLEY YOUNG had advertised a sale of a hundred horses in the yard of the Digby Hotel at Sherborne, Dorset. I booked in at the Digby, a red pile standing in its large garden between the railway station and the Abbey, a couple of days before the sale. Taking the list, I looked at almost every horse that sounded my sort, and I probably rode a dozen. While doing that, I had a close look at Sherborne and its surrounding farms and large estates. It is a small, predominantly red-stone town, well kept, well built. Even in those day, when British agriculture had not made the fantastic progress to prosperity that came with World War Two, Sherborne, like the majority of the farmers around it, was well-to-do rather than rich, 'comfortable' rather than prosperous. It made a good deal out of the two large public schools (public used in the English sense, which typically enough means 'private and fairly expensive'), one for boys and one for girls. The families around were in the main unshowy country people with a deep stake in the future of England, large holdings of gilt-edged, and sons in the services who liked to buy good horses and ride them hard. On the whole it would have been difficult (in the hunting season) to find two towns that less resembled each other than Sherborne and Melton Mowbray. From the moment I first set foot there I thought Sherborne just right.

A well-dressed crowd had turned up for Mr Young's sale, and needless to say I was there early, and had a stance among the dealers, close by the ring and under the rostrum. Prices, as I had profoundly hoped, were lower there than in Leicestershire, Rutland, Nottinghamshire, and Staffordshire. Also the West Country bidder is slower and stickier than the Midlander or the North Countryman. Noting these differences, I waited silently until the first horse I wanted came up. The bidding didn't fly, it crawled. They were about to third-and-last-time him at one hundred and fifty pounds when I slipped up into the rostrum.

'For heaven's sake, buy him in,' I said to Mr Young and the auctioneer. 'I can easily get two hundred and fifty pounds for that one.'

They held up the sale and, watched by the hard-eyed men round the ring, we went backstage for a short conference.

'I only met you for the first time the day before yesterday, so I can't say I know you,' Mr Young said. 'How long would it take you to sell 'em, and to whom would you sell?'

'To whom? Why. . . .' I gave them a list of a dozen names, including the Prince of Wales and 'Banker' Loewenstein, and I guaranteed to sell within ten days any horse I picked out. (I knew I wouldn't lose on them even if I had to take them to Tattersalls or Leicester.) The outcome was that they bought in eleven, two of them polo ponies. I sold every single one privately within the time limit, and all in the Midlands (though none of that batch went to the Prince or to the banker). My intervention had jumped up the sale's total by one thousand five hundred pounds and had given me an entrée.

I went in with Mr Young as a contact man, as a person able to sell as well as make horses. Our business arrangement was an entirely private one between the two of us. You see I wanted to work both for myself and for Stanley Young. I was no longer content just to be a riding personality, as with Mr Beeby. If I went in with Mr Young I had to be part of his organisation, and yet separate. He had a very quick understanding of such arrangements, and soon clarified the whole thing in a long letter to whose terms we stuck for years.

With some old friends from Long Clawson, father, mother, and three young children, I jointly bought The Malt House at Gillingham, the last house on the left going out to the Knoyles. We bought it for eight hundred pounds and, some years later, sold it (alas) for four thousand pounds. The stabling was good and the place agreeable. We were a happy household, I soon got hold of some paddocks, and there were other advantages. For one thing I was thirteen miles from Sherborne, and I wanted to be of use to Young, yet not too much in his pocket, and for another, Gillingham was an important rail junction.

Before Stanley Young took to horse-dealing he had been an auctioneer with the firm of Senior & Godwin at Sturminster Newton, great cattle people. He was very different from Harry Beeby, who was always in the saddle. I think in all the years I knew Young I only saw him once out hunting. He enjoyed his office work, and did it well. He was a business man. I often wondered why he'd got into anything as chancy as the horse trade, even though he had nerve, and took pleasure in the risks.

He had yards and boxes all over Sherborne, eight boxes at The Cedars, twelve at the Bulldog Tavern, twelve at the Lord Howe, twenty and a good schooling ring behind the Antelope Hotel, and twenty more at the Digby Hotel. In the Digby yard there were four sets of rooms, bedrooms, living-rooms, saddle-rooms, reserved for officers of the Home Fleet who would come from the great naval base at Portland or travel east from Plymouth and Devonport to stay for a day's or a weekend's foxhunting. He had developed a splendidly run and lucrative letting-out business, and the deuce of a lot of good horses were sold through his firm. All he had lacked before my arrival was somebody to pull the best animals out and exploit them, somebody with my show-ring summer connections and my Leicestershire winter ones. I'm not saying I was much more to him than a sort of mobile shop window, but if a shopkeeper wants to sell any-thing he'd better have a window. We understood each other, and then Mrs Young (small wonder, she was from Yorkshire) was an absolute dear. She was well off, too, and the greatest possible help to her able husband.

A chunk of his profitable trade was done with the Army when the troops were under canvas on Salisbury Plain. He would travel round his circle of farming friends, hiring horses from them at three pounds a week and immediately letting them out at five pounds a week, mainly I think to the gunners and the R.A.S.C. In those days, don't forget, the heavy horse was the motor of British agriculture, and Young did a very big business in the animals that drew the ploughs and the binders.

Those West Country farmers took some knowing. I heard a few of them say Mr Young was a sticky payer, but I would never agree with that. The boot was on the other foot, and too many, great as well as small, owed him money.

I was doctoring a swollen fetlock in the main Sherborne yard one sunny winter morning. Ronald Brake was prowling about, getting on my nerves. 'Anything I can do?' I asked.

'Where's Mr Young?'

'In his office.'

'But I've just knocked and there was no answer.'

'Then fling open the door,' I said. 'Breeze in, and say you've come for your money.'

When he came out he said, 'Blow me if you're not a queer cuss. How did you know what I came for?'

'I can look into a man's face and see £.s.d.'

'Leave that leg be, and come and have one with me.'

Dealing in any kind of animals from tadpoles to whales you must buy before you can sell. My experience of Stanley Young was that there was never his equal as a buyer. He would buy on his knowledge, of course, but he would also buy on his hunch, or mine, and he was seldom wrong. Many a horse we went to see together.

'How about it?'

'Have him,' I'd say.

'All right, come into the farmhouse,' and as we went in he was pulling out his cheque book.

Stanley Young's intake of quality horses came mainly from the Brakes of Limington, near Yeovil, a family as well known today in farming, foxhunting, and show-jumping circles as it was then. At that time the Brakes were bringing over from Ireland to a thriving hunt, the Blackmore Vale, any number of good hunters and jumpers. As each batch arrived they would sell a number to us to pay off at least their shipping and rail costs. Then the south-west corner of England with its green hills and Atlantic breezes was full of young horses, and many a good one we got from Devonshire and Cornwall. Still, all my life, I've had an extra fondness for Irish horses, such as one of the first to come into my hands at the beginning of my association with Young.

His name was Passport II and the Brakes bought him off an Irish peer (which one I forget) who'd taken a major toss with him in a banking race. That crash had given Passport his one blemish, a bad one. Where he'd run his forehead into a tree stump there was a deep dent. It didn't impair his courage or his good sense. Having bought him in, I put him out to grass at Gillingham. He came on so well that when the fly became bad in July I got him in by day and gave him a real school and polish. Then I showed him at the Bath and West Show in Dorchester on the first Thursday in September. By a piece of luck the Prince of Wales was at the show, and as Passport had won his hunter class it was natural that the Prince should take a look at him. It was a surprisingly long and thorough look, and at the end of it he said I would hear from him come the start of the hunting season, in two months time.

That was good enough for me. But he had thought of our horse as a potential point-to-pointer, rather than a hunter. So although I saw H.R.H. quite often at Craven Lodge, where I used to take batches of horses and where he continued to stable his, no mention of Passport was made until the New Year. Then it was arranged that I should bring my horse out with the Quorn the following Monday.

When we got to Melton, myself, the groom (not Tawny, he had stayed at Beeby's), and four horses, there had been a sudden frost and snow blizzard followed by an equally sudden thaw. The ground was a sticky pudding, and The Quorn announced on the Sunday that it would not hunt on Monday. But the Prince told me he'd got permission to remove the wire from the Melton Hunt Steeplechase fences on the Burton Flats. He was planning to take a few of his horses up there for a workout at ten-thirty, and would I be there with Passport?

It was raining like stink and the going was appallingly heavy when I got Passport out of his hired box. When we'd stripped him and I was on him the Prince of Wales and Major 'Fruity' had a good look at the horse and agreed, as anybody would who knew a horse from a vacuum cleaner, that he was a great sort.

'Well, Marshall,' said H.R.H., slipping out of his coat and handing it to the groom. 'I'll ride Son and Heir and you come with me on your chap. We'll go halfway round the course at about half speed. Happy about that?'

'You bet, sir.'

He turned his cap-scoop to the rear and we set off, going stride for long stride. Smooth as an oily swell on the Bay of Biscay, the two big horses swung along, neither more than a few inches in front in the air or on the flat. Great clods of stickiness, half-thawed clay, flew behind us. We pulled up and changed horses. He rode Passport over a few of the racing fences, then trotted him back to where Major Metcalfe stood silent, rather sad, his arm in a sling. They talked quietly together while Passport held himself dead still as I'd taught him. 'He's an absolute Bute,' I heard Metcalfe say. The Prince rode him away, then, on his own.

He took him to an open gateway, went through, turned him round, and then jumped the rails alongside the gateway, a sensible test.

'Marshall, I like this horse enormously and I'll have him led back to Melton with a message to Mr Glass to examine him right away. If you'd care to ride one or two more with me, by the time we get back he'll have your horse vetted and you'll be free, if all's well, to make what arrangements you wish.'

I got into the vet's yard slightly ahead of the Prince of Wales and Major Metcalfe.

'Why and when did you hit this 'oss over the head with your coal hammer?' Glass (who was examining Passport's forehead) called out to me in ringing tones.

'I'm very well, thank you. How are you?' I replied even more loudly, giving him a look that I hoped would freeze him to the marrow.

Passport moved about the yard well, using his hocks properly on the backing and turning. We then made for the field to gallop him and test wind and heart. Glass chose to ride himself, though he had grown stout, and now did little of it (I should have said *because* he did little). Water flew from his eyes and his face went from red to puce in the cold atmosphere. He was a passenger on such a horse.

'By cripes, can't he just gallop!' he said as he pulled up. 'It's many a long day since I was on one could shift himself like this 'oss.'

The Prince was listening carefully. A smile spread over his face. The sale was made. I was happy for Passport, for myself, and for Stanley Young, whom I'd had to persuade to fork out an unusually high figure in that case, and to wait for his return. He had gone to a true sportsman. I can say that in honesty because you can learn more about a man in five minutes in the hunting field than in five years on your flat feet. I saw him often, and he was great.

Some years later (I had better tell you the rest of Passport while he is in my mind) at the Leicester sale of H.R.H.'s hunters his sharp eye picked me out among the crowd at the other side of the ring. Over he came and held out a hand.

'I know who you're looking for, Marshall, but he's not here. I could not bear to think of anyone else having him. So I've pensioned him off and sent him down to the best of homes in the Duchy of Cornwall. I never won a point-to-point on him, though I was run out by a loose horse at the last fence of the Open at the Duke of Beaufort's when we were a long way out in front. But I had hounds to myself on him many a time, and I don't know any other horse that ever gave me such pleasure. Many a time when I was on him I thought of you, and d'you know what came into my head? When Major Metcalfe and I were looking him over at the Dorchester Show, you dropped his reins on his neck and stood well back, and then you walked round behind him, and his eye followed you round nearly all the way and then the other eye took over. It wasn't a hard or a frightened look, a "What's the beggar going to do next?" look. It was a look of faithfulness and affection. From that moment I wanted him.'

Stanley Young was beside me. 'Imagine that!' he said as the Prince left us.

Nearly all my life, let's be frank, I've sold horses for gain. It's a profession like any other, with its skills and risks, financial and physical, sometimes even legal. The client seldom knows as much as you, but he pays the piper and holds the power, and clients fall into severely differing categories. Many, as soon as you sell them a horse, take it that you're a rogue, and from then on claim if the horse is good that it's their doing, not yours, and if it's bad that it's your fault. From the downright dishonest client there are gradations to the other extreme, the type who will declare, 'I bought this horse from Richards, or Dixon, or Beeby, or Gale, and my money was never better spent; he wasn't cheap, but he was cheap at the price.' The Prince of Wales was in that generous company. Sometimes after the Abdication I heard people say he couldn't ride for toffee, and nonsense like that. I tell you now, and I ought to know, he went well in the best of country and the best of company. Of course he had falls. Who among all of us who like or liked to go in the front has not had crashing falls? They're an unwelcome part of the game.

* * *

Let me show you something to demonstrate Stanley Young's flair. One Monday morning he and I were at Tattersalls, looking round. That distinguished horseman Colonel W. E. Lyon was selling his horses, having left the Atherstone. When we came to the actual selling Stanley said, 'To my way of thinking there's only one horse here and his name's Prince Danilo. If we can have him, we will.'

He was a chestnut, aged six, a cheerful, willing-looking animal and a perfect mover. We were told (and personally I thought that suspect but Stanley overrode me) that he'd barely been proved with hounds—only out a few times and then never in a real hunt. We bought him for a hundred and fifty guineas and Stanley Young was delighted.

'He's the best-looking here,' I said. 'He should have made four hundred pounds. But at least we shouldn't lose on him.'

I hunted him through the following season with the Blackmore Vale hounds, particularly on their Tuesdays in the Sparkford Vale, a wonderfully clean training ground for a young horse. Danilo was hot, mighty hot. He was unsteady with hounds, and that was why we had had him cheap. When I came home in the evening Stanley would ask how Danilo had gone.

'Damn badly.'

'Stick by him, he's worth it. He'll pay a dividend one day.'

'Stick to him's more like it,' I'd say. 'I like to enjoy my hunting, not sit on a mad thing.'

During the summer we showed him for the first time

before Colonel Alexander at Shaftesbury. He won with ease, and we took him to every West Country show we could get to—Dunster, Dorchester, Yeovil, Exford and so on—and won every time. At the end of all that he was still unsold and Stanley gave me the job of hunting him again. We had now made Danilo into a valuable horse with a possible future in the show ring or on the race course. I agreed to keep him off the banking side of the country (where the best fun was to be had) and viewed the prospect of another season on him with distaste. Then one morning Stanley quietly announced that he'd sold Danilo, and as a hunter. I hardly believed him. It was a stroke of genius.

He'd sold him, subject to a week's trial, to Captain Esme Arkwright who hunted the Oakley. And do you know, the moment that horse found himself hunting hounds he was perfection. It suited Prince Danilo to go in front, and he had all the qualities required for the most difficult task that any horse is set, a task demanding courage, endurance, instant cunning, and good manners. Captain Arkwright, like many Masters, sold all his hunters every two years. We bought him in and then sold him to Lord Stalbridge, who hunted the South and West Wilts off him for another two seasons. When his lordship gave up the Mastership Danilo came up again at Tattersalls. At the sale Lord Stalbridge noticed me and came over.

'I suppose you've come to see your horse, Marshall.'

'Yes, my lord.'

He held out his hand. 'The horse of my life.'

Perversely enough, I have always regarded Prince Danilo, although I was unbeaten with him in the show ring, as one of my failures.

15

Not Quite the Genuine Article

I'VE been talking about two good horses, and you can see that selling even the genuine article often takes time and nerve. Now let me show you the obverse of the coin.

Among friends and acquaintances to whom I wrote when I had settled at The Malt House, Gillingham, was a London barrister, Alfred Montaigne. He had a place in Essex and a string of horses, some of them in training. I had known him in the hunting field when I was stationed at Colchester and had often met him since at Tattersalls. He immediately replied: 'I am sending you two horses. Please dispose of them on my behalf. Yours, Alfred M.'

There was a friend, thought I. The horses arrived, a most impressive pair. Yet in three days I was writing to Montaigne, 'Both your horses are all wrong. Why did you send them to me? I don't know what can be done with either. You don't expect me to sell them, do you? I've a good mind to send them straight to the kennels.' However, I liked Montaigne, and I thought I'd try that once to help him out.

His black by Cock-a-Hoop was *fat*. He looked a picture but he wouldn't move, had no wish to move, more than that—the poor horse couldn't move. If you trotted him a few yards he'd choke and then fight so hard for his breath that you had to get off. He was as bad as that and yet, if you looked at him in all his bloom, you said, 'That horse could win the Gold Cup.' I enlisted the help of an old man in Gillingham. 'Ride that horse about the place *at a walk*,'

I told him. 'Never out of a walk. If you drop your reins and send him into a trot he'll pass out. It must be his heart. It's a crying shame.'

Day after day the old man rode out on the black horse. There are few things better for a horse than steady walking exercise on hard roads, and the black became even more of a picture than when he arrived from Montaigne's. One afternoon two gentlemen, one named Salt, the other Doverdale, called on me at The Malt House.

'Captain Marshall, who's that old chap riding about Gillingham on a black blood horse?'

'Oh him,' I answered. 'You'll never chisel that horse out of him. He loves it. Never does more than walk it about. Of course he's an old man.' (Some old men are humdingers. That one was, but no need to say so.) 'And he may be ordered by his doctor any day to stop riding. Otherwise he'll ride him till he drops off. Never part with him.'

'What a crying shame!' Salt exclaimed. 'You see I reckon that lovely animal with his manners and temperament would be *exactly* right for an old man I know. He wants a horse he can just walk around Sussex on, looking the part. He won't ask the horse for a trot because trotting would disrupt his waterworks—not to be vulgar. He would pay well, too.'

'If that horse ever comes up for sale I promise I'll give you the office.'

They were both very grateful.

Next day the old man came in, madly excited. He and the black had met a traction engine steaming along the road by the entry to Sherborne Castle. The horse had turned tail and had actually *cantered* for fifty or sixty yards. The old man (who'd been round Aintree) said he had never had such a thrill in his life. Could the black be recovering? Hope springs eternal. I determined to take him out cubhunting the following morning early, when there was a near meet of the South and West Wilts. I walked him out and, there being no steam engines about the fields, the poor fellow was back in his old ways, and couldn't raise any semblance of a trot.

As we walked up to the covert the cry of hounds came from it louder than natural in the close humid air. A lithe red shape came from the thickets and slid down the line of a hedgerow near me. On a sound horse I'd have turned him, but I sat mum, hoping no one would find me out. Well, I got found out by the sharpest man in England or Ireland, the stupendous Mr Isaac (Ikey) Bell, M.F.H. He came galloping round the covert.

'Where's he gone, Marshall? Which way, which way? . . . *There* he is. Marshall, get round him, if you please.'

'I can't see him, Master,' I said, seeing him perfectly, but refusing to kill a sick horse just to get a cub back into a wood.

'As God's in his heaven, this is my unlucky day,' he cried. 'You're the only one that's seen fit to come out at this hour, and you've gone blind.' He looked then more closely at my horse. I think he twigged I couldn't gallop him. Mr Bell was a grand man, as every genuine foxhunter, or sailing man either for that matter, well knows. You'd have thought his hounds were tied to his saddle, he had such control, yet when he sent them in or on, what dash! what tongue! what venom! He sat his horse near me for quite a while, listening to what was going on in the covert. Then, as he turned to go elsewhere, he just said, 'Well, there's one cub gone. Don't let any more go this side if you can help it.'

Montaigne's other beauty was a different case. He was a real good'n except when he was standing in stable, when he would continually put out his stifle joint. You'd hear it go, click! and he'd stand with it out until you came round behind him with a broom and—pssst—shoved it back in. You couldn't leave him sixty seconds but the dratted thing would be out again, click! And it looked awful of course, as though he had a sawdust leg with a splinter of bone coming out.

I got the pair of them into Tattersalls on the same day.

The black horse was entered in the name of the old man at Gillingham, and he was No. 97 in the sale. Montaigne was present, as always, and gave me a judicious wink. So were Salt and Doverdale, standing bang beside the rostrum. I'd dropped Salt a line saying, 'I promised to let you know if the old man ever decided to sell that black horse of his, so I'll be as good as my word. He's coming up at Tattersalls on Monday the such-and-such, but I would particularly like him myself, so please don't go bidding against me.' I knew damned well he'd bid against me. After the scene was set I left the ring and hung about in the passage leading down to Knightsbridge with Tom Hill's boot and leather shop on the corner. I'd asked the man in the car park to give me a whistle when No. 96 came up.

Just as 96 was being third-and-last-timed I ran in, looking for the number and then at my catalogue and trying to seem flustered. I positioned myself near Salt without 'seeing' him, but making sure he had a good view of me. When the black entered the ring I heaved a great sigh of relief as though saying to myself, 'Thank God! I got back here in time after all.' What I was in fact saying was, 'Now's the day and now's the hour. I must get rid of this horse somehow, anyhow.' I started him at fifty pounds and went quietly up. Somebody else came in and I thought it was Salt. Then another bidder, close behind me. At one hundred and thirty pounds I very smoothly withdrew with a negative to the auctioneer that couldn't be seen by either of the others. He was knocked down for one hundred and fifty pounds without a warranty or any form of promise or guarantee. He couldn't be sent back.

'Did Salt get him?' I asked Montaigne when we came together in the crowd.

'No, the other I think. I don't know him. Howard, that was a canny bit of work.'

'We've still got your bay gelding to sell, you know.'

'Come and have a drink anyhow.'

'No fear. I've left my man to keep him moving over in his stall so he doesn't put it out again. Come and see him.'

'*God forbid!*'

I waited and waited. I'd made an appointment with Major Somerville, 19th Hussars, who was the Remount Buyer. 'This horse will make the deuce of a heavyweight charger,' I told him, choosing my words. 'If you get going on him in good country it'll take something fantastic to stop him. And wait till you see him.' He pointed out that he wasn't allowed to go above one hundred and fifty pounds for a charger. I replied that there were a lot of horses for sale, and not much money chasing them. We'd be satisfied with one hundred and fifty pounds.

Somerville kept on passing us, hurrying on other business and saying cheerily, 'Be with you in a minute, Marshall old boy.'

'Oh my sainted golly!' I said to the man in the box. 'How much longer do we have to stand keeping this stifle in? Pssst!'

Suddenly Somerville popped up again with a couple of others. 'All right, we'll have that horse out.'

They trotted him up and down. He went like a bird. He was splendid in action, a lowslung, long bay horse, and such a stride! He was a fine performer too. I only had one day's hunting on him and that was down in the vale on Christmas Eve. He'd jump on top of those banks with the withies on them, and stop, balancing, while I parted them. 'Whoa there, boy.' Then, having arranged things, I'd say, 'Go-o-o on then!' And he'd jump down and across any trouble on the landing side. Those withies could cut an eye out or lay bare your nose if you went right through them. It may be that in the Remounts they cured his stifle trouble by getting him hard and fit. He was a free-going, loose-limbed sort of animal.

'I never had to work harder to sell a pair of horses,' I said to Montaigne.

'You've done a grand day's work,' he said. 'Indeed you

have. Come home with me now and you'll see some genuine ones.'

We went out by car to his place in Essex. Next morning he showed me a brown horse turned out in a paddock. 'Here's a seven-year-old you ought to have, Howard. Never been handled.'

It was a beauty, almost perfection, possibly worth thousands. I'll have him just to please you,' I said quietly, keeping my voice like something bubbling out of the Dead Sea. 'Can we get a halter on him and just jog him up and down the road?' He moved even better than he looked. 'Why hasn't he been raced?' I asked Montaigne and McGinty, his groom. 'There must be something wrong with him.'

'Don't think so,' Montaigne answered. 'I bought him at Tattersalls aged three or four. Can't remember what I gave for him—shall have to look it up in my ledger, and we've had no time to work him.'

'No good having horses stand idle. I'll give a hundred for him.'

'Guineas,' he said. 'It's a deal.'

'Pounds.'

We were some way from the house and it was nearly lunch time. On the way back we passed a superb brood mare in a well-fenced paddock.

'That's what I call a mare,' I said. 'Magnificent.'

'Which reminds me,' Montaigne said, 'We've had nominations for her and two years running have forgotten to send her off. Better luck this year perhaps. Nice, isn't she?'

'Nice!' I said in disgust. In Montaigne's place I went nearly mad. By nature I am tidy and methodical. Is that only because I am and have always been poor? It hurt me to see them so casual about those lovely horses. He left it to the servants, and even in those days nobody could afford to do that. And yet . . . he'd had the sauce to send me those two horrors.

After lunch, which was perfection, he got out the book

in which he scrawled down details of his many horses and horse transactions. I waited with an apprehension that proved to be justified.

'You can't have him,' he exclaimed. 'You can't have that seven-year-old. On no account can you have him.'

I gave myself some more of his vintage port, dark as a moonless December night, neither sweet nor acid. 'I didn't ask for him. You offered him. The deal was struck. I want him.'

'No, by George! I made a mistake there. I sold that horse you want, and I sent on another, and it's even more complicated than that. . . .'

'You'd best leave well alone then.'

'Oh no, no, no, no,' he said. 'This is a real fix, mistaken identity. Shall look an ass, but not a knave. In the end it must all boil down to respect for the law. That's the important thing, don't you agree? I'm so sorry, my dear Howard.'

It turned out that the horse he'd sent on instead of 'my' one had been sold as a maiden, when he was not, had gone straight into training, and had won two races. They had to unravel all that, send back the stakes, get the seconds placed first, and 'my' horse went to take the place of the spurious maiden. It must have cost Montaigne a mint of money, but he had it to lose, and nothing upset him, nothing. As for 'my' horse, I saw him sold at Tattersalls for seven hundred pounds to settle a part of that endless settlement. I nearly had him for a hundred, and would have sold him for more than ten times that. I kicked myself because at luncheon I had not filled, refilled, and filled again Montaigne's port glass. Not that it would have made a scrap of difference. He had scores of bottles of vintage port standing on the windowsills of his handsome house. He had a theory that such unusual treatment improved the bottled wine.

I said I first met Montaigne in the hunting field. It was an odd meeting, but then he was never an ordinary man.

One day during a hunt over some horribly sticky plough

I came upon him standing in the middle of one of those enormous, flat, arable Essex fields. Montaigne was looking ruefully at the most splendid, raking four-year-old I ever saw. The young horse was pooped, rocking on his legs, head hanging, nostrils stretched to twice their normal area, eyes glazed, and flanks heaving despairingly. There was a grass field some way on, and the two of us pushed him there, a few steps at a time.

'He'll never get over this,' Montaigne wailed. 'Oh *why* did I let him go on?'

'Why indeed?' said I. 'He *is* in a bad way. I expect you'd be glad to take fifty pound for him as he stands, without the saddle and bridle.' I said in my flattest, casual, take-it-or-leave-it manner.

'Put a nought on the end of that offer, if one could call it an offer, and still you wouldn't get him,' he answered. 'His name's Morning Star and he's by Solus out of Andromeda.' A further stream of breeding followed.

It would have been the late Morning Star, I thought, if I hadn't chanced this way. But I couldn't see such a lovely horse come to harm. I rode off, searching for the hunt and its followers, and eventually I got hold of a bottle of Day, Son & Hewitt's tonic from Mr Taylor the vet. When the young horse had drunk it all he was still groggy. I persuaded Mr Montaigne, who at first thought me quite mad, that it was best to leave him there, standing untied, for the night. I feared for his heart.

In the morning he was a different animal. One of Montaigne's grooms picked the saddle and bridle out of the hedge, and rode him home. The owner was really overfond of that horse, although he had let him gallop himself into such a state of collapse, and as a result he became very kind to me. The following year I turned quite a few honest pennies on Morning Star when he won three or four point-to-points. The horse was then entered for the National Hunt Meeting at Cheltenham every year from the age of six, but he did not run there, or on any other course, until he was fourteen. Montaigne may have been a barrister, but he seemed to pass all his time with horses, and he could not bear to let Morning Star long out of his sight. He was always pulling him back to his own place near Colchester, and trainers do not take kindly to that behaviour. Morning Star was regarded as though he were a piece of Chelsea Red Anchor or some such precious rarity. He was becoming fat and idle, and I truly thought he would never race again.

I suddenly saw Montaigne among the ringside spectators when I was showing a splendid young horse for Constance, Duchess of Westminster, at the Agricultural Hall, Islington. His face was scarlet with excitement and his hair tousled.

'Can you be free tomorrow, Howard?' he said as I left the ring, and when he was sure that nobody could hear him he continued conspiratorially, 'Do come with me to Cheltenham. You're my guest. We're running Morning Star in the National Hunt, and by jingo! he's there with a strong chance and the odds will be fruity.'

What a day! Captain Cavanaugh had the ride. Even so ours started at eighteen to one, and he just toyed with very strong opposition. To think that he was fourteen and had never really been used! I made a humble one hundred and eighty pounds on that race and more on the others, thanks to Montaigne's good offices and advice. As for him, in addition to the one thousand pounds stake he did so well that when he got back he bought a whacking great new car without noticing any wallet shrinkage.

Alfred Montaigne was an unusual figure in the horse world, but like so many others, then as now, he was utterly and unselfishly devoted to horses, foxhunting, and racing. He was a bachelor, or so I always supposed, yet he was very popular with women, particularly young ones. And though he had tons of money he did not care about showing it. I always found that attractive, in man or woman. Your splashers are usually vulgarians or bores or both. For example, Montaigne won the Cesarewitch with Fundador, yet at that meeting his clothes were actually falling off him, moth-eaten and rotten. You'd meet him out hunting on horses worth a mint of money but wearing an old green swallowtail all torn at the back and its skirts unwashed, stained where horses had sweated into them. I saw him one morning at Tattersalls and I thought, My, Oh my, Mr Montaigne, we *are* smart today. He was wearing a most beautiful and expensive British-warm type of overcoat. Then he turned. The whole back of the coat was eaten out by moths.

18

Canute

IN a lifetime with horses I've known many good ones and some great ones that stand out like peaks from the level plain of the dull, the unsound, and the common. I doubt if a gamer little one ever lived than Canute, and it was by the merest accident that I got my hands on him. The horse that led me to him was an exceptionally poor one.

I was well dug in at Gillingham, happy, thoroughly interested in the people and the country, and dealing in a very satisfactory number of horses. I sold a horse that was a rough ride to some stables in Sherborne, and as I did not judge him fit for even a thirteen-mile hack, I booked a box on the railway from Gillingham to Milborne Port, which is three miles outside Sherborne. Apart from the movement of racehorses, and perhaps not even much for them, the railways are little used now by the horse fraternity. Yet rail boxes were much more commodious and more comfortable than the motor horse boxes in vogue today. I delivered my cheap horse to Tinney's Lane in Sherborne and had just left the stables with my saddle and bridle over one arm when I ran into an acquaintance, a Major Bernard, who lived at Oborne, to the east of the town.

'Marshall, I've wanted to see you for a longish time. Not anything vastly important or urgent. I almost hesitate to bother you with it. . . . Are you very busy?'

'Never more so, but if there's anything I can do. . . .'

'I wish when you have a moment to spare you could call

at Oborne and have a drink with me and look at a colt I have there, a bit of a problem. He's four now, and wild as an eagle. Let me tell you a little about him. He's by King of the Wavelets out of Excuse, a mare I won quite a few 'chases with. He hasn't been handled at all since he was castrated as a yearling, when he broke loose with the casting ropes still tied on his legs. He went mad and raced about until finally, completely blown, he fell over a field gate. He was held down, with a man sitting on his head. But when three of the ropes had been cut loose he flung us all from him and careered off with the fourth still made fast. There it stayed until it rotted off. Nobody has been able to get near him since with a halter or anything else. I wonder if I could persuade you to interest yourself in the colt, Marshall. I'd give one hundred pounds to see him carrying quietly, and another one hundred pounds to see his name in the list of runners.'

I answered him without enthusiasm. It sounded like a pig in a poke. But you never know. One of Stanley Young's drivers rolled up in a car to take me back to Milborne Port.

'I've got a young horse to look at,' I told him. 'There's no time so good as soonest, so go first to Major Bernard's at Oborne if you please.'

The moment I laid eyes on the four-year-old I knew he was good. I spent a long time observing him and his behaviour and his dam, and then I said to Young's chap, 'I'm going to put my bridle on that old mare and lead her on to Milborne Station. The youngster sticks to her like glue. Let him follow. You leave the car here, and when we separate the pair of them at the station you'll lead the mare back and turn her out quietly in her own paddock. All right?'

He agreed without much enthusiasm (as it meant a longish walk for him) and we set off, the unbroken one pottering about softly on the hard road with his unshod feet that had never been rasped or trimmed. . . . There was my empty box at the loading ramp in Milborne Station. I hung about for quite a time letting them nibble at the fresh grass in the sidings while two porters took out all the partitions in the box. We got both of them gently, softly and politely, into the horse box. The youngster was interested in some sweet hay and oats when, at a signal from me, Young's man led the mare away. The porters, as soon as she had crossed the ramp, lifted it and shut me in with the son, who in four years had never been away from her. He remained surprisingly quiet.

Presently, a porter came to the groom's door with a paper for me. 'You still in there and all of one piece, Captain?' he called. 'Sign, please. We can't shift you, not for two hours. Then you'll slip straight through to Gillingham.'

'Suits me,' I told him. 'Let me stop here alone with this colt as long as you possibly can.'

When he saw the halter in my hand, remembering his yearling days, he stiffened and trembled. I started gently rubbing him on his back and down his legs. Soon I could touch his skin with the halter. In little more than an hour I had popped it over his neck and, putting the end through the ring, fiddled it about. Presently Young's man spoke to me through the side of the box.

'Is that mare safe and quiet?' I asked.

'Yes, there was nobody at home. I left her in the paddock, grazing. What next, Captain Marshall?'

'Please drive to my place at Gillingham. Ask Bill Mason to meet this train with the brown mare and a long leading line. I'm going to travel with the youngster. I've got him haltered and he seems sensible.'

So he did. There was no blenching when they connected the engine with the usual concussion and noise. He only began to get excited when we had stopped in the Gillingham siding and he heard my mare's feet outside. We brought her in quickly, stood the pair of them together, and spent at least half an hour getting him used to the leading line. He took to the mare at once, madly, as I had expected. Eventually I hopped on her, rode down the ramp, and led him off home, where two boxes were ready side by side with only a low partition, so that he could watch her and learn by example. I made a point of going into her box first, whether it was to strap her, or water or feed her, or shake down her bed. He would stand with his head a little on one side, watching her and me anxiously. During his first morning at The Malt House, so steady had our progress been, I had got a head collar on him and a bit in his mouth. I telephoned Major Bernard.

'What about that nice colt of yours? I went to look at him in the field and I liked him.'

'Marshall! He's gone, clean gone. I'm organising a search, but we just don't know where to begin. He never left that field, and nobody could *take* a mustang like that away, we know.'

'The first one hundred pounds is nearly mine,' I said.

'WHAT?'

'He's here in my boxes. He's safe, and he's handling. I brought him on by train.'

'*By train!*'

I took immense care with the colt's breaking. He was edgy, naturally enough, about his legs. When I was long-reining I had to keep everything off his hocks or there was trouble. But he was no more difficult than any other to break, and very soon he was mouthing properly and carrying quietly. Major Bernard, thank goodness, left me completely alone for five weeks (if only all owners were so considerate), yet when he eventually telephoned I was a bit put out.

'Marshall, I've got someone interested in that colt. If I brought him along to your place do you think you could lay on some kind of a silly show for us?'

'That would be extremely unwise,' I said in my coldest voice. 'You ought to come along here tomorrow and see for yourself what kind of a "silly show" your young horse can provide. Hounds meet at Willoughby Edge Gate, and you can ride out with me. I'll mount you on a topper, a nice little Argentine mare that's going to be the best polo pony in Britain and that will stop at nothing in the hunting field.'

Out we went, the young horse as merry as a wagtail, and his owner astonished to see him so handy and so friendly. They found at the first draw, and ran out towards the vale. Not knowing the South and West Wilts country, since I did my local hunting with the Blackmore Vale and the Sparkford Vale Harriers (top class *riding* countries), I soon found myself going on my own with Major Bernard tailing behind me. All the field had swung off the line right-handed. Soon I saw why. They were making for a bridge, and in front of me was a gully, terribly deep, with precipitous sides. I was conscious of being in full view. The youngster's owner was coming up behind, and on my right the whole hunt, including Mr Bell himself just on the bridge, was watching me.

And that small moment of truth gave me the first indication I'd had that the colt was potentially a great horse. His head came up, and he pricked at what lay ahead.

'Go on then,' I said to him quietly, and he skated over the abyss. The little Argentine, La Loca, who loved my young one, bore Major Bernard after us and took the dread obstacle with ease.

'No more, no more,' Bernard gasped. 'This is an epic day. Never saw such a thing in all my life, and I've seen a woman eaten by a tiger.'

We hacked them quietly home, and got out a bottle of wine when we had left them in The Malt House stables. 'Marshall,' he said, handing me his cheque for one hundred pounds, 'I never paid up with less distaste. You've worked a miracle here. What d'you reckon the colt is worth as he stands?'

I advised him to ask four hundred pounds, then a goodish price, and not to think of taking a penny less. When, a few days later, he brought his interested party, it proved to be Major (later General Sir Richard) McCreery.

'Hullo, Marshall,' Major McCreery said. 'I didn't know you had Bernard's horse. He's asking a lot of money for him.'

'If I'd known it was *you* coming I'd have suggested he ask a little less, but I'll tell you one thing, at that price he'll be the cheapest 'oss ever you bought. I don't think Major Bernard will come down. He's seen the youngster, without a lead, jump the Hellespont.'

'So he told me. Can we have him out?' He rode him and finally jumped him from the orchard into a field, and back again. 'I'd buy this horse, now, Marshall, if I could think what to do with him. I'm off to Egypt next week on a staff job.'

'The best thing you could do for his sake is buy him and then leave him where he is. He's very young and there isn't much of him. Let him grow into his strength.' So I kept him, asking only three pounds a week for his keep and his training. It was like having a twin brother in the stables.

At the end of the year Major McCreery telephoned. 'Could you get Canute over to the Lytes Cary Meet on Tuesday?'

'We'll be there. Did you say "Canute"?'

'He's by King of the Wavelets out of Excuse. My wife has an extraordinary talent for picking names out of her head. I just put it to her last night and she came out with "Canute". Don't you think it rather neat, my friend?'

'It isn't neat. It's brilliant.'

'I want you to hunt him tomorrow,' he said. 'I'd rather watch him and see how he goes with you.'

'All I can say is, don't expect to be diappointed. If hounds run in that country as they usually do, *he'll go*.'

There's a good covert in the bottom near that meet, and it's called Yarcombe. Sir Walter Jenner kept it foxed. I went round the far side with Bunch, the whipper-in. The music came, and away we went to a splendid start. The brook opposed us and Canute sprang over it like a gazelle and then on over a perfect line of fences nearly to Bruton and

back. He was tireless, he was agile, he was clever, he enjoyed
every second of it, he was perfection. And all the time he was
in front, with never a one to guide or to give him a lead.
And then, as now, that field took some keeping in front of,
across the best of the Sparkford Vale. They ran into their
fox nearly at Castle Cary. Arthur Brake rode up with Major
McCreery, both on reeking horses.

'Don't they jump this country, don't they just?' Brake
said, pointing at Canute and me. 'Look at that young horse,
hardly sweating.'

'I never in all my life saw a horse go better,' Major
McCreery said to me. 'But the awful thing is, you agreed to
look after him for the year that's gone, and I can't even
take him now. It'll be months before I get back to soldiering
in England.

'Just you leave him with me,' I said, delighted.

But he returned sooner than he'd anticipated, and asked
me to take Canute to the Blackmore Vale Meet at Henstridge.
He got on him at the meet. I watched them have one busy
morning hunt. 'Marshall,' he said, when I came up with
them at a roadside covert, 'I think I'll just ride him home to
Stowell when they've done for the day.'

'Quite sure you're all of a piece with him, and happy
about everything?'

'Never sat on a nicer little horse. I'll bring your saddle
and bridle to Gillingham tomorrow, noon.'

Now I wonder if Canute heard him say that. . . . I left
them by the covertside with hounds chivvying about in the
thickets. I was home by two o'clock. Two hours later I
was at my desk by the window when I heard the one, two,
three, four on the hard road of a sound horse trotting fast.
It stopped in front of the house. Silence. I went to the
window, and there was Canute's comical face looking over
the wall.

'Hold up, boy,' I called through the open window.
'Don't move an inch, now. I'm coming to fetch you in.' I

got a bowl of oats and haltered him. 'What happened?' I asked him. 'Have you fallen with him? Never! Not a scratch on you anywhere.' Then I remembered that Major McCreery had a habit at any check or halt of getting off his horse, either leading it between draws or stamping his feet about. He did it partly to take the weight off the horse (which more riders could do with advantage in the hunting field) and partly because he had a wounded heel that stiffened up in a hunting boot. Horses very soon get to know such habits in their masters, and his regular hunters stayed with him if he dropped the reins altogether.

I soon telephoned Stowell Park. The receiver was snatched off by the Major himself, frantic with worry.

'Who's that?'

'Marshall here, did you have a good day? How did he go?' I asked in tones as flat as the floor.

'At the Compton Stud we lost our fox after a twisty run. The little horse went fine. I got off him at a check. He eluded me, trotted off into the blue, and hasn't been seen since. . . .'

'Oh, I've seen him,' I said. 'He just came on home. He hasn't a scratch on him and he's finished every crumb of his linseed mash. If I know him he'll be lying sound asleep when I go round the stable last thing tonight.'

'Keep him till you hear from me in about a month, and give him a few more hunts and as much steady roadwork as you or your man can spare time for.'

Roadwork? My heart sank, I confess, for since Beacon I had not liked to see a horse put to steeplechasing. Still, Major McCreery was a racing amateur and a most distinguished one, as his son was to be after him. When he bought the young Canute he had already won the Grand Military Gold Cup twice, riding a little mare called Annie Darling. Ah well, sellers can't be choosers. And in Canute's case, after all, I was never the owner, only the hired help. I soon received my second cheque for one hundred pounds from Major Bernard of Oborne, though, and that was pleasant.

A motor box was sent over to collect Canute. I never had him with me again, worse luck. He duly won that season's point-to-points (hence my second cheque), for he was so good that only class horses could live with him. Then he won the £500 United Services 'Chase at Newbury, and another good one at Sandown in the autumn, always owner-ridden. By that time the Major, good luck to him, was well in pocket. I next remember Canute running in the Becher 'Chase at Aintree, where he was second to Major Rushton's fine horse.

I went to see him run in the Foxhunters' at Cheltenham. Ambrose Clark (whom I had known in Leicestershire and on Long Island, you remember) owned the favourite, Chad's Ford, ridden by Reg Hobbs, the best amateur imaginable. Chad's Ford just held him. There was my dear little horse struggling away up that hellish long hill at the end of four miles at a hard gallop. Both game horses carrying twelve stone. Twelve stone! I met Lady McCreery as they left the unsaddling enclosure and I felt like saying, even to her, 'Twelve stone! You ought to be made to carry it round Cheltenham yourselves.'

Mind you, I'd never pretend that Canute wasn't lucky to land with such people. General McCreery was to prove himself time and again in two wars and in peace as a man and a soldier. He was a 12th Lancer. As for Lady McCreery, I always admired her from a distance. I knew her and her father, Lord Percy St Maur, well by sight because they had hunted from Loughborough. One Blackmore Vale Saturday Stanley Young had a colossal string of hired horses going out. Usually I rode the sale horses, and had nothing to do with the hiring side, but that day he asked me as a favour to ride one on and lead two, as he was doing himself. We were standing at the meet with our hirelings in a long line and Young ticking each one off as his rider arrived to claim him. I

watched the young lady and the handsome Major McCreery
(he may have been a captain then, or even a lieutenant)
alight from a car and walk down to the horses and hounds,
he in scarlet, she impeccable in black and white. I think
one of the most attractive things about foxhunting is that
people are spotless one minute, their clothes perfection, their
silk ties softly white, their tall hats gleaming, their breeches
London works of art, their ditto boots boned to a deep lustre
—and in five or ten minutes all that glory may be covered in
mud. But as I was saying, the young couple came down to
the horses, and they looked so happy, and kept gazing at
each other as much as to say, 'It's marvellous just to be alive
on such a nice, damp, good-scenting hunting morning.'

'She looks as though she's come to stay,' I observed to
Stanley Young. And so she had. And what wonderful good
sense she showed in picking one like Dick McCreery. I use
his Christian name without disrespect, because when he
raced that was how we all knew him. The urban masses may
not understand it, but foxhunting and steeplechasing, yes,
and racing too, are wonderful levellers. They don't pull
everyone down, as certain forms of Government do, they
pull everyone up. Anyway, we had a clinking good day with
the Blackmore Vale, that day I saw them walk down together,
and that would be one day her ladyship never forgot. I think
their engagement was announced about then.

The season after his honourable defeat at Cheltenham
(he was by then a famous horse), I met Canute in the hunting
field, Lady McCreery up. I ought to say now that she was a
star, on any horse. Many a time I watched her point-to-
pointing side-saddle, especially on her own good winner,
Bron. By golly she had guts and skill, and she could make
them gas!

'He's too good a lady's hunter to go racing,' she said to me
that lovely chill morning. How good, in spells, the English
winter is to the sportsman! And the little horse was looking
wonderful, plumped out and self-confident, ready to rob

the Bank of England or to help a lame hound over a nasty wire fence.

But that racing bug is powerful. Back Canute went into training with Ivor Anthony, one of the best, at Broughton. The two Bostwick brothers had horses with Anthony, they took a tremendous fancy (and who could blame them) to Canute, and they took him back with them to America. He would enjoy that country as much as I did.

And I suppose it was lucky for him that I had a railway box at Milborne Port that morning, and that Major Bernard ran into me and remembered his wild colt.

17

Problem Horses

WE bipeds can get about in cars or in bath chairs, but any horse is only as good as his feet. I'm going to tell you something now about feet.

My story begins (as so many do in the West Country) with those interesting people, the Brakes. A man went to their Limington headquarters looking for a hunter. He wouldn't fix on any of the ones they showed him so they said, 'We're just off for a hunt in the Seavington country. Come along. We'll mount you.' And they did.

Going through a deep ford the horse slipped, got into difficulties, and broke their client's leg. Just bad luck, it could happen to anyone. The Brakes then sold him another, a mare. He found her not to his fancy as a hunter, so he put her to a good horse, Rapier, one of the Hunters' Improvement Society stallions. His mare had two foals by Rapier, both strong and well-made, both brown.

I first saw one of those foals, fully grown, at the Light Horse Breeding Society's show. You beauty, you! I thought when I saw him standing at the head of his class. I was showing a tricky four-year-old, so I said to my niece, who was twelve at the time, 'Nip round to the sale ring and take careful note what that one makes and who buys him.'

When I left the ring she strolled up and in a low voice (she was a clever youngster) said, 'Mr Brake bought him and he made ninety-one guineas.'

'What!' I said. 'That sounds like an auctioneer creeping

up to a reserve one hundred pounds he failed to get.... Good girl, here's sixpence for an ice-cream.' He seemed a cheap young horse at one hundred pounds. It wanted fathoming.

Next morning I was out exercising near Limington and I saw Jack Brake on the horse sold at the show. I thought, Oh well, part of it's true anyway. He's here, and doesn't he just look a picture.

'Marshall, you'll like this 'oss,' Brake called. 'Just watch him lep a bit of timber.' We were in a wide grassy ride, wet and slippery, with ·a big gate either end. He jumped the two gates and came back over them. My God! I thought, that's a performance.

'Let's get on 'im,' I said. I had a ride, cantered him about, reined back. He went beautifully. 'Well, Mr Brake,' I said, 'I wonder if you'd consider taking twenty pounds profit on this youngster?'

'I just might, to do you a favour.'

'That'll be one hundred and ten pounds, something like that,' I said thinking he'd paid ninety-one guineas and that I was being businesslike.

'That'll do me,' he said. But I noticed an almost startled expression flit across his face, and I thought, Cripes! I believe I've set him too high.

As soon as I got back to the house I made enquiries. The Rapier horse had a reserve on him of ninety guineas. He had not made it and had been sold to Mr Brake for seventy-five pounds. So he'd jumped me twenty pounds. I thought, Damnation! to be caught like that. You deserve to go bankrupt. . . . However, he was still a cheap horse. Rapier stuff was in demand. I hacked him about to get him fit, and soon a Mr Lazenby from Lower Slaughter in the Cotswolds came to look at him. He liked him, jumped him, galloped him, had him passed by the vet, and bought him cheerfully for two hundred pounds. I felt, as one so often does, that I should possibly have valued him at three hundred pounds.

A fortnight later Mr Lazenby wrote to me: 'If I had to ride the horse every day of the week I would not ride at all, I would not hunt, I would not look at any horse again. It is purgatory to ride him. . . .'

Thoroughly puzzled, I at once picked up the telephone, and got my client to elucidate.

'You can't get on any road, even a side road, without him stumbling and breaking his knees,' he said. 'He'd catch his toes if you rode him round the Horse Guards' Parade. And him only five, and never done a smell of work. . . . Will you take him back, Marshall?'

'Yes I will, I must, though I was never more astonished in my life.' I thought quickly. Sir Arthur Cory-Wright had bought a decent horse off me for his secretary to ride. She couldn't get on with it, so Sir Arthur had asked me to sell it for him. 'I've got a nippy Cotswold hunter I can let you have,' I said to Mr Lazenby. 'We'll adjust the price as *you* see fit. This horse is extra handy over walls.' So I gave Sir Arthur's horse a school over every wall I could find, boxed him up there, and brought the Rapier one back. As for that lovely Rapier gelding, he stood eating his head off, and he could not stride over a straw lying on the road. He was perfect on grass, but take him on the hard and he would cut a pair of front shoes right through before you had gone a mile. It was a kink. There was only one thing for it. I arranged to sell him at the Leicester Repository. And thinking, I'll have to go high for this one, I put a two hundred and fifty pounds reserve on him.

He didn't make it. One or two people kept coming round me, as though they expected to get him for nothing. I stood my ground boldly, but of course I found it horribly difficult to face up to the expense and nuisance of taking him all the way home. In the end a genuine buyer, Mr Oliver Dixon Junior, came along.

'Is one hundred and fifty pounds any use at all to you, Captain Marshall,' he asked.

'You shall have him, Mr Dixon.'

And do you know what those excellent dealers the Dixons did? They sold him to an Italian princess as a show jumper, and he won just about every pot and jackpot in Italy, and ended up worth thousands.

*   *   *

How his younger brother came into my hands I cannot remember. At that time I used to buy batches of young ones and school and sell them as they matured. And him I sold and sold well, without difficulty or complication of any sort, to Major Morton, Master of the Sparkford Vale Harriers. He had passed the vet, of course, and within a fortnight of delivering him I received a letter, saying how well the young horse had gone out hunting. Ten days later Major Morton telephoned.

'Marshall, you'll have to take that horse back. He's dangerous on the road. Won't go a yard without tripping over his feet.'

'Well, I won't *have* to take him back,' I said. 'But I *will* take him back. I sold you the horse in good faith, as you know, and I certainly don't want you to have anything you consider to be dangerous. I'd taken particular trouble with schooling that horse for Mrs Morton, and I honestly thought he was letter-perfect. Of course I schooled him entirely on the grass. I don't, now I think of it, remember riding him so much as ten yards up any road.' That was the truth.

'Marshall, don't you think I might do well to buy that black mare I saw when I was last at your place?'

He referred to a nice black mare I had picked up at Peterborough Show. She was in a local class there, and she won it. When the man who owned and rode her had cantered her round the ring once, she took him out, *straight over the gate*. I followed him up like lightning—I've told you I was fast on my pins. I got to him just in front of three others,

two professionals and an enthusiastic amateur, but of course
the mare's owner didn't know one from t'other.

'How much?' I asked.

'One hundred pounds,' was the answer.

'Let me have a ride on her.' Up I got, rode her through
the crowds, reined back, and made straight for him. I could
see the others in the wings, pretending not to look at me.
'Knock me off a tenner,' I said to him, 'And I'll have her
for cash as she stands, without saddle or bridle. No vet. I'll
take a chance on her.' And I got her. . . .

I put a pair of kneeguards in my pockets and rode her over
to the Mortons' attractive little place on the Sparkford side
of Yeovil.

'What would you let me have her for?' Major Morton
asked.

'Two hundred guineas, if I take the other back.'

'There's just one thing I'd like to see her do before I have
her.'

'What's that?' I prepared myself to face some fearful test,
like jumping a pen with a sow and litter in it, or through
the fork of some giant oak-tree.

'Walk her down this steep hill where there are a few loose
stones,' the clever fellow said. 'Steep' was certainly no
exaggeration, and I could see nothing *but* stones. She picked
her way down like a cat. 'Marshall, I don't think you're
overcharging for her.'

'Well, I'm getting the Rapier horse back.'

'Oh, but he isn't worth tuppence. You'll never ride him from
here to Gillingham you know, never in a month of Sundays.'

'We'll see about that,' I said in my self-conceit, putting on
the kneeguards.

But by the time I had ridden the horse out of the Morton
drive he'd made three or four attempts to say his prayers.
'My Grandfathers!' I said to myself. 'I never knew a perishing
salaamer to equal this brute. The worst dodger on the road
I ever was on, and sixteen miles to cover between here and

home.' It isn't like the Duke of Beaufort's country or Leicestershire down there; the roads are either highways or narrow lanes, and there are no wide grass verges for the horseman. Through Mudford and Sherborne I rode him for all I was worth, holding him up on his feet, shoving him into his bridle. A bit of leg here, a bit of leg there, voice, backside, every blasted aid I could roust out. We were nearly at Gillingham and I was as tired as though I had carried him all the way. I was at the end of my tether. 'Dammit, I'm for a smoke,' I said to him. 'Take the reins and do your worst.' He walked on. Had I been fussing needlessly? I felt in my pockets for pipe, pouch and matches, and had just about lit up when he took a couple of extra-wonky paces. Down he went on his knees and slid on the gravel for yards. The knee-guards rubbed clean off. The roadway was covered with blood and bits of knee. 'Now you've done it,' I told him. 'Not a sixpence back out of you. Damn Rapier and damn the mare that bore you. . . .'

But the habits of a lifetime hold firm. I led him home, made him comfortable, bathed and bathed his knees with brine, and put big pads of lint all round them. There in his box he remained until three weeks before Christmas when, that year, the trade in hunters was hotting up. He had decent clean hay to eat and bran, nothing else, and he came up glossy and fat as one of Mr Bentley's lovely oysters. He looked so wonderful I began to think there *must* be an outlet for him, perhaps on the stage or in pageants. When the shoeing smith came on his regular round I had him make a set for that one, and in the course of stables we did his mane and tail. He looked like a thousand, no a million, dollars.

I had a couple of horses to show to the Member of Parliament for Battersea North, who turned up driving a comfortable horse box with a hunter inside. He also had with him a gentleman in hunting clothes whom he introduced as Sir Adam Hamilton, M.F.H., from Scotland, a young and extremely personable spark. I don't know when I saw a handsomer man. The horses I had ready for the M.P. to try were exceptionally good ones. But a buyer always has a picture in his own mind, or if you are lucky, several pictures, and unless you can put horseflesh to a picture you're wasting your time and his. I twigged immediately that when the M.P. had said *he* wanted a horse he had meant that he wanted one for his friend, Sir Adam, who was the kind of client to make a coper's mouth water, madly enthusiastic, almost certainly a horseman, and last but not least (I could tell it by a glance at his boots and breeches) *a spender*.

'What a disappointment, Captain Marshall,' he said. 'Neither of these is my horse, and that's flat. I'd hoped you'd have one I could buy outright and ride straight on to Mr Bell's Meet at East Knoyle. Sorry, too, that you've gone to all the bother of having them vetted. . . . What in heaven's name is that lovely horse over in that box?' he suddenly asked, looking at our Rapier friend.

'Well,' I said, the warhorse in me hearing the distant roll of drums and tramp of infantry, 'that's a very well-bred horse by Rapier that's been carefully mouthed and broken. He's only four. He had a bit of an accident with his knee but he's mended well. He's done some work, but not lately. He jumps and he gallops, but as you can see, he's been standing in for weeks and he's butter fat. . . .'

'Can I throw a leg over him?' the young M.F.H. asked sharply. I could see he was thinking, When is Marshall going to cut the cackle? If only he did I might yet get in a hunt today.

'Certainly,' I said, my heart warming to him.

His friend the politician had meanwhile started up his luxurious horsebox. He lowered the window of the cab and called, 'Adam. I can't be so infernally rude as to be late for Ikey's meet. Are you coming or are you stopping here?'

'I'll ride on and pick up hounds if I find myself a horse,' Sir Adam said. 'Otherwise Captain Marshall here has been good enough to say he'll take me on in his car. Be sure to find Ella at the meet, though, and tell her what's happened. If she knows there's a horse in it I expect she'll understand. . . . Right, Captain Marshall, let's have him out, shall we?'

The horse, absolutely delighted to be out, carried him well in my paddock and when he tried him at three or four schooling fences jumped them keenly and impeccably. For a Scotsman he rode well, with a nice long leg and light hands.

'He's my sort,' he said. 'If he fences like that when he's let down and in the coldest of blood, he might make into a jumping star. He stands back at 'em. I like that. I think I'll buy him. Have you a certificate?'

My man handed him a vet's certificate. I wished the earth would open and swallow me. It was the certificate for one of the others, of course, a bay gelding, and the Rapier horse was dark brown. Sir Adam looked at it quickly, said, 'It seems perfectly clean,' and thrust it into his pocket. He had been riding in a covert coat over his hunting things and a tweed cap. 'Have you something to ride, Marshall? Now that I've bought him, the pair of us could cut across country and find Ikey Bell and his hounds. What a lark!'

'Take your coat, Sir Adam?' asked my man. 'I'll bring it on for you in the car. The other gentleman left your velvet cap, whip, gloves, and sandwich case. I have them in the harness room. . . .' As he took the coat he swiftly removed the certificate from the pocket. I was considerably shaken by his leger-de-main (if he did that to others what might he not do to me?), however I decided I might as well stay with it on the principle of in for a penny in for a pound.

'Now look, Sir Adam,' I said. 'You wanted to pay for this horse before you took him, and I think that might be satisfactory. I don't know you, do I?'

'Yes, yes. But I haven't got a cheque book here.'

'That's all right. Come into the house and have a port-and-brandy. I can provide a cheque. Let's have it settled once and for all.'

'Fine.'

Frank as I am by instinct and by nature, I won't tell you the price of that horse. You see, he was so good-looking, and jumped so well, that to put a low figure on him would have been suspect. I silenced my conscience by the thought that if anything went wrong I would take the horse back off him. He *was* a nice young man.

We rode off, the pair of us, through the viaduct and over the road. I was racking my poor brain, already reeling at the turn of events, to make out a line to Mr Bell's main draw without any hard road at all in it. We jumped out of the first field into a grass ride, and after following that jumped into a wood, burst our way through that, jumped out, and I could see the covert I was making for, set on its eminence, still distant. It was a glorious late morning with brittle sunshine and a crackle in the air, yet I perceived that the Rapier horse was getting fussed at having another with him, and was beginning to catch his toes even on the grass. A fair amount of the going was ridge and furrow, and we did a lot of jumping. 'By gad, Marshall, you really are the hell of a fellow,' the baronet said. 'I declare I've never been taken on to a hunt like this. It's almost as good as hunting. Do you make a habit of it?'

'I want you to get to know him,' I said. 'We may not have a hunt, you know.' I fervently hoped we would not. His horse was lathering up the neck, yet he clamped on him and stuck him at a big open ditch. At least that horse could jump, and so could mine, one of the two they had rejected. 'Let's stand absolutely still a minute and have a listen,' I said, realising that his poor horse would blow up if he didn't get a breather. We heard nothing, and went on, but more steadily now. He and the horse were not doing at all well. They were soon going to be properly at odds with each other. I strained my eyes into the distance.

'THERE HE IS!' I cried. 'There's Mr Bell. See the red coat beyond those conifers? He's still drawing. Now you're all right. STAY HERE. They'll push him out and run this

S

way, fifty to one. And when they do, *get after them*, waiting for neither man nor angel.'

'Now isn't this a bit of luck? I don't know when I've enjoyed myself so much,' said the charming young man.

And as soon as that horse heard and saw hounds he changed one hundred per cent. He came on his toes and went well into his bridle. He'd simply hated that long and energetic hack at a sharpish pace because, as I again warned his new owner, he'd done nothing for months. 'You might as well have pulled out Sophie Tucker, popped a saddle on her, and expected her to give you a great ride.'

'Marshall!' he said to that, 'What utterly miraculous ideas you have in that head of yours.'

We had our hunt, short and sharp, with both of us right in front and cutting out the work until they checked on a quiet country road. The fox had gone to ground in a bank. Up came the car followers, a string of them, and the most beautiful dark girl got out from behind the wheel of an open Bentley.

'Captain Marshall, Miss Rothschild,' my companion introduced us.

'You've ruined my day,' she said to me. 'I'd arranged to find him at the meet and take him hunting in my car. Instead you kept him hidden away all morning and then put him on a horse.'

'You can't expect to see much of him on a hunting day,' I said. 'Unless you buy yourself a horse like this one I'm on and then you could stick to him like glue.' The lady's providential arrival showed me an immediate way out. I had visions of the prince charming and M.F.H. sprawled all over the road and his horse too, and everybody saying, 'Who sold him that brute? Why, Marshall.' Easing myself up to him, I said that his horse, completely unfit, had done more than enough, and that I would lead him quietly back to my place and send him the following day to any address he might name.

He thanked me with his boyish charm and vivacity. I never thought there were Scotsmen like that. He was no haggis. The horse was put in a railway box and taken all the way to Perthshire. When I had seen him on his way (and the farther he went the better, I felt) I telephoned Sir Adam at the mansion near Tisbury where he was staying.

'That horse of yours. . . .' I began. 'He's a bit peculiar sometimes on the hard high road. It's not as uncommon a peculiarity as you might suppose. I remember a star hunter with the Quorn, belonging to Lord Ivor Churchill. . . .' He listened to me carefully, said he would ride the horse about his estate, do some show-jumping with him, and when he hunted him he would have him either boxed or led.

He kept the Rapier gelding for several years, and I sold him other horses. That lameness on the road must have been hereditary. The odd thing was that both those horses, full brothers, came separately into my hands. They were good sorts, exceptionally good, except for their one dreadful failing.

18

Satisfying A Difficult Client

SPEAKING as one horse-coper about another, I would say Commander McCowen was pretty smart. I met him often in Sherborne, where he used to buy too many outstanding young horses for my liking. His strategy was to make up a good string in our part of the country and then, choosing his time, sell the lot in a batch at Leicester. He enjoyed it, for selling horses in those days could be fun, and there were all sorts of us at it, from the very influential in court circles to the lowest in the East End of London.

On one of the Commander's trips to Leicester he sold sixteen hunters and he would have averaged four hundred and fifty guineas if he had accepted a bid for four hundred for a grey cob on which he had a five-hundred-guinea reserve. I know the figures because I was at that particular sale, chasing one of the cheaper hunters, a mare called Moonbeam. The Commander (playing a more or less legitimate fast one on me) had bought the mare from Stanley Young, who found her on an Exmoor farm. Her age was eight and she stood fifteen hands three inches. I knew privately, having once been lucky enough to have a day's hunting on her in the Sparkford Vale, that she was a ride and a performer second to none. And in her pocket-sized way she was as good-looking as Eclipse.

I had a new client whom I prized, Mr Hartley of Billesdon Coplow, seven miles east of Leicester, in the Quorn country. He was a small, spare gentleman, mild of manner, invincibly polite. He favoured Lovat-tweed knickerbocker

276

suits worn with greenish stockings and the high-backed spats then called Duke of Connaughts. I met him by appointment at the Repository before the sale, introduced Moonbeam to him, gave him a little show on her, and then put him in the saddle.

'*Most* attractive, I should like to have her bring me my breakfast in bed.' That was his comment. 'And you say she really gallops, Marshall?'

'None better. But you'll have to bid up, mind. This is a mare who's been going in front in the Sparkford Vale over those spread fly fences and sizeable brooks. There must be a tidy few who, like me, have noted her and who'll think a journey to Leicester no waste of time or money to make her theirs.'

At the mention of money an uncomfortable look occupied his face. 'It's so good of you, Marshall, to recommend her. After all, you're making nothing from it.'

'She's a great mare. I want you to be well-horsed and satisfied.'

'What should she fetch?'

'She'll go over three hundred guineas, of that I'm sure.'

'Never! Then I'm done. Such an attractive mare, and you say she gallops.'

I found my way to his side as her number came up. She was rapidly started at two hundred guineas, and, looking pale, Mr Hartley came in at two hundred and eighty. But it was filled in up to three hundred much too fast for his liking, and she was knocked down to the people who had the Craven, Woolland I think was their name, for three hundred and twenty-five.

'And dirt cheap at the price.' I said as she was led out.

'I do regret that. Oh, I deeply regret I did not go on,' Mr Hartley said. 'You don't think they'd sell her to me now if I made them an offer.'

'Not them. It's the mare they want. They've got fids of money. When you had it recommended as that mare was by me to you for a man of your age, weight, and experience, you should not have hesitated. Mares such as that are as scarce as cucumbers in the Kalahari.'

'Look here, Captain Marshall, could you not find me her equal at the money? You know exactly what I want, same age, same height, the galloping Somerset stag-hunting sort bold and easy at her fences, must have a limpid eye and small, perfect feet.'

'I know where they are, indeed I can say I know of THE MARE, but if you mention buying them, up goes the price. There's not much you can do with a West of England farmer except have a wad of money in your fist and say, "Here you are then, money down, take it or leave it." '

'You've actually got one in your mind's eye that would do me, Captain Marshall?'

'I have.'

'Then I'm going to trust you,' he said, producing, his cheque book and a Waterman pen. 'I'm making you out a cheque for three hundred guineas. I shall expect you to deliver the mare within one month, together with her vet's certificate.'

'Mr Hartley,' we shook hands. 'lose no sleep over your mare. She's as good as in your stables at Billesdon, and you'll love her.'

As I left the Repository through the small door in the big one I ran into Harry Gale, that dear old friend of my boyhood who worked for the Drages of Chapel Brampton, Northampton, deans of the horse-dealing world. Harry was doing so well for them, buying in Ireland, that they'd bought him a house there.

'You're wasting your time, yoong Marshall,' he said. 'We've sent Mr Hartley doozens of horses and he never keeps one. Right fussy, he is.'

'Perhaps you don't find him good enough ones, Harry. Just take a decko at this, for a horse he hasn't even seen (and nor, between ourselves, have I) and made out to me, whom he scarcely knows.' I showed the cheque for three hundred and fifteen pounds.

'Woonders never cease,' Harry said. 'He moost feel sorry for you, lad.'

I went home and began to feel sorry for myself. No horse I had on my lists would do. One had gone, one was lame, and a third, no matter how much I stretched the measure, would not stand higher than fifteen hands. I heard of a brilliant fifteen hands three inches mare in the Wylye Valley country. The owner was an old auctioneer who would change his mind about selling the moment he saw you were interested. I paved the way, dangled the money, had everything fixed and then when I saw the mare I knew she did not fit the bill for Mr Hartley. Time was running out and I was desperate. To cheer myself up I went hunting a lot and sold three other horses, but his three hundred guineas weighed on me like half a hundredweight of suet pudding.

Out with the Blackmore Vale one day I spied young Norman Richards on a mare that looked just about the sort. Norman was only fourteen then, I believe, and he was often in my pocket in the hunting field for he went really well and, young as he was, he already had an eagle eye. He rode every horse his father acquired in the Blackmore Vale country before their very successful·move to the Duke of Beaufort's, where they established themselves as top-class dealers in hunters.

'How old is that?' I asked the boy.

'Six.'

'How much?'

'One hundred and fifty.'

'Change over,' I said, and at once knew that the mare would do. It was important not to show young Norman I liked her. He was sharp as sharp.

Next morning I telephoned a vet. 'I want you to examine a mare I hope to buy. If she isn't certified as eight years and fifteen hands three inches and sound you'll be wasting your time and mine. I'm in a hurry to get her off to Leicestershire, as it's a special order and it's taken me too long to find her. *So bring your official-headed writing paper*, and you can make out the certificate on the spot.'

He hummed and hawed in the stable, and kept starting to make out a certificate and then defacing it or tearing it up.

I said, 'Can't you write a certificate? All you've got to get down is, "I have today examined this horse and have found it to be eight years old, fifteen hands three inches, and sound." That's all. Surely there's no need to go growling and groaning over anything as simple as that.'

'But she isn't eight. She's six by her mouth. And no matter how I try I can't make her stand much more than fifteen hands one.'

'Never mind. Put down the correct height. And if you think the age is six, say six. I'll just have to change the buyer's mind for him on those points. At any rate we're agreed that she's sound?'

He continued to make heavy weather of it until, would you credit it, he ran out of paper. I then, unseen by him, picked up one that appeared to have been completed but with which for some reason, he had been dissatisfied. It got lost. He couldn't find it anywhere, the reason being that, carefully folded, it reposed in my pocket. As soon as he'd gone I posted that certificate off to Mr Hartley, pointing out that whereas the mare I was sending him behaved in every way with the maturity of an eight-year-old, he was getting her with a two-year bonus, two more years of life. And whereas she was a shade under fifteen hands two inches, she was in every other respect a big fifteen hands two inches. What I did not mention, naturally, was where I had found her, nor that Richards had been good enough to knock a chip off their asking price.

That night the vet telephoned to say the mare had spavins and he couldn't give her a clean bill. I could have killed him. Meanwhile my letter was hurtling north to Mr Hartley, so there was nothing I could do. The mare was boxed up to her new and comfortable home at Billesdon, and very

shortly I received a charming letter from her owner, thanking
me for taking so much trouble to find exactly the right
animal. . . . It had cost me a lot of worry. I was thankful
that it ended well.

Four years later Mr Hartley asked me to stay at Billesdon
Coplow to see a mare he wanted to sell. He was still hunting
the mare I had bought for him from young Norman Richards.
'She's great,' he said. 'And so fast that if I don't like the look
of a fence made for the youngsters to break their necks at,
I can cut round and still stay with the hunt.' And she looked
as though he had done a good deal of 'cutting around'.
She was jarred, but sound. (That vet and his spavins!)
She was a game little sort, if not exactly in Moonbeam's class.

I told Mr Hartley I would take his other mare off him.
But I could not pay much because she had a blemish I had
not seen before on any horse, a nest of warts on the seat of
curb on each hock. When she lay down she would rip the
tops off them, and the straw would stick to them. A horrid
sight. Yet she was a fine specimen, good clean head and
neck, well ribbed up, and plenty of bone.

On the Sunday, after a traditional English luncheon
terminated by a glass or two of vintage port, Mr Hartley
asked me to walk out with him across the park to his famous
Quorn covert, Botany Bay. He confided in me that he had
always been proud of his hunting noises—not an unusual
form of conceit, unfortunately—but that of recent years, when
he had viewed a fox away from Botany Bay, hounds had not
seemed to come to his halloa. Would I help him test the matter?

He stationed me at the bottom end and walked away from
me up the long ride through the middle. He soon disappeared,
there being bends in the ride. The arrangement was that
when he had climbed to the top of the covert, which is a big
one by Quorn standards, he would give tongue an unspecified
number of times and would then come back and ask me how
many halloas I had heard. When he disappeared I sprinted
after him. Peering cautiously round the first corner, I saw

him just about to disappear again. So I followed him on, a long way farther. Presently I heard something like a tin trumpet. It sounded three times. Concluding that that was all he could do without straining himself, I hared back to my original position.

'Well, my friend,' he said when he at last arrived. 'I don't suppose you heard me at all. Let's face it, I'm an old man and it's a long covert. If the wind's wrong you can scream yourself black in the face and nobody will hear.'

'I heard three halloas, no more, no less,' I said truthfully.

'Good, good. I dearly love to see them come streaming to me when I hold my hat in the air.'

As for his mare with the warts, when I got her home I kept her in hock caps at night, well padded out with cotton wool and treated with a secret ointment an old Somerset man used to sell. They said he could charm warts away. Anyway, when the ointment had seeped well in he appeared one afternoon and just picked the warts out by the roots. They obviously intended coming again, so I decided to get the mare fit and then sell her. But for the warts she would have sold many times over, for she was a grand ride and hunter. She had the loveliest, clearest bay skin that ever I saw.

I was standing by her stall at Leicester when Mr Parry from Cheltenham came dodging along, looking carefully at everything for sale. 'Now, Mr Parry,' I said. 'Here's the mare that'll just suit you for your letting-out business. A real good sort to go handily down those hills and pop over the walls in the bottoms. A nice nippy mare and a hard mare.'

He stood, feet apart, squared up to her, looking her over. Even in that poor light you could see all the pretty little hammer marks in her coat. Finally he gave tongue; 'I'd like the saddle that's on her back and the man that clipped her.' All the time he never took his eyes off her hocks. I suspected he'd been pumping Mr Hartley's groom, or mine.

You meet some hard people in the horse world. Often I wonder how I have survived so long among them.

19

Lord Hindlip's Daughter

IF ever you wish to win with a horse in the show ring I advise you to listen to this story from the 1930s, which mainly concerns (apart from myself) Lord Hindlip and his attractive daughter, the Hon. Diana Allsopp.

Lord Hindlip had first seen me riding in a hack class at Olympia and had liked the way I appeared to let the horse alone, to carry its head free of all human encumbrance. He made enquiries about me there, and again in Derbyshire, where he had a country place, and the following May he sent a chestnut mare down to me at The Malt House. She was a nice-looking, straight-moving, clean-bred mare, aged six and standing fifteen hands two inches. I was asked to prepare her for the hack classes at Richmond and Olympia. Show hacks, as you know, have always intrigued me, and I sized that one up in the first minutes of our riding acquaintance as being nowhere near Olympia standards. She was a flighty mare. You know what I mean by that? You'd only to bring a gelding near and she preened and forgot the task in hand. A proper flibberty-gibbet. Worse, she loathed noise, any noise, and misbehaved when she heard it. I didn't take her very seriously, and I was still less keen on her when I showed her at the Bath and West and she completely lost her head in the ring, doing her best, or worst, to make an ass of me. Soon after that exhibition Lord Hindlip telephoned.

'How's my mare progressing?'

'Moderately. She gets upset. I don't think she'll ever do

any good. I've put in the dickens of a lot of time and work at your expense, yet she doesn't begin to be even a *promising* novice.'

'Are you there, Marshall? Now listen to this. She's entered in every novice and open hack class, first at Richmond and then at Olympia, *and she's going to win them all*. Don't interrupt me, please. This has nothing to do with silk purses and sows' ears, and anyway what the devil d'ye mean by that—that our mare looks like a pig? You mean she'd lose on looks.'

'No, my lord. Her looks are improving, and her action. It's sense and poise she lacks, and to get both into her would take weeks of solid work, and then nobody could guarantee success. Those hack classes are the hottest in the world. They're desperately hard to win.'

'She *must* win,' he said. 'She must *win* every class right to the top, the Balmanno Cup. Are you there? My daughter Diana will ride her. It's her coming-out year. . . .'

'But my lord, it's a question of time. . . .'

'Are you working on several other horses just now?'

'Naturally, I can't afford to concentrate on one rather dubious show hack.'

'We'll make you eat that "dubious", my friend, and from now on you *can* afford it because *I* can afford it. Are you listening? I want you to set aside your other horses, do your packing, and bring the mare to London tomorrow. We'll put you up here with us in the London house. You'll have the run of your teeth, and every possible consideration, and as soon as you arrive we'll come, the pair of us, to any terms within reason that you think suitable.'

'That's extremely handsome of you, but. . . .'

'But what?' His forceful tones made the receiver throb.

'I could put the others out to grass for a spell, but I'd have to bring one, a young grey horse, with the mare. Anyway she'd travel and do better with company.'

'Bring your grey, man, for God's sake. I'll ring Horace Smith now and tell him both animals will be standing with him and are to have the best of everything at my expense.'

'Another thing. . . .'

'Out with it.'

'We shall have to work her really hard and yet it's vital that she should keep her spring bloom. It's a shame we shall have no paddock to turn her in for the dew on her back and a bite of fresh grass with some earth on it.'

'I take your point, Marshall, and it makes sense. I can't get hold of a grazing paddock in Mayfair nor yet Belgravia, but I'll order a ten-pound package of fresh grass to be sent daily from Dovedale. *You* order the horse box right away and leave your place after breakfast. You'll be able to get the horses settled in at Smith's place during the afternoon. We'll start work on the mare the following morning. There's not an hour to lose.'

'Again I must warn you that I feel it would take a year to bring your mare to Balmanno Cup standards.'

'Warning registered, now stop moaning. The English are always moaning nowadays. It's a disease. When you reach Hill Street we'll agree on our plan of campaign.'

'Very good, my lord.'

At Horace Smith's in Cadogan Square the red carpet was out for my pair of horses. I could see that Lord Hindlip had borne down on them as on me. I put my bags in one of the few hansoms that were still plying London as curiosities and was driven to Hill Street. It proved to be a splendid and comfortable house. I had been allotted a bachelor's apartment: bedroom, dressing-room, bathroom, and sitting-room. Fires glowed in both sitting-room and bedroom, and nothing, from the newspapers and the whisky decanter and the airtight case of Havanas to the pleasant footman from Dublin, had been forgotten. Looking around me and appreciating the thought, the organisation, that had gone into it all, I regretted that the chestnut mare was not a better prospect.

She appeared to have settled when Lord Hindlip and I went to see her in her box that evening before dinner (Miss

Diana was dining out and going on to a dance). We arranged for Smith's grooms to feed her and muck her out the following morning, and I would ride her at seven.

It was a heavenly morning and London was looking its best, but the mare had never imagined that any such hellish place for a horse as London could exist. What a ride she gave me from Cadogan Square to Rotten Row, shying at every lamp post, turning tail and bolting from almost every 'bus or milk cart. Eventually, though, I had her on the tan, with other horses working, and all the spaces of Hyde Park round us. I really set about her, steadily and tightly schooling, then a long jog, and then a walk to cool her off before I met the others by the Achilles statue.

Punctually at eight-thirty Lord Hindlip, Miss Diana, a diminutive and charming figure looking awfully sleepy, and a smart chauffeur in dark-green breeches and tunic, emerged from an enormous car. The chauffeur carried a side-saddle on his arm. I put the yawning Miss Diana up (light as thistledown), and off she went at a trot, then a slow canter.

'Brigson will drive you to Hill Street now for breakfast, Marshall,' Lord Hindlip said. 'And he'll bring you back here to take over from my daughter at eleven o'clock.'

Two and a half hours seemed a long time for a girl aged eighteen to be riding in the Park after dancing till four in the morning. However, at the end of her stint she looked fresher than at the beginning. She rode well, but I decided to vary the routine by joining her on my grey horse so that we could work together and practise the movements, stillness, and details in which a champion hack and rider must be perfect. The grey was a promising creature, more of a jumper than a hunter and just too young to jump at Olympia that year. I'd brought him to London because I felt there would be time on my hands with only one to school, though in that I'd underestimated Lord Hindlip.

'What d'you think of her?' I asked as Miss Diana slid to the ground and I changed saddles again.

'She's sticky. She doesn't like the tan underfoot and she simply hates the traffic. Yet at Dovedale she was a good ride.'

'If we can make her float on this soft tan she won't know herself in the show ring,' I said. 'I'll keep working her now until noon and this afternoon I'll lead her from my grey horse. By the end of tomorrow morning she should be steadying, for I suspect she has some sense in her somewhere. Then we'll have her out tomorrow afternoon and give her a reception committee.'

Next morning I briefed the chauffeur for the afternoon show. He went off to Hamley's toy shop in Regent Street and bought a trumpet, a couple of big rattles, and a snake that, when you blew into its tail, shot out a yard or more and emitted a whistling hiss. He was an ingenious Londoner, and he played his part well. As I walked the chestnut mare round Rotten Row he would race ahead with the limousine. Before she could shy, a green-clad figure would dart at her from behind a tree-trunk and give her the trumpet, the snake, or the rattle treatment. Meanwhile I would sit as easy as circumstances permitted, and soothe her with hand, voice, and leg. On the fifth afternoon she had so steadied that when Brigson and I spied and heard a Salvation Army band playing in Connaught Square, just across the Bayswater Road from the park, we simultaneously had the idea. There were eight bandsmen and two straw-hatted lasses with collecting boxes. I fished a pound note from my pocket and Brigson soon fetched the Army over. We stationed them at five-yard intervals, double ranked. They struck up *Shall We Gather at the River?* Each of the girls whirled a rattle, and Brigson shrilled his tin trumpet. I walked, trotted, and cantered the mare in and out among them as though they were the posts of a bending race. She simply hated the trombone, but after a few passes she would face even that. As a final test I stood her absolutely still and had them form a wide circle, start playing *Onward Christian Soldiers*, and close the circle on us at a steady creep. She trembled, but stood fast. They slowly

receded. Then we thanked them, and they us, and I got off
to let her eat a little grass and slithers of apple.

There's nothing like hard, regular work, the best of rations,
and a healthy coat. After only a week of our treatment the
mare had become placid and steady, and far from losing
condition, she was thriving and turning into something of a
beauty. In all my life I had never, I think, been able to spend
so much time and, let us be frank, money, on one small horse.
The progress made by the mare and by Miss Diana amazed
me. Indeed, I worried more for the girl than for the mare,
for like most top-class débutantes she was up dancing nearly
every night, and rarely got a proper sleep. She was a delightful little person, and it hurt me to see her unstifleable yawns
and the pale violet marks under her eyes.

'I'm so *tired*,' she would say. 'No sooner do I crawl into bed
than daddy pulls me out again.'

'You simply must cut a few engagements if you and the
mare are going to do us all justice,' I kept telling her. 'It
means so much to Lord Hindlip. You can't ride if you're
tired out. To be relaxed on a horse you must have steady
nerves and complete health.' All the same, she had the nerve,
and she was a natural rider. Then her smallness and neatness
suited that mare. But would she cut any dances? Would she
hell!

On June 12th when they walked into the Richmond ring
for the Novice Lady's Hack they were both letter-perfect,
and when the routine had swum past us several times our
chestnut was called in first. I approached and, with suitable
decorum, assisted Miss Allsopp to the ground. 'You rode her
well. But perhaps a shade more relaxed next time.' I was
answered with a cavernous yawn of fatigue or nerves or both.
I changed the leather and helped the judge into the saddle.
She also rode the mare well, and was obviously delighted
with the ride. I helped her down, handed her her leather and
iron, and raised my hat to her as she moved on to the next
ride. I off-saddled and got ready for the run out.

'Captain Marshall, I don't know how to keep awake,' Miss Diana said in her small, pathetic kind of voice. But she pulled herself together and gave a very good show with the mare in hand. As quickly as possible I saddled up and got her mounted again. I pinched her thigh until she gave a little yelp and hissed at her, 'Wake up. Ride her forward into her bridle, and at the slightest sign from judge or steward make straight back here to the top before anyone can say you nay.' Back she came, though I, sharply on the look out, never saw any signal at all. And there she stayed. Surprising how often that works.

Our chestnut mare had enjoyed herself. Everyone admired her healthy, at-home head carriage and calm gaze. If they could have seen her a fortnight previously! The Champion Cup next day was similar to the novice event except that the judge did not ride her. A quiet but faultless show brought the chestnut home quite comfortably. We had crossed the first two obstacles.

Olympia began on June 23rd and as usual clashed in its first week with Ascot. There was a particularly strong field of hacks even for that show of shows. I spent much time with our mare in her box, and was surprised at the regularity of Lord Hindlip's visits to the same unusual boudoir. Nothing was too much trouble for him, and not for one second did he lose his conviction that his daughter would emerge victorious. The mare won both Novice classes, though neither was easy, leaving us with only the final pinnacle to climb.

On the Thursday morning at ten the Champion Hack Class, no fewer than thirty-six of them, began its trials. At noon they were still not finished with the preliminaries. Then all of a sudden they filed out. I was waiting for the mare, and Lord Hindlip at my side was waiting to haul Miss Diana off to a luncheon party in Hill Street. The judging proper was due to begin in the main ring at two-thirty.

'How do you think you stand?' I asked Miss Diana.

'Haven't the foggiest,' she answered cheerfully. 'I leaned

on the mare and dropped off for quite a while, lulled by the tinkling of their bits, so soothing. Then that charming older judge said, "What's the matter, young lady, bored?" And I said, "Not on your life. I'm adoring every second of it, but I haven't been to bed for four nights." And he said (what do you imagine he meant?), "If every pretty girl in England could say the same the outlook would be bleak." '

'Come along,' her solicitous father said. 'You must eat something and put your feet up.'

'If I might suggest a pint of black coffee,' I said.

She had woken up. 'While I was drowsing in there, Captain Marshall, I somehow became aware of a lot of whispering going on and I saw people looking sharply at our mare. I feel, I just feel, that something's gone wrong.'

They had scarcely left me to find Brigson and the car when a steward came up with a note signed by both judges: 'Lord Hindlip's mare to be examined for her wind in the interval.'

'What rot is this?' I asked indignantly. 'Our young mare has already won three Novice classes and one Championship.'

'I assure you it's just a matter of form. I am merely transmitting the judges' instructions, and there is a vet here, Mr O'Hegan, to get on her.'

Attendants in livery were already spraying the ring. 'I never heard of an examination with water hoses playing about,' I said. 'I absolutely refuse to allow it, and we can only agree to an examination before a proper quorum and with our own vet in attendance.'

'Where's the owner?'

'Where d'you expect at one-fifteen? Lord Hindlip has gone home to Hill Street to eat, and has taken Miss Allsopp with him.'

'It will look bad if you refuse the examination. All we have to do to clear her is to get O'Hegan's signature, and he says he only needs to sit on her while she walks across that section of the ring and back.'

I legged the fellow up, resisting the temptation to pitch him right over the back and break his neck. He smelled of spirits though he did not look drunk. After I'd got some of the hoses cleared, I walked the mare across the ring and back, and out of it.

'Let me off,' the strange vet said, waving the steward away. 'No, no, can't zign that. Whizzler in her zlow pazes.'

A friend of mine from Melton was standing near us. 'We're in trouble, Dick,' I said to him. 'Take this mare and put her in her box, Lord Hindlip's box, and don't leave her for a single moment until I get back to her.' I ran to the telephone boxes. 'Is his lordship in?' I asked the footman.

'Just sitting down in the dining-room. There's a biggish crowd of them.'

'Ask him from me to get up mighty quick and come to the 'phone.'

'What is it, Marshall?' Lord Hindlip asked. Note that: no complaint about being disturbed.

'They've spun her for wind. A vet I don't know and smelling of drink. It's a frame. I advise you to get back here immediately and bring Miss Allsopp. Time's short, so go straight to the secretary's office. You should ask for Lord Lonsdale too. He won't be farther off than the Pillar Hall.'

So during the luncheon interval it was thrashed out in the secretary's office. I saw Lord Hindlip wade in there, Miss Diana in tow, and I watched silhouettes for a time on the glazed panel of the door. I had seen Lord Hindlip's determination make a super mare out of an ordinary one, and provided he had the time I believed he would triumph. I went to get the mare ready to perform again. The remarkable Man in Green was standing by the box with a flask of the blackest coffee and some foie gras sandwiches for the rider, who presently appeared.

'Marshy, we go in. It's all right.'

'Drink that coffee and eat your sandwiches while I shine up your boots, Miss Diana.'

When the horn blew for 'Finalists' the double doors opened
and Miss Allsopp, now as determined as her father, sailed
in first. After the show of walk, trot, canter, stand, rein back,
and walk, she was called in first, and there she stayed until
the numbers were taken and the rosettes and the Cup
presented. It was over. We had won the Balmanno Cup.
No, that is incorrect. The lady, the mare, and I had played
our parts. Lord Hindlip had won the Cup.

During Olympia some French officers from Saumur had
begun negotiations for my grey (well, you know me, I had
begun the negotiations). The night we won the Cup I rode
him in white tie and tails from Cadogan Place to Knightsbridge where I cantered him in and out of the traffic while
the foreign officers in their be-roped, be-frogged, and be-
tasselled uniforms made a grandstand of the Hyde Park Hotel
steps. I sold him, and I sold him well. He too had greatly
benefited in steadiness and wisdom from his sojourn in
London during the season. Next morning I saw the little
chestnut off in her box on the long journey to Derbyshire.
I never heard of her being shown again.

Horseless in London, and feeling lost and depressed, I
went back to Hill Street. There was to be a big dinner party
and dance that night. The valet was working on my tails,
removing the signs of my midnight ride. I suddenly wanted
to be back in Dorset among the slow-spoken but sharp-
witted farmers.

Years later I found, between the lining and the material
of the tail coat given to me by Mr J. Hyams, three pale grey
hairs. It took me a long time to remember the horse that
had left them there.

20

Constance, Duchess of Westminster

An increasing number of people seem to find the English summer unsatisfactory. They beetle off to countries where it's so hot that the grass doesn't grow, the sweet rain doesn't fall, the sky is a brazier without a lovely cloud from one rim to t'other, and to enjoy your drink you have to put ice in it. As something of a dealer, I looked forward to the summer because it provided me with grass, and a cheap means of keeping temporarily such horses as I was able to buy in. As a riding man and, I hope, a sportsman, I've never seen much wrong with our weather except that we get too many floods and frosts in winter, and National Hunt racing seldom gets a fair crack of the whip. I've been abroad quite a bit, and I'm perfectly aware that we English live in a perpetual mist. I'm not talking now of our talent for self-deception and self-congratulation, but of our weather. And in my opinion it's the mist, the thickness in the air, that makes an English summer's day so wonderful, so uncloying an experience.

It was on such a day, and it was at Hurlingham, watching a game of polo between Eton and the Jodhpurs that I saw Constance, Duchess of Westminster, for the first time. The light through the trees was a warm gold in colour. The ponies quickly grew tired, as though they found it hard to breathe. Spectators moved slowly, not listlessly, but as though all movement had been retarded by the warmth, the texture of the afternoon. Noises seemed muted. The Duchess's son-in-law, Captain Filmer-Sankey, was playing exceedingly well

for Eton, who in the end just won a great struggle. Lady
Ursula, one of the daughters, was walking about in a hat
as big as Bedfordshire. But it was the Duchess who took the
eye. What poise, what breeding, what unstudied elegance
and authority!

At that time of course I did not know her, except by sight,
and never for a second imagined that I would. I met her,
however, as soon as I began to work with and for Stanley
Young because she lived in our country with her second
husband, Captain Lewis, her daughters, Lady Mary and
Lady Ursula Grosvenor, and Captain Filmer-Sankey. They
were at Hazelgrove House, Sparkford. The driveway ran in
under an arch at the Yeovil side of the village, or you could
walk straight into the park from the back yard of the Sparkford Inn. The Duchess sized me up remarkably quickly
as a nagsman who, if he did not improve every horse he rode,
at least would not harm any horse, and when you have said
that you have said a lot. From my first ride for her she used
me increasingly. I employ the word 'used' in its accurate sense
because wherever horses were concerned the Duchess was
not like the other rich men and women with whom my trade
brought me in touch. She knew everything and she saw
everything. Without being autocratic she was authoritarian.
I think you know me well enough by now to see that I was
always what some people would call 'fussy' about horses.
I liked to have every horse under me fit and comfortable and
happy and perfectly turned out. I had little to fear and
much to gain from an employer as expert, as demanding, as
she. I wish she had employed me more, but of course she had
her own staff, and I was only there for special horses, special
occasions, shows, hunter trials, breaking, schooling. The
Duchess, and I mean this emphatically as a compliment,
could have been a horse dealer. Horses were in her Irish
blood (she was Miss Cornwallis-West before her marriage).
I never met a more interesting person, and from our first
meeting to our last I found it incomprehensible that her

marriage to the Duke had packed in. The Hazelgrove contingent helped to enliven the already lively Blackmore Vale scene, particularly on those Tuesdays in the Sparkford Vale. Both Lady Ursula and Lady Mary went extremely well, as did Captain Filmer-Sankey, though the Duchess liked to poke fun at him and at his two 'screws', as she insisted on calling Croft House and Aubretia. Screws or no, each was good enough to win the Grand Military Gold Cup.

On the day Queen Alexandra died, the Sparkford Vale (which, like the Cotley and other notable packs of harriers, hunts the fox) met at Kingweston, near Somerton. The sad news came when we were all mounted, and the Master about to move off to his first draw. He decided, in deference to the memory of so gracious a lady, not to hunt. You know what it is when you are keyed up to perform in a sporting country such as that, and mounted as we were, when fog or frost or anything else intervenes. The let-down is intolerable. Well, that morning our party decided to ride straight home to Hazelgrove, seven miles across country, without using a gateway or a road. I was on a promising youngster that Her Grace had just bought off Joe Hogan of Limerick. He was 'proper Irish' as I soon found out. Once he began to 'gas' he'd have jumped into the pit of hell and out again. Lady Mary was on Philipino, on which I had many show ring wins for Her Grace and also won the Lord Tredegar Hunter Trials, and the four or five others were just about our equals. Off we set, cantering steadily on in extended order, sweeping over that lovely bit of vale. And it ended just right. We came to the brook, the last obstacle before Hazelgrove. Lady Mary, for once, took Philipino over the bridge, but I had a go and the young horse made a mess of it. In we both went among the mud and weed. I had a job to get him out, but he was all right, and none the worse for it.

He was a typical Irish middleweight, and we won a good few prizes, he and I, that summer. He was queer about mounting and nothing I could do cured him, so I got very artful with a silk handkerchief, which much amused the watching Duchess. That was how I used to get the judge safely in the saddle when we were showing, just flick a big coloured handkerchief across my horse's nearside eye at the moment of danger, as though flicking away a persistent fly. It was quite exciting and, remarkably enough, it always worked. As autumn approached, though, Her Grace decided to have a deal with him and she sold him to the Master of the Quorn, Major A. E. Burnaby (the one who *began* to curse the heir to the throne). I should think the little horse went wonderfully well in front of that galloping field. The Duchess liked to ride him. We could never get her up on him side-saddle, he just wouldn't have it, but she rode him a lot cross-saddle. I was surprised that she sold him but goodness, she did enjoy a deal! Everything in her stables got sold in the end, and of course that's the way it should be—keep bringing on new blood. Philipino and Twink were sold, after we had done well with them, both showing and hunter-trialing. There were no Three-Day Events then or we should have been doing that like mad. I was told to take Philipino to the Whaddon Chase to show him to Lady Rosebery. And she bought him at the Duchess's figure (unless there was a secret knockdown between them).

I rather think Twink went to the same knowledgeable buyer. He was a grey, up to weight, and a beauty. What a horse he was in the deep! He had the strength, the quality, and the brain to cope with any obstacle and to survive any hunt. Yet even he, whom the Duchess and all of us loved, had a small vice. You'd be hacking him home in the network of small roads that criss-crosses the favoured Sparkford Vale. You would come to a crossroads and know that home lay to the right. Twink would decide it lay to the left, and he'd take you that way whatever you did. I had ways and means of persuading him, and even then it was difficult. I believe it took Lady Mary, one evening, an extra six or seven miles to get him back to his stable.

I remember The Sheik, another good-looking horse belonging to Her Grace. He wasn't the easiest of hunters, but he showed extremely well, and had one of the handsomest blood heads in England. I soon won a Novice class at Olympia with him. The Duchess had been waiting for that.

'Sell him if you can, the sooner the better.'

My wartime friend, the aristocratic bookmaker Tommy Graves, took me to Buck's Club that evening, and he was asking around if anyone wanted a really lovely lightweight blood hunter for his girl or his wife. A tall young man came up and asked where the horse might be seen. He was Lord Haddington, who'd recently married a Canadian, Miss Cooke. Soon we were out in the night air, had collected Lady Haddington in his car, and were on our way to Olympia. I got the Duchess's show hunter into a bridle and a side-saddle, thinking the lady would be satisfied with just sitting on him in the collecting ring. Like her husband, she was wonderfully good-looking, and she wore that night a silver sheath of a dress. Diamonds shone in her hair and at her throat.

Lord Haddington gave her a leg up, and somehow she adjusted her evening skirt to the saddle. She felt his mouth and rode him straight off, out of the doors and into the Addison Road. It was the most exotic sight imaginable, both horse and woman dressed for great events, not a hair of either out of place, jewels, dress, and horse's bright chestnut coat all gleaming under the lights of Olympia. Tommy begged her to ride him into and round the main ring, but of course she refused. She cantered him in the collecting ring, did a couple of figures of eight, reined back and pronounced her verdict in one word.

'Divine.'

'Is the Duchess here tonight?' Lord Haddington asked me.

'Yes she is. I'll just see this horse back in his box and comfortable, and then I'll take you both to Her Grace.'

'My wife adores your lightweight,' Lord Haddington began

when we were seated, 'but I fear that you'll want an awful lot of money for him.'

'Oh no, especially not off you,' the Duchess said, thoroughly in control. 'In any event, if you really want the young horse you can always sell a jewel—there are any amount of those in your family. I've sold most of mine. I'd much rather have horses than,' she glanced at Lady Haddington, 'emeralds or rubies.' She sold him the horse for six hundred pounds, and Lady Haddington found it too much of a handful in the hunting field. However, the last I heard of the Sheik, he was winning hunter 'chases with Lord Haddington up.

That particular horse originally came from Mr Tom Richards, and I truly believe Her Grace had only paid one hundred pounds for him. When he had won at Olympia and had been well sold she asked Mr Richards to visit her at Hazelgrove in order to 'make an adjustment'. She was fair and straight, but never soft. There was method in everything she did. It was an education to observe the fun she managed to derive from running her good, but after all comparatively economical, stables. . . . As for that Olympia deal, I don't remember getting anything out of it—except enjoyment.

In the year Sir Arthur Cory-Wright nearly swept the board, at Olympia 1932 it would be, I rode another good light-weight for the Duchess, and again won the Novice class, but got beaten in the Open by Sir Arthur's Home Rule. Sir Arthur won the Heavyweight with Cinnamon and the Ladies with The Duke. Cinnamon was a strapping great brute with collar marks on him from the plough in Ireland. That did not stop him from being the star of the show. My God! He was a horse, and he just suited Harry Gale who had the ride. I remember Harry asking Mr Tom Hobbs, Sir Arthur's stud groom, 'Have ye got him nice and coomfortable inside then, lad?' Mrs Alfred (later Lady) Munnings had the ride on The Duke, and that was a combination and a half. She was one of the world's real topnotchers in the saddle, not surprisingly since she was the daughter of 'Odol' (of the snow-white teeth) Haynes who had the big livery stables in Oxford Street. I always then thought I'd rather see Mrs Munnings in the saddle than look at her husband's paintings, and I still would.

Most of the foreign officers competing in the jumping events gravitated round 'Banker' Loewenstein, and he decided as it was a vintage year, to buy the best four hunters in the show and to take them and a big bunch of the foreigners straight up to Thorpe Satchville after Olympia. Hearing of this from a reliable source, I reasoned that he would be torn between my mount, the Duchess's chestnut and possibly two others. I'd known the Banker hunting in Leicestershire since I was a nipper, and I took care to give him one or two special little unofficial displays. I could make that horse do *haute école* or anything, bar blow his nose.

'We've got a lovely young horse here, Captain Loewenstein,' I told him. 'He's for sale, you know, if Her Grace could get the right buyer.'

'Would you happen to know what sort of figure the Duchess might be prepared to consider?'

'I should think around the two thousand pound mark.'

'So. With the Duchess's permission, please contact Mr Hobbs with regard to transport. I should like to take your horse with the Cory-Wright trio to Melton the day after the closure of Olympia. The following day, if you will accompany the horse, when we have tried him and the others we shall discuss terms. If we fail to agree on a sale I shall send you and the horse at my expense back to the Duchess's place in Somerset.' That was how he talked, rather like a dictionary.

I hurried to Her Grace with the good news and she gave me her lowest figure on the horse and urged me to take the greatest possible care of him until the deal was struck and Captain Loewenstein's cheque was in my pocket.

'I don't trust Continental stable management in the English climate,' she said. Note that.

It was an experience, nostalgic yet pleasant, for me to stay at Thorpe Satchville Hall. When we were boys Otho Paget lived there, and we loved him, and his hospitable house. During my last year at Hickling, Mitchell and I had gone down regularly to school hunters for an American, Mr Mendelsohn in the Cottesmore country. He was elderly, had taken to hunting late in life, and was doing well at it. On the way home we usually dropped in at Thorpe Satch-ville. Mr Paget would show us his beagles and always give us something to eat and drink. He was a man who got on with boys.

In the course of time he sold the house to Captain Alfred Loewenstein, 'Banker' Loewenstein as we knew him in the horse world. He was a Belgian, dark and foreign-looking, married with a boy at Rugby. He hunted with three packs, and went like a whistle mounted on the best blood horses that money (and I mean money) could buy. Beautifully schooled, they would stand right back and jump for miles. Many a time I watched him in the hunting field. He held his whip in his left hand and shoved the other hand right forward on the wither. He rode into all his fences like that, never touching the horse's mouth at all. Horses went well for him. I should have liked to have had the supplying of them, but never had the luck to sell directly to him.

He had acquired, in addition to Thorpe Satchville Hall, Croxton Park near Waltham-on-the-Wolds. Many a day's fun we had as boys on the pretty, heart-shaped race course in the Park, little meetings with five flat races and two over hurdles and everyone knowing everyone, except for the cotton people out of Nottingham. But the Banker bought (or possibly rented) that remarkable stretch of grass as a landing ground for his private aeroplane, a very unusual possession in the early thirties. And he was to end his life from it. He fell out of the blinking thing, crossing the Channel to Belgium.

On that Sunday morning at Thorpe Satchville the

foreigners had all four Olympia champions out for a trial under the park trees. The jabbering, cackling, and laughter seemed extraordinary to me in that setting where I would keep remembering Otho Paget's broad figure. Strange yellow and scarlet and milky drinks, drinks seldom then seen in England, were carried round. All four horses were as genuine as they were handsome. They were quickly sold. The figure I got for ours was one thousand eight hundred pounds. He was six, but very much a lightweight, and the Duchess had reckoned his value to a shilling. I knew she would be pleased. I don't know what the others fetched. Cinnamon's price must have been astronomic.

All four horses were sweating. They were led about under the trees with their saddles off. I saw our chestnut with his coat beginning to stare in the damp, chilly atmosphere. So I went over, took him from the stable boy who had him, led him into the sunshine, and whisped and rubbed him until he was dry, talking to him all the time to settle him down. While I was busy with him (though it was no longer my job, since the horse was sold) the Banker's stud groom, a Belgian, came up, breathing heavy. He disapproved. A fat lot I cared.

'I'd let this 'oss go inside if I were you,' I told him. 'You'll find he always needs extra clothing, for he's the thinnest-skinned, chilliest cuss you can imagine.'

I gathered from his reply that he did not believe in coddling, and that our horse must take his chance with the others. If he got cold they would improve his circulation with exercise.

Within a month he had died of pneumonia.

One Horse Leads to Another

I SUPPOSE the horse trade, like the slave trade, goes far
back into pre-history, yet it has this in common with nuclear
fission, it's quite easy to start a chain reaction. Often it starts
unexpectedly, one horse leading to another. Take that
lame horse of Arthur Brake's for example, the one from
Skibbereen; he wasn't mine, I wasn't trying to sell him,
and yet I can count up to twenty direct sales resulting
from him. I'll stick to the facts, and give you the beginning
of it.

Limington, not far from Yeovil in Somerset, is a pleasant
village; but far more important, it is the seat, eyrie, or H.Q.
of the Clan Brake, who have brought so many fine horses
to Dorset and Somerset, and who always had and have the
knack of making horses go. For a spell in the 1930s I had
some boxes in Limington, and I was at Arthur Brake's house
one night after hunting, both of us in slippers before a wood
fire, when he jumped to his feet.

'I wanted to do some dressings,' he said. 'And I've let the
boys go. Will you come with me and hold one or two?' He
picked up a tin of powder and a spatula. When we got to
his stables he walked up behind a horse and began dabbing
at his heels with the powder.

'For heaven's sake!' I said. 'Let me get a halter on him and
hold up a leg. You'll catch yourself a kick and a half if you
go on like that.'

'People have been telling me so for twenty years, my

friend. But I haven't caught your kick yet, and maybe I never will.'

Next morning I was jogging past his house when he hailed me from the far end of the orchard. 'Just set that gate open, will you, and cup-cup this horse out. He's footsore and won't lead a step. I want to work him into one of those boxes at the end of the yard, don't matter which.'

The horse came quietly enough on three legs. He was carrying his off hind. I left, intending to put my own horse away and fetch a halter so that I might be of some help. When I got back I found Arthur Brake leaning against the yard wall, standing on one leg, and groaning. In the few minutes that I'd been away he'd gone fiddling with the lame leg and the horse had pasted him a real broadside, right on the muscle of the thigh. I fetched my man, Walter Travers. We carried him into the house and propped him on a couch. He was a strong man, and knew how to wear pain. That's something of an art, you know, and it's one that has to be mastered by devotees of the horse and the hound. Anyone who rides a great deal and goes well will feel grand for most of the time, but he'll have to pay for that extra well-being with the occasional breakage.

As we emerged from his house, fortified by a little of the Highland medicine he had prescribed to be taken orally for his damage, I said to Walter, 'Mr Brake's horse isn't footsore. If he were he'd be lame on the other hind as well. You hold him for me and we'll get a bran poultice all round that foot and coronet.'

In the evening I called again, thinking to cheer up Mr Brake. As I left I noticed that our horse patient was standing squarely on the foot. The pain had gone from it, and that could mean only one thing. Calling Walter to hold him, I took the poultice off and out popped a great thorn from the front of his pastern where the hair joined the hoof, and following it a fair amount of blood and matter. We fomented it clean, and left it to drain naturally. By morning it was healing, and the horse looked utterly different from the day before.

'Feeling any better?' I asked the human patient.

'By the Lord, I'm still queer with it. And it has turned all the dark and lurid colours in the spectrum.'

'Then the pain will lessen. He struck you on the strongest part of a riding man's frame—so soon after my lecture, too. If he'd had shoes on, you'd be in Yeovil Hospital and they'd be having a conference as to the wisdom of sawing off your poor old leg.'

'Cheerful beggar! If I feel there's something needs doing to any old horse I just can't wait, that's all. But I'll see they're held or tied up in future, if I remember to. I fear we won't get shoes on that one for a long, long time.'

'Would it do you any good if I were to prop you in that window and jog him past, and he going dead level?'

'You're joking. It was an ill-luck day I bought that horse. I was in Bandon Market and met a dealer who said he'd mount me on the best horse in West Cork. The meet was along Skibbereen way, and he went well up and down those crags and rocky outcrops and over the turf banks. But he came off the Fishguard boat hopping lame and he's drawn nothing but wrong numbers ever since.'

'Let's have him out then,' I said, when Walter and I had carried the invalid to a chair where the sunshafts slanted through to him. 'And here's a bit of a present for you.' The thorn was an inch and a half long. I'd put it in a matchbox and wrapped the box in coloured paper. (No doubt the festering had been coming to a head anyway. Moving the horse had loosened the thorn, and the poultice finally drew it.)

'Surely you're not going to ride him,' Walter said as he saw me pull on my gloves. 'He won't have been backed for months.'

'I want to give Arthur a show,' I answered, 'and in any event I saddled him up before breakfast and hooked him to the chain, and he looks a reasonable sort.'

That horse from Skib trotted out fine and utterly sound on the gravel before Arthur's window, so much so that I took him into the paddock, also visible to Arthur, and after giving him ten minutes of flexing exercise to take the stiffness from him I let him whisk round the set of small schooling fences. The Irishman was delighted with himself, and at my signal pulled back into a comfortable walk. I had intended just walking him in the sunshine till he cooled off.

'What horse is that?' A man was leaning on the gate, a tall fellow, slightly built, with a Norman sort of face. I recognised him with difficulty, for I had never before seen him except in hunting clothes. It was Captain Vivian, R.N., who lived at Clinger Farm with his unusually charming and intelligent wife, one of the Holfords of Duntish Court and County Meath. 'Is he one of Arthur Brake's? Is he for sale? Are you buying him, Captain Marshall?'

'No, I'm not buying. You'd best see Arthur himself. He's sitting in that window.' And I thought to myself, Now there's a bit of slow business. I believe I've gone and made a sale for Arthur, whereas all I really needed to do was put the Captain off, buy the horse, and then take my profit on him. I'm sure he wants him.

Almost every day hounds met, Captain Vivian was out hunting on a little black horse not absolutely up to his weight. He wasn't much of a horseman, but he had the heart of Nelson, fearless. He galloped it and clattered it about, pasting it over every kind of fence, and he fairly made it into an accomplished hunter. The trouble was that it grew bare and stale, a Rosinante. Even then it was allowed no respite from its tasks.

'You know, this little horse would do you, Marshall,' the Captain said to me out hunting a day or two after we had met at Arthur Brake's.

'I'm not sure I want to be done, sir.'

'Rest him and new him up a bit. You're bound to do well on him. I'll take a mere one hundred pounds on him because but for you I'd never have found that one of Brake's, which is more up to my weight.'

I bought him, and I can't remember any adjustment in that price, which in truth seemed reasonable, almost suspiciously so. Captain Vivian liked to have a deal and he was a hard man. It didn't take long, either, for the Captain's treatment of the horse to be explained. With more food and less work he came on, hand over fist, and got so full of himself he would buck until he dislodged his rider, no matter who. In those days I fancied I could sit on almost anything, but he had me more than once. And when you have to watch for a buck every instant you're on top there can be little pleasure in riding.

At that time I was living at Haydon Lodge, close by Evershott Station, and a few of my horses were stabled at Maiden Newton Rectory.

Mr Michael Hornby had a ride down the street on the ex-naval horse one day.

'I like him,' he said.

'That's half the battle,' I said.

'What would you take for him?'

'I'm asking one hundred and fifty pounds, and that's giving a horse like this away.'

'Seems reasonable. Does he kick hounds or is he yellow?'

'He has perfect hunting manners and he never turns his head. No, he's cheap because he's a young man's horse. He can be a shade cold-backed in the early morning. He needs masses of hard work.'

'Sounds just the job,' he said. He was hunting with the Cottesmore, and I let him take the black up there for a day's trial. He could ride, yet he got dislodged in no uncertain manner and I don't know whether only once or several times. He told me he thought the horse had a screw loose, and very properly he returned him to me.

Tattersalls with a full warranty was the answer to him. I sent up three. They were stabled overnight in stalls, and

when morning came Captain Vivian's black horse had
contrived to rub himself behind the knee. He was sore on it,
and a little inflamed, so I withdrew him.

In the course of the sale a sporting-looking customer
approached me, very tweedy.

'Pity about your black one,' said he. 'I was hoping to
put in for him. Looks as though he might suit me in Essex.'

'He'd suit you in Essex or any other country. There's
nothing he won't do.' (Except stop bucking.) 'Write his own
name if you ask him. But this is a horse that has been asked
some very *serious* questions without ever being found wanting.
A captain R.N., a rare good'n to go, has been hunting him
with the Blackmore Vale and the South Dorset three days a
week all season. He's never missed his turn. He's a really
clever hunter, and you won't find a harder horse in England.'
(Too true, you won't.)

'Well, Captain Marshall, if you can get the ache out of
that leg and can send me a clean vet's certificate in a week or
so, I'll give your reserve price for him.'

He had not asked me what my reserve price was. I had
in truth been hoping for one hundred and fifty pounds, and
would have accepted one hundred and twenty, but as things
had developed it seemed only wise to hold it up a bit. I
told him that two hundred and twenty guineas was the
reserve I put on him.

'All right then,' he said. 'But you must take one from
me for fifty pounds. He's a blood horse aged five and standing
sixteen hands.'

'Done,' said I, thinking, Talk about a pig in a poke?

My vet's certificate on the soundness of Captain Vivian's
little horse (by George! He was sound if ever horse was) soon
went off by post, and the horse himself by rail, to Essex
the following day. And the next day but one I got a message
that a horsebox had been drawn into Maiden Newton station
and that the addressee was me. I hung a bridle over my arm
and began to stroll off from the rectory stables, past the war

memorial to the station, when Mr Higginson happened to pass in his car. He had a friend with him whom I also knew.

A. H. Higginson, an American of the upper crust, was Master of two Dorset packs of foxhounds, first the Cattistock and then the South Dorset. He was a keen and in many ways brilliant foxhunter, and willing to spend his dollars to show other people sport. He also wrote books on hunting. Some of his hunting contemporaries thought him the oracle and others thought him half-cracked. That's life for you. He enjoyed himself, and I had any amount of fun out of him and with him. I even sold him a quad or two, and when you sold to him you had to be extra thorough and careful. He had not only an eye but also a nose for anything the least bit 'off'.

He was the last person I wanted to see that particular morning as I ambled towards Maiden Newton sidings to pick up a fifty-quid question-mark of a horse.

'Why hello, Marshall. Where are you off to with that bridle?'

'Got a new 'oss at the station, Master. Arrived from Essex.'

'Essex. If they can go on those ploughs they can go anywhere. Jump in,' he said, flicking open the door behind him.

It was only a couple of hundred yards to the sidings, and I dearly wanted to inspect the newcomer quietly on my own. I parried a dozen questions, to none of which could I put answers. Was ever a seller in an odder position? I expected the fifty-pounds throwout to be chronically unsound, or a roarer, or a devil, or all three . . . yet anyone who sells horses must be an optimist. My best bet was to be completely evasive, and of course not to breathe a suspicion of the origins in a swapping deal. I *was* evasive, and the volatile American responded in inverse proportion.

'Is he sold then?'

'No, he's not.'

'Then why don't you want me to have him?'

'I want you to have any horse you fancy.'

'Rot, Marshall. You're hedging.'

'I can't sell you a horse you haven't even seen.'

'Is he my sort? What hunt's he from?'

'You'll see him in a second,' I said. If only the ground would open and swallow him. Steeling myself for an encounter with a mystery animal that might well be vicious and was probably the ugliest horse west of a line drawn from Oxford to the Isle of Wight, I kept talking as I fiddled with the door. 'Hullo, my little fellow, what have they got you imprisoned here for, in this nasty box on wheels? . . .' I kept the patter going while I looked him over, surprised at the tame way he thrust his head into my bridle. He was charmed to see me, sniffed at my sleeves and gave me a soft, dreamy stare. To my way of thinking, he *looked* as nice a blood horse as you could want; clean legs, good feet, pleasant expression, sensible eye, deep chest, narrow but plenty of heartroom, a proper front on him. Heavens! I thought as I led him out, I bet you make a noise like a bull.

'Good looker,' A.H.H. said at once. 'Let's see him move.' I ran him up and down the road. One, two, three, four, just like clockwork. 'Moves fine,' he said. 'Let's have a saddle on him.'

I now had concluded that the strange horse must be either a rearer or affected by the bucking mania of the one I had just off-loaded. I fully expected to measure my length in one of Maiden Newton's delightful streets. He saddled up quite kindly. We could see no sign of nappiness. 'Lead him out, Walter, while I get my stick and gloves,' I said in undertones to my man. 'Hold him tight against the mounting block and don't let him so much as blink till I'm on.' There was no need for precautions. He stood still, then walked like a lamb into Mr Hawkins's Manor Farm stackyard and back past the doll-sized post office to the Dorchester-Crewkerne road. He trotted back to our observers, then repeated the process at the canter and came to a quiet halt just beyond them at the double gates in the high rectory wall. I reined him back five paces. I felt as though I were dreaming. Why in the world should anyone want to get rid of him? Perhaps he wouldn't jump, or was a crib-biter, or kicked hounds, or was unshoe-able?

'What's the lowest revenue required on him then?' Mr Higginson asked when he had ridden him about a little.

'Two hundred guineas to you, Master. Two hundred and forty to anyone else.'

'Hounds meet at The Acorn, Evershott, the day after tomorrow,' he said. 'If you ride him over to Cattistock to-morrow some time, after satisfying yourself that he's reliable over timber, I'll ride him on to the meet. Provided he goes well and is quiet with hounds I'll take him at two hundred, but I won't pay you for him until the first of May.

'It's a deal,' I said. 'Subject to his performance in the hunting field, and I've no worries on that score, none at all.'

I took the horse out to the paddocks and without over-facing him soon found that he jumped very nicely. Timber was the main thing for Mr Higginson. Many a time he said to me, or in my hearing, 'I like timber, I like an obstacle I can see through.' He'd go to considerable lengths to avoid jumping a Dorset bank, although it can be one of the more interesting obstacles. I made a fuss of the horse, kept him curious about his surroundings and his food, and saw to it that he was well strapped and that his shoes were one hundred per cent.

When I rode him at a walk over to the next village, Catti-stock, it was a warm April day. The farmers were at their spring sowings and all the countryside was in the waking bustle of growth that spells the end of another hunting season. I gave him plenty of rein as he ardently paced through the sunlight, moving his head slightly from side to side in the unforgettable manner of the English or Irish blood horse, curious, friendly, yet aloof. 'What's wrong with you, my beauty?' I kept asking, but he would not answer. Soon I was handing him over to the American stud groom at the hunt stables.

I was too old a hand to go anywhere near the hunt. I made myself scarce, saying, after Mark Antony, 'There let it rest. Mischief, thou art afoot, take now what course thou wilt.'

The telephone did not ring until well into the evening. 'Marshall?'

'Evening, Master. Hope you enjoyed your day.'

'I did.' A long and incredibly boring list of names and hunting clichés followed. That always happens after a day's hunting if you are unlucky enough to tap a Master of Foxhounds in full spate. God! It's hell!

'And the horse?' I prompted at long last.

'He went well, very well. In addition I was much amused.'

'How so?' I did not like his tone. I did not like it at all.

'A gentleman from Essex was staying at The Acorn to have a look at my hounds. There was a big turnout at the meet and that fellow came up under me, close to my boot and said, "I see you're on my horse." "You're mistaken," said I. "This is one of Captain Marshall's." "Don't I know it," said he. "I sent him off by rail to Maiden Newton two or three days ago." I need hardly add, Marshall, that I soon had it out of him how much you paid for that horse— fifty pounds it seems. That's why I told you I was much amused.'

'Did he not tell you that there was another horse involved in our deal?' I asked quickly. 'But in any event, if you don't want the thoroughbred I'll gladly have him back here first thing tomorrow morning. There are plenty of others who. . . .'

'Hold hard now,' he said. 'I happen to like that horse, and I'm keeping him according to our gentlemen's agreement. If you can turn up another like him for me, please do, but I warn you, your asking price goes under the microscope, you Shylock.'

I had hardly put down the receiver when the thing rang again. It was the man from Essex. *L'audace, toujours l'audace.*

'How's that nice little black horse?' I asked before he could get a word out save his name.

'Our hunting was just over when he arrived. He's turned out till the spring, and doing really well. I've wormed him. He had a high red-worm count. . . . I say, I fear I may have put my foot in it with your M.F.H. I had no idea you'd make such a quick sale. I thought you'd just loaned the horse to him.'

'Foot!' said I, 'foot! You put the whole ruddy leg in it.'

'But you weren't there. I had a childish hankering to be recognised as the former owner. I mean, it's pretty darned exciting to see a famous American M.F.H. on one that you foaled yourself.'

'Between ourselves,' I said, taking a pull at myself, and in truth quite overcome by the fellow's ingenuous approach, much as an old roué might suddenly succumb to a débutante, 'between ourselves, what's the matter with your horse, and why did you sell?'

'I took a fancy to your black one, and I like to ride a different one every season.'

'Now listen,' I said, scenting business, 'if you have any bother at all with that black horse, get in touch with me, and I'll either come and sort him out or I'll take him back. And be sure . . . what sort of saddles do you use, leather or linen lined?'

'Leather.'

'Well get some good sheepskin numnahs made to fit 'em, and ride that 'oss in them, even at exercise. He's got no flesh on his back at all.' That notion had just come to me while I talked on the telephone. And the ex-naval black horse went so well in Essex the following season that I developed a lucrative one-man trade in hunters there. It was a rich field.

That's what I mean by chain reaction.

With the Meynell

Soon after that wonderful young huntsman and hound-breeder, Sir Peter Farquhar, gave up the Mastership of the Meynell Hunt which he shared from 1931–34 with Sir William Bass (there's an evocative name!), I moved north to that country.

I'd seen an advertisement in *Horse & Hound*. The proprietors of the Dog & Partridge at Tutbury wanted an expert to bring on some show horses. For one reason and another I applied, and got the job. A part of me had hankered for the bracing air and the great foxhunting spread of the Midlands. Yet after Dorset which was, and indeed still is, unspoiled much by man except in suburban Poole, I saw with dismay in the Nottingham, Derby, and Burton-on-Trent areas the spread of shoddy building over some of the best of the heart of sporting England. Still, the townspeople in their cars and with their extraordinarily fixed ideas about houses and gardens were in truth just beginning to seep out into the countryside, and the hunting remained very good.

My re-entry to the Midlands was unpropitious. The north-country horses I'd been engaged to show were nowhere near the quality required. I never relished the comforts of inns and taverns, and to live even in so distinguished a one as the Dog & Partridge was not to my taste. However, I'd taken the job and I fulfilled my contract, and in truth the summer passed like lightning, since year by year I seemed to get more rides in the show ring.

At the Burton-on-Trent Show, which was held in the park
of Baroness Burton at Rangemore, I had just shown a good
quality hunter belonging to Captain Maurice Kingscote,
and had won with him. I was standing hat in hand, enjoying
the sun on my head and the familiar sounds and smells of a
country show, when I saw a flurry of movement behind the
stands. It was made by the most handsome young horse I'd
seen in a year of handsome horses. Looking up his number
in my catalogue, I found that he was by Farman, a sire
available to local foxhunters, and that his owner was Mr
Edward Major of Castlehays Park near Tutbury. I knew
Mr Major by sight. He was a sporting farmer, one of the
spearhead brigade of the Meynell; I'd always liked the cut
of his jib, and by George! I liked his horse even more.

They were at loggerheads. That horse, if he felt like it,
could be a terror, a headstrong swine. It's no use a rider
relying on strength with such a one because a man's
physical strength as compared with a horse's is like a
Georgian teahouse compared with the Empire State Building.
Quite soon Mr Major was in the saddle, but the young horse
put in a ripsnorter that would have dislodged Mr Sponge
himself. By that time I was near enough to catch the loose
horse. I began to soothe him in the usual ways, hand and
voice. The owner however (who had soon righted himself
after a dive into the hard summer turf), had other ideas.
He was a regular grenadier, an Empire builder, a thin-
red-liner, a lash-me-to-the-master, a death-or-glory wallah.
You see, many of the best people in the world, the very
best, treat the horse as a challenge to their own courage and
willpower. And of course with every man (or woman) on
every horse there come moments when determination is
vital; but there are other and more frequent moments when
only the wily ones may find the answer.

'He'll have you again,' I warned Mr Major, looking at
his horse's rolling eye, masterful expression, and hunching
back. Everything about him said. 'If a fight's in the offing,

314

lay on, MacDuff.' There was more than half an hour to
go before the start of their Novice Hunter class. I wondered
if that noble specimen could not be wooed out of his fret.
'If you could get him going quietly he'd win that lot,' I said.

'Going quietly, says he! They're all the same, those Farman
brutes. He's set on making a fool of himself, and of me.'

'Why not let me see what I can do? I'll try it with pleasure,
Mr Major, free, gratis. It's my job, d'you see, to find the key
to any horse, and this one is worth a lot of trouble.'

He looked hard at me. Some owner-riders might have got
their dander up, not he. 'That's handsome of you, Captain
Marshall,' he said. 'I reckon you won't do any harm, so go
ahead and see if you can do a bit of good. What can *I* do?'
he added.

'Sit down on that bench. Light your pipe. Keep quite
still, and silent.'

He laughed. 'You imagine that young horse understands
English?'

'You bet he does. . . . I'll see what I can tell him.' I led
the horse quietly away from Thermopylae, undoing his girth,
moving his saddle back a little, loosening his curb chain and
his bridle, talking to him softly. We walked about, the pair
of us, his rein hooked loosely over my arm. Occasionally I
would stop to pick him some grass. Then on we would go
through the crowd again, like a boy walking his girl in a wood
and making up to her. Round behind the stand, in full view
of the pipe-smoking owner, I rubbed the young one's ears
and jaw, and put his saddle exactly right. That kind of thing
is vastly important with a difficult horse, and few amateurs
understood it. A little more talking and then, gently, gently,
I eased myself into the saddle until I sat there, feet dangling,
his reins lying among his plaits. He turned his strong head
and looked at me with a smile. 'What? Are you there? You
are a joke.'

I watched our class getting ready at the far end of the stand.
They entered the ring. I let them go round once, then joined

in in front of them and went on. They were all behind me, and that was the place for them. How he strode out! He was the Emperor after Austerlitz, he was the band of the Royal Scots Greys, he was a mackerel sky scudding before the westerlies over Bantry Bay, he was magnificent. We had the best of judges, Major Cantrell-Hubbersty of Raglan Hall, and by jingo! we were going well. He had eyes for none but us. The front was the place for a mettled youngster like him. He'd have fretted himself hot elsewhere. We cantered. We galloped. Shades of Sam Marshall of Hickling, how we tore round that ring! 'Easy boy, easy there, see, I give you your rein. You can have your head, my lad, it belongs to you, and the judge has called us in.'

'Now then, Marshall, I saw that bit of a performance behind the stand. Between ourselves, what did it mean?'

'There's nothing at all the matter with him. He'd got a piece of wheat straw no bigger than my thumbnail under his saddle and, you'd hardly credit it, it was driving him nuts.'

'Will he carry me? Is he quiet now?'

'He will, he is, I guarantee it.'

'God help you if he isn't.'

He had a ripping good ride and when he came back he said, 'Marshall, you stop there. *Don't move.*' And he put them all below us. Some of them were annoyed at it, but none of their mounts could hold a candle to him for looks, presence, and style, once he had simmered down. What appealed to me about him, and it was typical of a Farman animal, was that he looked a proper workmanlike, hard horse, ready to win a steeplechase or to charge at Balaclava. Baroness Burton's Farman was by Velocity, who won the Cambridgeshire, and of course he was put to many a top-class hunter mare because the Meynell was, and is to this day, a rich country of good dairy farmers, of brewers, and of established landed gentry.

Not long after, and not by accident either, I went exercising from Tutbury and negotiated the long slope to Castlehays, a tall red-brick house standing two miles up its own private road with a great range of farmsteading to one side of it. Open to the winds of nature, with views for miles nearly all round, it was a proper Wuthering Heights in bad weather and, to my mind, a paradise in good. As I drew near the buildings I came on a man ploughing behind a pair of heavy horses. The share grunted as the mould board turned the heavy, waxy soil with round pebbles in it and the field was coming up a teapot-brown sort of colour. Strong land. I'd have asked him where the boss was; then, to my surprise, I saw that it was Mr Major himself. He'd be thirty-one years old then, neatly put together, and with the expression and quiet manners of the Englishman who is neither from the south nor the north, but nearer the north in spirit. He showed no sign of stopping the plough just because I'd appeared, so leaving my horse standing at the edge of the field, I walked up the furrow with him.

'Why not tie him up?' he asked curiously.

'Because I've trained him to stand untied.'

He looked hard at the horse. 'Well, he has a leg in each corner,' he said in disparagement.

'How many more of those young Farman horses have you got on the farm?'

'A few, why?'

'I'd like to have the handling of them.'

'They *take* handling. How d'you make your living?'

'Breaking, making, and selling horses.'

'Is that the way of it? If you asked me the most difficult way to earn money I'd say that was it.'

'Oh, money. I never have any of *that* stuff.'

'That makes two of us then.'

'When could I have a squint at your youngsters?'

'Not today. I'm ploughing and I won't finish the headland till dark or later. Tomorrow's Sunday. I should get back to the house by midday. Come half past twelve and I can give you a bite to eat. Simple fare. I'm a bachelor.'

317

'So am I. . . .' I waited for a bit, listening to the slow surge of the heavy horses laying into their collars. 'I've got to leave the Dog & Partridge soon. They need my room. So I won't be around much longer.'

He said nothing, concentrating on his ploughing.

When I got inside the house it was even bigger than it looked from a distance, a solid pile, the King's property. My host was a tenant of the Duchy of Lancaster. His father and mother had been well-known farmers in Cheshire. They had taken Castlehays for their son, had left him to make the best he could of it on his own, and had themselves moved to yet another farm, on Epsom Downs. . . . There were boxes and buildings galore at Castlehays and he had numerous horses that needed working. He had not the time required for the job. It was enough to make one's mouth water, but I sized him up and kept mum. He was not the sort that any man could push. After lunch, excellent fare and plenty of it, prepared by Mrs Farrell, his housekeeper, we moved to the sitting room, where we sat before the fire, smoking our pipes. I was thinking that I should not outstay my welcome, when suddenly he spoke.

'Would you like to hang up your hat?'

Just like that. I was almost too taken aback to answer. It seemed too good to be true. That wonderful great place, all the room in the world, a bustling farm and one's forage right on the spot. . . . I said yes, and it was one of the best yesses of my life.

I went to lunch and stayed three years.

We fitted together like lock and key. I was able to have my own furniture, some of it from Hickling, around me. I was a lot older than he, and that made it easier. There was never, that either of us can recall, a harsh word between us.

On the nights before hunting I'd plait up both horses in the stables a few yards from the front of the house, and then go into the kitchen where the pair of us would pull all our tack to bits and clean it thoroughly and our boots and clothes until both we and our horses were completely ready for the morrow's sport. The Meynell was, and I believe still is, a splendid country to ride over, but hunt followers were rather more carefully organised than usual, to avoid giving umbrage to the farmers over whose land we rode. It was the practice of the Field Master to hold us on any road that ran parallel to the track of hounds, and not far from it, to one side or the other. That was where I ran into trouble. I was there to sell horses or to show how effective my schooling might be. On such occasions I found it more than flesh and blood could bear, to stick to the road. Ted was ploughing one hunting day when hounds ran towards Castlehays, and he saw the whole field bottled on a small road while fifty yards off the line of the road I was coming towards him on his own Farman horse, jumping something like twenty perfect (and quite easy) fences. After that I received a severe wigging from one of the Joints, Sir Ian Walker, and Ted also was told that if he could not keep me in better order, and teach me some hunting manners, he had better get rid of me. He did no such thing, and incidentally that little foray clinched a deal, and we sold the horse.

When Ted was working on his farm, and by Jove he was a worker! He would scarce lift his head when the hunt passed, let alone jump on a horse or into a car and follow. Yet when he was out hunting he was hunting, and if hounds ran over his own farm he would not stop even if there should be a crisis.

He was a warrior of the hunting field, the sort who was full-stretch all day from the meet until they said, 'Good night, gentlemen.' He was determined to be in what he called the first eleven, in other words the first flight. He would come home in the evening, happy, and his voice would be gone and his horse cooked. You never saw such a fellow for love of foxhunting. His coat was all scarred and his breeches and boots and hat. I said when I first stayed at Castlehays, 'By Heaven! Here's a coat's been in an argument with a bull-finch.' But it was always the same, and if he bought a new

one and the hounds ran he'd get it straight into battle.
It was his nature to treat hunting as a personal physical
challenge. There are many fine foxhunters like that. They
enliven the hunting field and they step up the prices and the
demand for blokes like me, for they *use* horses and they have
to be well mounted. Young horses, especially out hunting,
were merely a nuisance (as they can be). He would not ride
a young one if he could help it, and if he did he would get
impatient, fearing that the necessary fiddling about might
cost him a good hunt.

'Don't cuss him, you're spoiling him,' I would say.

'I hate riding these young'ns.'

'Change over. I like 'em.'

Ted Major was all alone with the hounds at the end of a
famous run when they killed their fox in Hanbury Churchyard and I expect (knowing him) he jumped the wall to get
in there. When he really got going nothing would stop him
until he was floored, and then he'd be up and asking for
more. One evening when he had some people in playing
bridge I sat listening to their talk, and heard him give this
description of a run:

'They were drawing Birchwood and it was blank. The
field were all waiting on the road, while hounds just feathered
across in front of them and into a thicket. Charlie was in
there, and away he went, hounds with him, on his brush,
catching all the field flat-footed. Young Captain Jaffray,
hunting hounds, was in front of me by a length and we
galloped down a short lane. Then we started to jump. Sixteen or eighteen fences we took at racing pace. Not a strand
or wire, not a gap nor a gate to go at. Everything we did was
right until we jumped into a four-acre field. The boundary
was a brook with a stiff fence either bank, the far one a black
bullfinch. With the brook there you hadn't a hope in hell.
Captain Jaffray went out through the gate, but I didn't. I
drove him at it with a roar. He landed in the gravel in the
water, sliding and splashing about, scrambling somehow up

the bank and, me still roaring, either crawled or jumped or tore his way through the bullfinch. We stood on the other side, in the clear, and we were shaking. Then we were off again, and as good as before, fence after fence, until he got into Baggot's Park, a big place. They pushed him through that and then we ran on over the banks, pretty good, but not so good as the start with that wonderful gallop. . . . Well, quite two months later we met at the Spurrier place, Marston Hall, and at the meet Mr Cedric Boyd from Hollybush Hall came to me. "I've asked everyone who hunts with us in a black coat, bar you, Ted, this question," he said. "Who was in front of me that glorious run from the Birchwood spinney?" "You've found him," I said. "I was in front with Captain Jaffray." "Then how did you get out of that four-acre field? I looked at that obstacle, and I looked again, and I'll swear it was impossible for any horse to get over or through it." "Well, it's not much good *looking* when hounds are on," I told him.'

The only way I could help Ted on the farm, I felt, was by concentrating on the horses and making a job of them, making them pay. Horses take time, time, and more time. And when Ted had seen how I went about them he let me alone. Occasionally I'd help him with his sheep when he was castrating or separating lambs or some such easy jobs. He was very conscious, much more than I, because he was so determined to succeed with his farm, that there was a second war with Germany in the offing. In spite of his passion for hunting he thought as much of his heavy working horses as of the hunters and young stock. The first task he gave me was breaking in a whacking great Shire mare, Smiler. I put the long reins on her and broke her in the classic manner. Ted was much amused. He really was good company and because of his popularity in the neighbourhood and my skill (if I may be so bold as to be honest) our combination went well. They used to send him all sorts, hunters, show horses, polo ponies, and I would give them their lessons. It amused him to see me riding a polo pony or even a hunter about his farm with stick and ball. Ah, those were good days! And I was and am grateful to him.

Our friendship was the more unusual in that our tastes after dark were entirely different. The accommodation at Castlehays included a billiard room with an excellent table. Ted liked a game of billiards or snooker, but I would never play with him.

'Why not give it a try, Howard?' he must have said many times.

'Sorry, I hate ball games, except cricket.'

'But you knock a polo ball right round the farm. If that isn't a ball game, what is? You've obviously got an eye. . . . Oh well, if you won't, you won't.'

His idea of a pleasant evening was to have three people in and play cards. I always hated cards. I'd sit beside them, if I wasn't out elsewhere, listening to their talk or reading a book.

As we came to know each other, Ted and I did a bit of dealing in combination. We went once to see a horse near Melton. In the dealer's yard Ted nudged my arm and pointed at a clipped-out chestnut in a loose box. 'That one looks like going hunting.' But the one for sale was in a near-by paddock, unclipped. He was, as Ted said, 'A good-lived 'un.' The fellow got on him and took him over a couple of fences at a very slow pace. He was a grand sort and up to weight, and the price was very much right. I advised Ted to buy him without further trial. For once he jibbed at my advice. 'I asked him to rein the horse back,' he said. 'And he pretended not to hear me. We ought to see him reined back. He may not have a mouth. Or ride him yourself, Howard.' There was little time, and he paid up; I was sure that horse was genuine, and so he proved to be but for one embarrassing fault that we soon discovered. When put into his fast paces nobody could turn him. I don't think it was his mouth, I think he had a bee in his bonnet.

'I left it entirely to you, Howard,' Ted said. 'When I'm with you I reckon to know all about cows and nothing about horses. And you sailed in and bought him without even giving him a gallop. Remember how that dealer just crawled him over those fences? No wonder he was unclipped and turned out. The fellow had no customers—bar you, sucker.' He was right, of course. He had been intuitive enough to suspect the horse while I'd been too taken by his scope and strength. I got on the telephone and I gave Mr X the works, urging him to take the horse back and refund Ted his money. Would he do that? Would he hell! I'd known that man since Hickling days, and liked him. I've never spoken to him since. When I was with Beeby, too, as I pointed out to him, I put many hundreds of pounds worth of business his way. In the end I told him what I thought of him and slammed down the receiver. What to do? I clipped out that horse, worked on his coat, mane, and tail, took him to Leicester Repository, and sold him without warranty for a good deal more than Ted had paid for him. The buyer was a heavyweight from a Scottish pack. I hope the horse didn't gallop him slap into the side of a Cairngorm. So, I got Ted his money back, but he used to tell the story against me.

While I stopped in the Meynell country I got in touch with the Bellvilles of Papillon Hall, who had been so very kind to me when I worked for Geoffrey Brooke. The Bellvilles still hunted a lot in their own country, the Fernie, and with the neighbouring Atherstone. Major Frank, the senior member of the family at Papillon, asked me to look out for any suitable hunters. I judged the Farman stuff too hot for him, and it was some time before I arranged to take him a horse. He was nine years old, had mouth, manners, and was an impeccable jumper. As it was rather more than thirty miles from Castlehays Park to Papillon Hall, and I had another horse to drop off in the Pytchley country, I left home early in a hired box.

Meanwhile Major Bellville had sent me a wire (but it missed me) saying, 'I've had a fall and am hurt. Don't come today.'

When we drew up on the gravel sweep before the house young Mrs Bellville appeared in something of a fluster. She had begun to explain that her father-in-law was in a bad way, when he appeared with short, tottering steps, dressed as usual in tweeds with a braided Homburg hat. He was a very tall person, something of the London lawyer type. Nothing would do but that, as I'd had the nuisance of the journey, I should produce the horse, and the young lady was instructed to bring round a car. He got in with the greatest difficulty and was driven by her to a vantage point. I knew the park well, and my mount was a winner of hunter trials. He sailed round that lovely place at a brisk canter. When we stopped at the car the invalid had worked himself up into a state of excitement.

'They're taking me to London in an ambulance to put me to rights,' he said. 'But I can't let this horse go back, Marshall. I won't be longer than a day or so. You stop here till I come back, there's a good fellow. You must hunt tomorrow, we've plenty of horses for you to ride. My daughter-in-law will look after you. But I don't know that I often saw a hunter go better in cold blood, and he isn't leaving here until I've ridden him.'

While we were talking the ambulance arrived, and he was taken away. I enquired about his accident. . . . He had been going through a heavy self-shutting gate, following other riders. The gate was swinging at him on the off side, so he slipped that iron (they were only walking through) and stuck his foot out to take the weight. His foot and spur went through the bars of the gate. Meanwhile his damned horse got frightened, and backed, and the toe of his hunting boot and the spur held like a fishing hook entangled in the gate. He was torn apart. We had no news of him that night, at our rather sombre dinner party. The operation was to be the following day.

I had a roughish day's sport with the Fernie. Major Bellville's brother was out, and he could scarcely see. 'Is that you, Marshall?' he asked, riding up to me and putting his face about two feet from mine. 'Oh yes, I see it is. How nice to see you again! What's that you're on? Oh, one of Frank's, I see. . . . I can't see the hounds. Is that them, down there?'

'They're just coming up through the farm. They'll be with us directly, if we stand where we are.'

'I can hear 'em,' he said, cheerfully. Such a game and tragic figure. He was killed later in the hunting field.

We were dining that night when young Mrs Bellville was asked by the butler to go to the telephone. It, or at any rate the nearest one, was in a recess near the dining-room. I heard her cry, 'Oh no!' Then she burst into tears. It was a long time before she managed to come and face me with the news. He had died under the anaesthetic. Operations were more dangerous then.

So I telephoned for a box, and took that hunter back to Castlehays. He sold within the week to somebody else, and I was glad to see the back of him. I was fond of the Bellville family and of their house.

During my time at Castlehays I took to riding for Mr Harry Frank, who kept a fine lot of hunters at Wooton-under-Edge on the Duke of Beaufort's boundary. I'd have one Frank horse over at a time so that I could really concentrate on it, and they did well at Wuthering Heights, I can tell you.

In 1938 Mr Frank was good enough to send me a really tremendous My Stars gelding called Jupiter II. He had been hunted before he came to me, and was said to have gone extra well. Then he'd been put into some small show where he had moved so freely that he knocked over a judge and also the table holding the silver cups. Jupiter really was the hell of a big, quality, Roman-nosed thoroughbred, with a front on him such as is seldom seen, indeed it looked as though the Creator had thought he'd been over-generous in the matter of front, so had rubbed off the end of the horse's nose. He was a headstrong and bold horse by temperament. I judged

there was only one way with him, and that was to start
him again, right from the beginning. That I did. I mashed
him until I had him let right down. I stood him in a box
and mouthed him until he gave with pleasure to his bridle
and his head carriage came right. Then I drove him, to
Ted's amusement, all over the farm in the long reins. My
favourite place with him was the stackyard. I could in the
end manœuvre him any way I wanted. He'd do everything
for me but stand on his head. Then I backed him very very
slowly and carefully. It took time, and it took most of my
time, but by the end of it that horse and I went together,
and when we started showing him I could put any judge on
him with confidence that he would have the ride of his life.
We went through the chosen range of shows like a dose of
salts, winning everywhere, and at the International Horse
Show at Olympia we were Champion Novice and winner
of the Middleweights, and finally Champion Hunter. I
reckon that Championship if it was won anywhere was won
in Ted Major's stackyard, just as those wonderful multiple
centuries of the great Don Bradman were really made when
as a boy he used to bounce a golf ball against a wall, hitting
it time after time with a cricket stump. Mr Frank had sold
Jupiter prior to Olympia to Mr J. E. Ryan of Unionville,
Pennsylvania. The price was a good one, naturally, but it
would have been very much better had he waited until we
won, and I told him right along that nothing would touch
his horse in any show in the world. He was regal. Yet he was
a strange, standoffish sort of horse in his box, even with me.
Interesting.

And who should be there at Olympia with Mr Ryan than
my own brother Mitchell, looking even more of the dashing
hussar than ever he had. And what stories he had to tell
me, and how he could ride, the so and so! I put him up on
Jupiter, to show him how the English show horse had pro-
gressed, and he put me up on Over There, a Canadian-
bought thoroughbred that would jump six foot and more.

I took him a round of A-Class fences, and I never had a better ride. Mitchell had only had a third on him, but in a very big class, time counting, and only a second and a half between first and third, on a horse that was far from fast. That was the difference, as we then saw it, between our supreme horses and theirs on the other side. Ours were the faster, then.

Still a bachelor, very prosperous, fantastically handsome, Mitchell was a quandary, so far as I was concerned. He apparently was working for an American millionaire, Mr John McE. Bowman who ran the Goldens Bridge Hunt, a newish country. Three years in a row Marshall had won the Hunt Team jumping at Madison Square Garden with Dansant, Over There, and Waterway. It sounded a great life. I quote from a letter of Marshall's written at that time:

'After we'd won the Hunt Team, Jack (Bowman), who loved a party, took about fifty of us to his apartment at the Biltmore Hotel. It was a great do. I was talking to Mr Bowman. Everyone else seemed to be asleep on a chair or a sofa. He pulled up the blind. It was daylight. "It's six o'clock," Jack said. "Hounds meet at Percy Rockefeller's at nine, and you'll have to hunt them, Marshall." "Well," I said, "I'm ready dressed," (I hadn't had time to change after the Show) "and if I can't stand, I can surely sit on a horse." "O.K. I'll call Murray to take you there, and we'd better have some coffee or tea." All I wanted was a nice easy day, but it was not to be. Hounds got on a deer and ran to Rye Lake very fast. We tried to stop them, but it was an avalanche. Tommy Wallace, whipping-in, and myself got to the lake, and we saw a sight that could only happen once in a lifetime. The deer, a fox, a bunch of duck, and lastly the pack of hounds, were all swimming to a small island in the middle of the lake. Hounds were there all night, and they were short of sleep when we collected them by boat in the morning. The deer was still there, unharmed. The fox and the duck had gone. Our hounds were complete.'

Back at Castlehays, I saw Ted Major's Cubitt being pulled to pieces, and the wheels being scrubbed inside and out.

'Hullo, is there a girl, then?' I asked him.

'I'm off to Cheshire tomorrow,' he admitted, shuffling his feet. 'I hope to be spliced within a year.'

'You're dashed cocksure. Is washing the car supposed to help?'

'I certainly hope so.'

He was so modest, so good-hearted, and so serious that I had no doubt of his success, should he have chosen wisely, and I truly believe I hoped he would succeed, if that was what he wanted, even though that would undoubtedly mean another shift for me. By then I had stayed with Ted for two years, and there was quite a spell yet to go.

He came back smiling all over his face, engaged to Miss Joan Eardley. Her people were farmers, and she was a charming, good-looking, and efficient young woman. I've always noticed that a farmer is only as good as his wife, and it was clear that in his choice Ted had chosen prosperity and, with any luck, happiness. I heard from him only the other day, and he said he was sending a turkey for Christmas, and that they'd reared a thousand turkeys on the farm as a sideline. Funny what a wife can do to change a man. When I lived at Castlehays the only kind of fowl he'd allow near the place was a dead one for the table.

Whether getting engaged had made him think of matrimony for me as well, I don't know, but suddenly one evening he announced, 'I've taken tickets for the Meynell Hunt Ball in the Grand Hotel, Derby, next week. My cousin Muriel Bates is driving over from Cheshire for it, and I count on you, as a dancing man, to come. It's a must.'

There were a lot of rich people in the Meynell. If they put on a show it was always well done, and that Hunt Ball was no exception. He had told me his cousin was very pretty, and he had not exaggerated. She was also small, light on her feet, and an exceptional dancer. When she and I got going on that floor we danced until breakfast. . . . I did not see her again for nine years, and then I married her.

I have to end this description of my time in the Meynell country pretty well as I began it, with the splendid-looking Farman horse that bucked Ted off at Rangemore. When you jumped that one he often bucked like the dickens and he did it on landing which was, many thought, an unfair trick. To cure him I carried a little wicker bottle full of water. As he landed (and bucked) I just dotted him one between the ears, sprinkled some water in his eye, and scolded him. We thought I had him cured. Time and again I rode him, with and without the wicker bottle in my hand, and he never bucked. Ted rode him, jumped him in cold blood and with company; no bucks. So we sold him to some Meynell people called Boyd. They were good customers and we let him go for three hundred pounds, which certainly was not over-dear. A week later he was bounced back at us. Bucking.

I worked and worked on him. Why did he buck? Surely I could find a cure? Ah. what a ride! You would never get to the bottom of him. Then he was so cunning. He was an actor. He would lay his nose in my two hands and look dreamily into my eyes. I rode him without a single buck. I asked him to buck. I took him out on the downs where all horses got over-excited. I walked him downhill in a cold wind, his coat staring, his rein lying on his neck. Would he? No.

'Let him go back to them,' I said to Ted. 'There's no sign of a buck in him. I can't make him buck.'

'I don't trust him,' he said.

In my heart I agreed with him. 'I'd take him back today,' I said. 'Only it's such a filthy morning. I suppose I'll just have to ride him out exercise.'

'Watch yourself, Howard.' He finished his breakfast and got up, stretching. 'It's too horrible outside to do any good on the farm. I'm going to have the morning at my accounts. See you lunchtime.'

It was raining in torrents and blowing a harsh east wind as we left the stables. The Farman horse felt uncommon fresh under me, a great bunch of muscle. We jogged down the two miles of private road. On the corner by the public road stood the farm of a friend of mine called Walker. He hailed me as I passed. He was in a barn where his men were turning over some potatoes.

'Are you riding that way?'

'Yes, but I'm not taking this horse in any mud.'

'As you pass by, just glance over the hedge and see if any of my ewes are on their backs—rain like this in their wool, and them heavy in lamb.'

I should have said, 'Look, I've got my horse to see to, and he can be a holy terror. You look after your sheep, and I'll look after this horse. . . .' But I shrugged my dripping chin into my upturned collar, listened to the howl of the east wind and the hiss of the rain spears, and said nothing.

'There's a hundred and fifty of them,' he shouted after me.

Count as I would I saw no more than ninety-eight ewes. The field was a big one, and full of dips. I couldn't go through the gate. It was off its hinges and tied up either end in a sea of poached mud. I thought I'd ride down the hedge until I found a jumpable place, pop over into the field, and make a job of the counting. I always hated leaving anything like that half done (my father's training, I suppose). At least it would pass the time. I left the road to look for a place, and then— he put one in. Quick as light, down went his head until his nose violently struck the grass. Up went his heels sky high. His back was a catapult. I took a dive, a lurching dive, and landed on my right shoulder, breaking everything. I heard it crunch.

I knew I'd bust my collarbone, for I'd often done that before, and I'd plainly damaged my shoulder. There was another pain as well, as though a rib had broken and was poking into places where it was extremely unwelcome. Now and then I managed to get on my feet and make a feeble attempt to catch my horse, fishing for him with the handle of my Swaine & Adeney hunting whip. He stayed near, but would not be caught. Over in the distance a farm hand was spreading manure from a cart. I tried to make him see me by waving a wet white silk handkerchief. Would he look my way? Not he. He forked out the contents of that cart, drove back to the farm, loaded up, and eventually returned. I'd been there for hours. Now the manure cart was nearer than before. At last he saw me, the ox-eyed creature, and came over. He caught the horse and made me to my direction a kind of sling that eased the shoulder and collarbone, though the rib hurt more than ever. Back to the manure cart he went, and fetched me a Guinness bottle with a screw cap, full of cold tea. Strangely enough, it revived me no end. We got the horse back on the road and I led him from the off side, letting him pull me along by my sound left hand, twined in his mane. I fainted as I walked and came to, still walking. Now that he had beaten me that devil of a horse took me home.

Ted had gone out on the farm, but his man drove me straight to Derby Hospital in the Cubitt. They doped me, set my collarbone, and worked on the shoulder, but did nothing about the rib. Back at Castlehays I said to my friend Major, 'You know there's more pain than ever a broken collarbone and a few odds and ends in the shoulder would create.'

Ted drove me straight back to hospital, but the doctor refused to do anything more, so Ted hurried me home and put me to bed with hot bottles, aspirins, and brandy and water. I lived with that pain for the next eight years, all because I had tried to count Farmer Walker's ewes, and also because, let's face it, I hadn't listened to Ted when he said at our very first meeting, 'They're all the same, these Farman brutes.'

The Rose-Bowl

'WHAT *shall* we do with all these show horses when we get them home?' Lord Stavordale enquired of me and of the mellowing afternoon.

I was riding for His Lordship at Windsor in July 1939, and had been so busy about my duties that I was at first puzzled by the question. He knew he could trust the horses to Mr Ball, his stud groom.

'There's to be war,' he said. 'Within the week we shall be at it against Germany, us and France.' He handed me a dry biscuit and a glass of champagne. We were standing at the open boot of his car. His face was very sad; it was a young face, and gentle. There was not a more delightful owner to work for in all England. He was very tall, and had the languid stoop that was fashionable in the beautiful London of the 1920s. His voice, slow, unforced, had that tenuous lingering cadence that I, coming from the harsh north, always found so attractive. He was dressed in London-season light clothing, while I was booted and spurred, black coat, tall hat. Tendrils of Havana smoke hung round us in the sunshine. Nestling in my pocket alongside my old pipe was a new gold lighter from Dunhill's in Duke Street, a present from a grateful owner. His Lordship wore a waxy, heavy-scented gardenia in his buttonhole. It was browning at the edges, as gardenias will. Bursting bubbles in the champagne tickled my nose. 'We going to win this class?' he asked.

' 'Fraid not, my lord. Jack Gittens has that extra good

galloper in, and Captain Wickhouse-Boynton dearly loves one that can fly. Although ours is a mare with potential, Gittens will scorch us with his gallop. And he knows it.'

So it proved. I walked back to Lord Stavordale.

'She went well for you,' he said, 'and she's a taking mare, but he was right to stand us second. Well, that's the last of the very last show.' He closed the boot of his car with a clonk. 'I shan't be here tomorrow. I've a horse, Flickermouse, in the three o'clock at Salisbury and we think he could just about win. It's a bumper's race, though, and you never know with them, do you?'

While I was in the ring on the mare I had seen Geoffrey Brooke's daughter, Mrs Lloyd-Thomas, among the onlookers and she had waved ·to me. Her husband, an equerry to Edward, Prince of Wales, had been killed race-riding. I wanted to see her, and soon I found her, and learned that she had been looking for me.

'They say it's to be war, Captain Marshall.'

'Yes, they all do.'

'I want your advice, and if possible your help.' She spoke of a batch of exceptional young horses she had recently bought in Ireland.

'Don't let 'em come over,' I said. 'They'll be better off in Ireland than here.'

'It's too late. They've already made the crossing, and they'll be turned out at my place near Shrivenham when I leave this show. I shall desperately need some expert help with them, and if you could possibly come up and look after them I'd be eternally grateful. Can we exchange addresses?'

'The general isn't here today?' I asked.

'You mean daddy? No, he's in London today, at the War House. They're still living in Malmesbury House in the Close at Salisbury. He won't get back there till tomorrow. You can imagine what sort of a stew he's in.'

'Stew?'

'Yes, of course. Job-hunting. He'd come out of the Army, and now he's finding it awfully hard to get back in.'

'That's my problem too,' I said. 'I'm fifty, but fit. There must be a place for everyone in such a war as we're going to have. That's why I had hoped to see your father. I was his soldier-groom when we were both in the early twenties. I thought he might help me get back in, if it's only firing a gun.'

'A lot of his old cronies are after him, and he can't even get a fighting job for himself.' she said. 'But I'm sure he'll do his very best for you, Captain Marshall.' She sounded remarkably, I would not say insincere, but unconvincing. 'And don't forget,' she added as we parted, 'if your entry to the Army is delayed, come to Shrivenham and give me a hand with those six young ones. They'll all want careful breaking.'

Back at the horse lines, I asked Mr Ball about Flicker-mouse. 'Oh by Jove!' he said, 'I wish I could get a fiver on him, Captain Marshall. But as you know I must stop here tomorrow with three horses in the parade. So no Salisbury for me, worse luck.'

'Lord Stavordale's talk of war has knocked the wind out of my sails,' I said. 'I don't see any worthwhile rides coming my way tomorrow, so I'll push off for Salisbury in the morning, and I'll lay your fiver for you if you wish.'

'Here you are then,' said he, pulling out his wallet and abstracting a large white note.

It was unusual for me to decide to go betting. I expect I was really going to Salisbury because the Brookes lived there, and if I wanted to bet it was because the thought of a War in which I as yet had no part to play was unsettling.

Flickermouse took the eye in the paddock. I got thirty pounds to five pounds on him twice, just as the amateur jockeys were mounting. Lord Stavordale's horse ran game enough, and was beaten a short head, so goodbye your fiver, Mr Ball. I wished I'd had the sense to stop at Windsor where

I belonged, and where I pretty well knew what was going to beat what. A farmer friend from near Sherborne, Mr Greenham, a racing man, came up to me.

'Now then, now then, Captain Lugubrious. What's done can soon be undone, as I can prove.' He held the card for the next race under my nose, covering one number with his thumbnail. 'You'll get it all back and more on this one if you make haste. Nettleweed, Steve Donoghue's Nettleweed, *and it's tens.*'

I hurried to the place where Dutton and the others stood silent. 'Hundred pounds to ten pounds Nettleweed,' I said, and I was on. Just then a sudden rush of punters caused them to close their books with a unanimous snap. Nettleweed won easily, and the valuable Mr Greenham came back at me with, he swore it, an even better proposition.

'Play it all on Musical Queen if Carslake has the ride. Otherwise don't touch it.'

Carslake rode her to a good win, and by the time I had bought my farmer saviour a drink and paid my expenses I went to the car park nine hundred and ninety pounds richer than when I arrived. Not that I thought of buying myself a better car than my little Ford. If ever I had any money it went on horseflesh. I would rather sell a horse any day than have a successful bet. Nor would I wish to moralise about betting. I just never could afford it, worse luck.

Dear little race course, Salisbury, especially when the sun shines. I always had a soft spot for that place.

It seemed only good manners not to barge in on the Brookes. I parked at the County Hotel in Salisbury, and telephoned. The General himself answered.

'Marshall! Where the devil are you?' he barked in his old impersonal way. 'Come right round, and I'll give you a drink. Hurry now. I've got a Territorials' meeting at seven-thirty.'

I walked towards the Cathedral, and in the jeweller's shop near the corner I recognised a second-hand silver

335

rose-bowl that was being offered for sale at thirty pounds. It was the bowl I had won at Lord Harrington's point-to-point in 1903. No doubt of it at all, because there, bang in the middle, was engraved the badge of the South Notts Hussars. Nor was there anything more than coincidence in its presence in that window. I never could bear having anything about me that was not properly kept, and when I set up half a house at Gillingham I got tired of seeing my silver trophies in the office because they were nearly always tarnished. So I sold them to a Sherborne dealer, thinking I'd seen the last of them.

I stood blinking at the rose-bowl through the plate-glass window, remembering Lord Harrington's white whiskers, Danny Maher's slender hands, the foaling box with the one-eyed mare in it and the damp little black foal, and my father bidding me leave it and go to bed.